DOING ECONOMIC RESEARCH

ECONOMISTS OF THE TWENTIETH CENTURY

General Editors: Mark Perlman, *University Professor of Economics, Emeritus, University of Pittsburgh* and Mark Blaug, *Professor Emeritus, University of London; Professor Emeritus, University of Buckingham and Visiting Professor, University of Exeter*

This innovative series comprises specially invited collections of articles and papers by economists whose work has made an important contribution to economics in the late twentieth century.

The proliferation of new journals and the ever-increasing number of new articles make it difficult for even the most assiduous economist to keep track of all the important recent advances. By focusing on those economists whose work is generally recognized to be at the forefront of the discipline, the series will be an essential reference point for the different specialisms included.

A list of published and future titles in this series is printed at the end of this volume.

Doing Economic Research

Essays on the Applied Methodology of Economics

Thomas Mayer

Emeritus Professor, University of California, Davis, US

ECONOMISTS OF THE TWENTIETH CENTURY

Edward Elgar

Published by
Edward Elgar Publishing Limited
Gower House
Croft Road
Aldershot
Hants GU11 3HR
England

Edward Elgar Publishing Company
Old Post Road
Brookfield
Vermont 05036
USA

British Library Cataloguing in Publication Data
Mayer, Thomas
    Doing Economic Research: Essays on the
    Applied Methodology of Economics. –
    (Economists of the Twentieth Century
    Series)
    I. Title II. Series
    330.072

Library of Congress Cataloguing in Publication Data
Mayer, Thomas, 1927–
    Doing economic research : essays on the applied methodology of
    economics / Thomas Mayer.
        p.   cm. — (Economists of the twentieth century)
    Includes bibliographical references and index.
        1. Economics—Methodology. 2. Economics—Research.   I. Title.
    II. Series.
    HB131.M448   1995
    330'.072—dc20   94–40772
                                                                                  CIP

ISBN 1 85278 939 5

Printed and bound in Great Britain by
Biddles Ltd, Guildford and King's Lynn

To Dorothy

Contents

Preface

Here is a set of essays roaming over various topics in the *applied* methodology of economics. I stress 'applied' because most do not deal with the important and fundamental issues that most methodologists and philosophers of economics focus on, such as instrumentalism versus realism, or how to determine the truthfulness of statements in economics.

Instead, I concentrate on problems that I hope are more germane to the working economist, to whom this book is mainly addressed. I hope that they will not be put off by the word 'methodology' in the title. I am by trade a macro-economist specializing in applied monetary theory and monetary policy, who writes on methodology out of a dissatisfaction with some aspects of the papers that he reads on macroeconomics, rather than from a wish to apply lessons garnered from reading philosophy of science to economics. The latter is surely worth doing, but it is not my area of comparative advantage. It is, moreover, well ploughed ground, on which several excellent books are available, while applied methodology is a much less cultivated area. Except for Chapters 3 and 11, what I discuss are more mundane issues, such as whether in regression analysis one should discard variables that have insignificant coefficients, and whether the failure of consumer choice theory on experimental tests matters. I hope that the book will be easy reading for economists unfamiliar with the literature on methodology.

Not surprisingly, this book shares a common outlook and some ideas with my previous book on methodology, *Truth versus Precision in Economics*. But it is not a sequel in the sense of developing further the argument presented in that book. In the previous book I described and evaluated two methodological perspectives that shape the work of practicing economists. In this book I claim that there is a middle ground between the abstruse methodological analysis that most methodologists favor and the unreflective attitude of 'let's grind out a result, and never mind what it signifies', that so often shows up in the work of practicing economists. Most of the book then illustrates that this middle ground is worth cultivating, mainly by looking at problems that practicing economists have dealt with. These problems cover a wide range, and are just a sample of the issues that low-level methodology can deal with.

Anyone writing on methodology is likely to be told that he is naive if he thinks that he can change the way the profession operates, and is therefore just wasting his time. I have three answers to that. First, whether something is worth doing depends on the opportunity cost. I have spent a substantial part of my professional life working on monetary policy issues, thus, in effect, telling the Federal Reserve what it should do: to no effect whatsoever, so my opportunity cost is low. Second, I do not see myself as a Martin Luther sweeping away the old. If I can change to a small extent the research practices of a few economists I will feel that my attempt at reform has been worthwhile. Third, professors are supposed to profess what they believe.

Chapter 7, 'On the realism of assumptions', covers some ground I previously covered in a paper on Friedman's methodology (Mayer, 1993a), but I am now less dismissive of realistic assumptions than I was in that paper. Chapter 8, 'The monetarist debate and the new methodology' is a revised version of a paper published in Thomas Mayer and Franco Spinelli, *Macroeconomics and Macroeconomic Policy Issues*. I am indebted to Avebury Press for permission to reprint it.

While writing Chapter 4 I was a guest at the Center for Economic Studies at the University of Munich, and I would like to thank the Center and its director, Professor Hans-Werner Sinn, for its great hospitality. In connection with the survey results reported in Chapter 9, I am indebted to Mary Jackman for help in constructing the questionnaire, to Colin Cameron for advice on the econometrics and Edalati-Sarayani Abolghasem for tabulating the data, and to all the respondents for answering the questions. I am greatly indebted for helpful comments on all or some of the chapters to Jordi Cat, Joseph Bisignano, A.W. Coats, Daniel Hammond, Kevin Hoover, Terence Hutchison, Liang-Yu Liu, William Milford, Patrick Minford, Steven Sheffrin and Nancy Wulwick, and for editorial assistance to Judy Kim.

I am also indebted for excellent copy editing to Mr A.J. Waterman.

THOMAS MAYER

1 Introduction

Economics has become an unreflective discipline. As Bruce Caldwell (1992, p.146) remarked, 'economics is a discipline in which the absence of methodological self-consciousness is considered a virtue'. We value certain types of work because that is what our colleagues value; since they value that work there is no need to inquire any further. There seems to be a pronounced reluctance to consider whether we are moving in the right direction, as long as we are moving fast enough. Perhaps for some, perhaps even for many, economists this reluctance arises from an underlying sense of unease and uncertainty, a feeling that, despite the substantial resources and great ingenuity that we are investing in economic analysis, our progress in understanding how the economy works, as distinct from understanding the implication of certain axioms, is disappointingly slow.

Whatever its cause, the consequence of this reluctance and the resulting reliance on our colleagues' views of what are the correct procedures, we face the dangers of complacency and of what social psychologists call 'group-think'. One way to ameliorate such group think and complacency is to open communication with other speech communities, such as methodologists. Or perhaps all that is needed is something simpler: just standing back and reflecting on what we are doing.

Accordingly, in this set of essays I ask some questions about the utility of some of our procedures and perspectives. This is therefore a book on methodology, but to a large extent my emphasis is on useful heuristics rather than on the more fundamental issues that methodologists usually deal with. In that respect the word 'methodology' is inappropriate for what I am doing, but there is no such word as 'heuristology', and it should not be invented.

My other task is to narrow the gap between methodologists and practicing economists, something that would help to make economics a more reflective discipline. Economists not only acclaim the division of labor, they practice it. A.C. Pigou (1877–1959) was the last great economist to master almost the entire subject, though J.R. Hicks (1904–89) also exhibited a remarkable range. Modern economists, or at least those most actively engaged in academic research, form a set of speech communities whose members write primarily for each other, and whose language is sometimes incomprehensible to members of other communities. Given the stream of research papers that inundates our mailboxes and the resulting inability to keep up, this incomprehensibility may be inevitable, but it has an evident cost. This cost is particularly obvious for the methodological speech community, which sees its task as advising the other communities.

These other communities, even if they were to read such advice, could often not comprehend it and, what is more, would be disinclined to pay attention to such critiques by outsiders.

I try to narrow the gap between methodologists and practicing economists in two ways. One is by discussing some low-brow methodological ideas that are directly relevant to an economist's day-to-day work. The other is by appealing to methodologists to place more emphasis on the problems that practicing economists face.

At first glance the latter may seem unnecessary. Don't methodologists, just like other suppliers of services, have an incentive to meet the needs of the customers who will use their products? No, they do not. They do not operate in the usual type of market that is responsive to customers, but in academia, and academia places other desiderata ahead of meeting the customer's wishes, or, put differently, in academia the producers themselves are their own customers. What counts in that market is in the main the demonstration of brilliance and of technical skills. These characteristics are displayed better by addressing one's own speech community than by addressing a broader public. In saying this I do not accuse methodologists of careerism; they are merely acting in accordance with the values with which their surroundings imbue them.

Moreover, since our intellectual climate values abstraction highly (see Klamer, 1987), it is not surprising that methodologists pay more attention to the abstract philosophical aspects of their subject than to its more concrete and practical uses. I suspect that the typical methodologist would be pleased if someone would mistake her for a philosopher of science, just as the typical mathematical economist would be pleased to be mistaken for a mathematician.

In any case, practicing economists generally pay little, if any, attention to the work of methodologists. There are several reasons for this besides the just discussed abstract and philosophical bent of methodologists. One is that, since everyone is busy with his own work, practicing economists do not want to take the time to learn what methodologists have to say, particularly since that would require learning a specialized language. Second, some, though certainly not all, practicing economists believe that economics is making excellent progress. If economics ain't broke, why fix it? Isn't it better to participate in the triumphal march of progress than to stand on the sideline and ask what it all means?

Another reason is that what methodologists and philosophers of science say often rings strange to the ears of the practicing economist. I remember my own reaction when I first heard about the problem of induction, and was told that, even if one has seen all swans except one, and all of them are white, one cannot conclude that 'all swans are white'. This seemed bizarre to me who felt happy if he had, say, a hundred observations, and often had to make do with much fewer. Economists, like other practicing scientists, are not all that afraid of being wrong. We shrug our shoulders about the problem of induction, and worry instead about the small size of our sample. And rightly so. In their applied econometrics economists do things that they know in principle to be questionable, because that is the only way they can obtain notable results, so why not do the same with respect to the strictures of methodologists? Science is a messy business. Applied mathematicians provide answers to mathematical problems despite the foundations of mathematics being unsettled (see Kline, 1980).

Moreover, philosophers of science and therefore methodologists sometimes pay much attention to a problem that is important for many sciences, but inconsequential for economics. For example, philosophers of science are surely right to worry about the inseparability of observations and theory, and about advocates of different paradigms legitimately reading the same data differently. These are fascinating issues that every educated person should know about. But do they matter all that much to us as economists? I have the impression that, when economists who advocate different theories interpret the same observation differently, this is often something we can readily deal with without invoking philosophy of science or methodology. When a Keynesian ascribes a recovery to expansionary fiscal policy, and a monetarist puts it down to the expansionary monetary policy that accompanied it, we know how to deal with that disagreement, at least in principle. If we cannot resolve that debate, it is so for much more mundane reasons than those that interest philosophers.

Similarly, disagreement among economists who belong to different schools does not often seem to turn on the interpretation of a text in the philosopher's sense. To be sure, post-Keynesians and neo-Keynesians disagree about what Keynes *really* meant, but, at least explicitly, that is a disagreement about the history of economic thought, and not about how the economy functions. Implicitly, it may be an attempt to invoke the authority of Keynes to buttress one's view of the economy, but that is a questionable argument in any case. Hence, despite their importance for philosophy of science, the methodologists of economics probably should not pay much attention to these problems of interpreting texts.

Another problem that inhibits the interaction of methodologists and practicing economists is that many practicing economists consider methodologists to be arrogant outsiders who wish to assert an authority that they do not possess. Doesn't it take great presumption to tell one's colleagues what they should do? (Of course, we economists have no qualms about telling policymakers what to do, but let's pretend that this is another matter.) What makes it seem particularly presumptuous is that in the pecking order of economics methodologists rank at or near the bottom.

Still another reason is the wish to preserve human capital. Someone who takes the methodologist's 'you can't do that' seriously may have to admit that his previous papers in which he did just that are of questionable value.[1]

The reasons just cited for disregarding methodology may seem weak and unsatisfactory. But Donald McCloskey (1985, 1994) has presented a much stronger case for disdaining methodology. He argues that the Tablets of the Law that methodologists bring down from the Mount Sinai of Philosophy of Science have no authority over economists. Following Rorty (1979), he argues that philosophy is not privileged, that philosophers do not have a set of epistemological principles that amount to a philosopher's stone, able to turn the dross of social science into the gold of true science. He therefore advocates abandonment of what he calls 'methodology with a big M' in favor of 'methodology with a small m', that is the giving of practical advice on specific day-to-day problems. (Much of what I do in this book is such methodology with a small m, or close to it.)

McCloskey is not the only one who refuses to grant philosophers of science the status of law givers. Daniel Hausman (1992a, p.21), himself a distinguished philosopher of science who specializes in economics, wrote, 'those interested in economic methodology must use their own judgment and their knowledge of the practice of economists to formulate and defend rational standards for the practice of economics'.

I agree with McCloskey and Hausman: economists should not bow down before philosophers of science and their messengers, methodologists.[2] But that does not mean that they should disregard entirely what philosophers and methodologists say; there is a middle ground between unquestioning obedience and total disregard. Philosophers of science and methodologists do not hold a God-given commission as taskmasters of us lesser folk, but they can be helpful advisers. Hausman precedes the just quoted passage with 'there is still a great deal to be learned from the judicious study of contemporary philosophy of science'. Philosophers have studied the success of knowledge acquisition in various fields, and unlike most practicing economists they have thought long and deeply about such issues. Their views and advice therefore deserve a respectful hearing. Thus one can make a strong case that the introduction of Popperian philosophy of science has done economics much good, even though it was misunderstood, practiced at most half-heartedly and, according to some methodologists (Caldwell, 1993; Hands, 1993; Mäki, 1993a), it is just not practicable in economics.[3] *Perhaps* one can make a case that, with respect to methodology, at least for practicing economists 'a little knowledge' is not 'a dangerous thing', but the appropriate thing.

Subsequent chapters
The following chapters are written so that they can be read independently of each other, hence the reader can omit some chapters or read them in any order. This independence required a few, but not very many, repetitions since they deal with different topics. Their common thread is not a specific topic, but a focus on low-brow, instead of high-brow, methodology and a wish to show that

it is useful to stand back and reflect on the practice of economists, even if one does not summon the heavy guns of philosophy of sciences. The only material that requires even a slight acquaintance with methodology or philosophy of science is Chapter 3. A glossary explains the few specialized philosophical terms that I use.

The next chapter urges methodologists to spend less time talking among themselves and to communicate better with working economists by paying more attention to their concerns and needs. That is not an easy thing to do because our prevailing intellectual climate values specialization and narrow expertise so highly. Reflectiveness is praised less than the flaunting of state-of-the-art techniques. But if methodologists do step out of their narrow disciplinary boundary they can make a valuable contribution to the progress of substantive economics.

Preaching such generalities may be good for the preacher's soul but is less likely to convince anyone than is a demonstration that it is possible to say something about topics that lie in-between the methodologist's usual concerns and the issues practicing economists deal with. Accordingly, in the following chapters I have tried to plough such a middle ground. Chapters 3 and 11, and to some extent Chapter 7, are closer to the traditional concerns of methodologists, the others are closer to the concerns of practicing economists.

Chapter 3 is addressed perhaps more to methodologists than to working economists, though I hope that the latter will find it easy going and useful. Although positivism is still the religion, or at least the Sunday religion, of many (most?) economists, among philosophers of science positivism is essentially the discarded belief of yesteryear. Economists, too, have criticized positivism (for prominent examples see Caldwell, 1982; McCloskey, 1985, 1994). However, in this chapter I argue that, despite the fundamental philosophical weakness of positivism, it does provide a useful guideline for working economists.

Chapter 4 takes up a problem to which working economists have devoted much attention. This is whether macroeconomics needs firm microfoundations. I argue that the participants in this discussion have overlooked important methodological aspects, and conclude that macroeconomics does not *need* such foundations, although they are a desirable characteristic of a macro theory.

The next chapter discusses Ricardian equivalence, a topic usually treated as an issue purely in substantive economics. But it turns out that a significant part of this dispute arises from a methodological disagreement. Owing to their dismissive attitude toward methodological considerations, economists have not realized this. As a result, proponents and opponents of Ricardian equivalence have talked past each other.

Chapter 6 deals with the confusions caused by the loose use of words, or with the inappropriate meanings that are read into some words. I do not develop a theory that explains such confusions, but instead take up several concrete instances where confusion about the meaning of words has inhibited economic research. Among them are the distinction between science and non-science, the meaning of the term 'theory', the dual meaning of 'Neo-Walrasian research program', and the confusing use of the term 'democratic'.

The topic of Chapter 7, the appropriateness of unrealistic assumptions, has been much discussed in economics since Friedman's (1953) famous essay in which he argued that assumptions need not, and often should not, be realistic. It is an issue on which many economists seem to have strong opinions; some claim that assumptions *must* be realistic, others that they should never be realistic. I argue that both extremes are wrong: that although assumptions *need* not be realistic, there are some important advantages to their being realistic.

Economists are proud of the extent to which their techniques have improved in recent decades. Is this pride justified? Techniques are inputs into the research process, not outputs. One should therefore resist the temptation to use the sophistication of techniques as a measure of the value of the research output. Hence it is legitimate to ask whether the employment of sophisticated modern techniques has brought us any closer to resolving the issues that matter for the general public that pays our salaries. The only way to answer this question is by a series of case studies. Chapter 8 presents such a case study, dealing with the Keynesian–monetarist debate.

The next two chapters deal with econometrics. Each year a vast number of econometric studies are published. Do their results make much difference to what economists think? When economists read econometric papers that contradict their priors, do they change these priors, or do they dismiss the disconfirming results on the argument that econometric studies are polluted by data mining? Chapter 9 presents the results of a survey asking economists how common they think data mining is, and how this affects the credence they give to econometric results. While to most respondents data mining does appear to be a problem, they do not consider it a serious enough problem to invalidate econometric results entirely.

Chapter 10 deals with the appropriate treatment of regressors that are not statistically significant at the usual 5 per cent level. It is a common practice to rerun the regression without these regressors, and to treat the new regression as the valid one. I argue that this is not necessarily the correct procedure. Judgement, not a mechanical rule, is needed, and even if a mechanical rule were appropriate, it would not be to eliminate all variables insignificant at the 5 per cent level.

In an important recent book a philosopher of science who specializes in economics, Alexander Rosenberg, tried to answer the question whether economics is an empirical science or a mathematical science. With some sadness he concluded that economics is a mathematical science, not an empirical science. In Chapter 11, I challenge this conclusion, arguing that Rosenberg has greatly underestimated the empirical successes that economics has scored. Moreover, he focuses excessively on economic theory, particularly the theory of consumer choice, and pays too little attention to the less abstract work that most economists do. Since the relation between the underlying theory of consumer choice and the other parts of economics is not nearly as close as Rosenberg assumes, the failure of consumer choice theory on experimental tests that he cites does much less harm to economics than he claims.

What is our knowledge of economics based on? At one time most economists would have answered that economics consists primarily of a set of valid deductions drawn from premises that are self-evident and are also the stuff of everyday observations. Although this view is less widespread now, many economists, at least implicitly, adhere to it in the sense of taking rational utility or income maximization as a solid rock upon which they can build their theoretical structures. In a brief chapter, Chapter 12, I examine this position.

The final chapter deals with the proposal of another philosopher of science, Daniel Hausman, and of many institutionalists, that economics should abandon its stance of splendid isolation, along with its simplistic psychological assumptions, and pay more attention to the findings of psychology, sociology and experimental economics. I argue that the failure of consumer choice theory on experimental tests does not provide a strong case for such a change. Instead, it is the inability of neoclassical economics to explain certain types of market behavior that shows that the thin neoclassical theory needs to be supplemented – but not replaced – by the type of richer theory that the new institutionalists are developing. With such a theory economics will be less isolated from the other social sciences.

Notes

1. Bruce Caldwell (1993) lists – and refutes – some additional reasons that practicing economists give for paying little attention to methodology.
2. Hausman (1992a, p.234) compares the relation of philosophers of science and methodologists to that of scientists and engineers.
3. In economics Popper is known primarily as the advocate of falsificationism. But, while Popper advocated falsificationism for the natural sciences, for the social sciences he advocated situational analysis, a methodology similar to Lionel Robbins's deductive method (see Caldwell, 1991). Moreover, many economists probably think of Popper's teaching as just an insistence on empirical testing, but it goes much beyond that. Furthermore, as Blaug (1992) argues, while many economists claim to follow Popper, they generally avoid the hard testing that he advocates.

2 Methodologists and the practicing economist: a plea for collaboration*

Economic methodologists have two main tasks, to bring insights from philosophy of science to practicing economists and to bring insights from economics to philosophers of science. I will deal only with the first of these. In this task methodologists are greatly hindered by the low regard in which practicing economists hold methodology. What methodologists write can help practicing economists only if they read these writings. To persuade them to do so, methodologists must first demonstrate that they *can* help practicing economists in their day-to-day work. That will require that they spend more of their effort on applying methodological insights to specific substantive issues, and less on the more subtle and abstract issues that pervade the philosophy of science. To do that they will have to curb the pervasive impulse to conduct their discussion at the highest feasible level of abstraction and technical sophistication.

In echoing Polonius's plea for 'more matter with less art', I am not arguing for the elimination of highly abstract methodology, but am pleading only that it be accompanied by more emphasis on the practical uses of methodology. Methodologists should model themselves less on the missionary who preaches to the natives the commandments of an alien god (epistemology), and more on the peace corps worker who shows them how to plant better crops. Clive Granger (1991, pp.10–18) rightly complained that abstract theorists talk too much to each other and not enough to applied theorists. Methodologists, too, need to spend more time talking to their clients, practicing economists, and less to each other. Methodologists and high-brow economic theorists are probably no worse in that respect than others; it seems a common failing of homo academicus. But since methodologists want to influence the work of other economists they cannot afford the cost of this failing, which is that those who should be their customers usually ignore what they have to offer. And when they do not ignore it they sometimes scorn it, so that it is first necessary to defend methodology against the charge of being useless or even a hindrance.

In defense of methodology
That scourge of conventional methodology, Don McCloskey (1985, p.25) calls methodology (with a big M) comical, something that stands between:

* This chapter is a revised version of a paper given at the luncheon meeting of the International Network for Economic Method at the 1993 Allied Social Sciences Meetings; hence its informal style.

the cool majesty of sprachethik and above the workaday utility of method with a small *m*. Because it cannot claim the specificity of practical advice to economists or to the lovelorn, it is not method. Because it does not claim the generality of how to speak well ... it is not sprachethik.[1]

In calling methodology with a big M an unnecessary layer of management standing between the top executive, sprachethik, and the production worker, that is the practicing economist, McCloskey may well describe the current work of some methodologists, but he is not describing all the work that methodologists can and should do. Those on the assembly line of economic research cannot be entirely trusted to evaluate their own work, and sprachethik is too distant an executive to do such an evaluation. For example, does sprachethik as such tell us what the limits on ad hocery are, or just how much data mining is permissible? No, it does not, unless the term 'sprachethik' is broadened, so that it includes much of what we now call methodology. To be sure, methodologists do not discourse on the details of the appropriate methods in the small; they do not tell us whether to use two-stage or three-stage least squares, or whether it is legitimate to assume extrapolative expectations in a particular model of inflation. But in-between such specifics and grand pronouncements on the validity of instrumentalism, or falsificationism, there is a middle ground where the methodologist can and should help the workaday economist.

McCloskey also criticizes methodologists because they second-guess scientists who know more about the science than the methodologists do. However, as Steven Rappaport (1988, pp.113–14) points out, economic methodologists need not impose rules derived from outside economics. They can employ the rules that economists themselves have developed. In addition, as discussed below, methodologists possess distinctive skills and knowledge that can help practicing economists. Moreover, economics is a rather unreflective field, where the emphasis is on techniques and on doing what one's colleagues are doing, only doing it a bit better. In such a situation outsiders who ask critical questions can be extraordinarily useful.

McCloskey also claims that methodologists do harm by imposing artificial and unnecessary rules that interfere with day-to-day work. This may be a fairly common view. Practicing economists who produce a result they feel confident about are likely to be annoyed when a methodologist rules it out of court on a (to them) obscure philosophical argument. But while one cannot deny that some methodologists do act as though their lofty perch in the eyrie of philosophical doctrines entitles them to lord it over lesser folk, methodologists need not behave that way. They can be liberating instead of constrictive (see Coats, 1987, p.306). They can sing the arias of Wagner's young Walther instead of Beckmesser's.

Here are four illustrations of methodologists as liberators rather than as pro-scribers. New classical economists have persecuted their opponents by accusing them of ad hocery. Most economists know in a vague way that ad hocery is bad, so that calling Keynesian or monetarist theory ad hoc discredits it. It needed a professional methodologist, Wade Hands, to rescue Keynesians and monetarists from this persecution. As (Hands, 1988) pointed out, there is a basic distinction between Popperian ad hocery and Lakatosian ad hocery. Only the former is clearly a sin against scientific method. To accuse those who do not accept your theory of asserting something that is ad hoc with respect to your theory, that is of Lakatosian ad hocery, is just to accuse them of not accepting your theory, and of nothing else. By thus protecting Keynesians and monetarists from the charge of methodological error, Hands, far from constricting the freedom of practicing economists, has opened up space for them.

A second example is the assertion of many new classicals and other formal theorists that theory must be built 'from the ground up', that only rigorously established foundations can carry the weight of scientific analysis. By showing that this is just not so, that empirical science is better described as a continuous interplay of observation and theory, so that the Cartesian vision is not good history of science, methodologists can liberate economists from an inappropriate and stifling demand for rigour. By pointing out that the new classical debate is a manifestation of the old debate of rationalism versus empiricism, methodologists can show that the new classicals' peculiar criteria for 'serious' economics do not require unquestioned obedience.

As a third example consider the emphasis economists place on theory. Many practicing economists seem to believe that unless a piece of economic research makes explicit use of economic theory it is worthless, or at least that it lacks claim to the exalted title of 'science'. Hence, *mere* data gathering is not a scientific activity. By informing economists about the high repute in which physical scientists hold Tycho Brahe and other gatherers of data, methodologists could bolster the prestige of those who gather data, and thus induce more economists to do so.

My fourth example comes from the theory of demand. Nobody can deny that indifference curve analysis and revealed preference theory have been fruitful. But a mechanic's tool kit usually contains more than one wrench, and an economist's tool kit should often contain more than one theory. I don't know about others, but at times I have found it useful to think in terms of cardinal utility. Not that one can say anything that is valid with cardinal utility that one cannot also say in terms of ordinal utility, but sometimes it is more convenient to express some ideas in cardinal terms. Yet I would not want to submit to a leading journal a paper that talks explicitly in terms of cardinal utility. A referee would probably reject it out of hand because he or she knows that it is 'wrong' to do that. Why is it wrong? Isn't it largely because Paul Samuelson and other respected economists taught us many years ago that scientists should not refer to entities that cannot be observed? Philosophers of science have long ago rejected this brand of positivism. Yet it still constrains what we economists are allowed to say. By getting rid of such outworn dictates methodologists can enhance the freedom of practicing economists, a freedom that is threatened by the methodological decrees issued by economists who are not professional methodologists.

To be sure, methodologists should not be flower children who proclaim, 'if it feels good, do it'. We do need rules for validating knowledge claims. Is the development of such rules a task for professional methodologists, or can we leave it to practicing economists, as the prevailing disdain for methodology suggests? Methodologists have three obvious advantages. Being outsiders rather than specialists in the particular field, they may be more objective and less affected by 'group-think' than are the insiders. Second, they are more familiar with the rules that scientists in other fields have found useful. Some writers, such as Weintraub (1989) have argued that this familiarity is not helpful, that valid rules for economics can be developed only within economics. But the natural sciences are one of the great achievements of mankind, so it seems worth seeing whether they have something to teach a less developed field such as economics. Third, methodologists have thought longer and more deeply about the validity of knowledge claims than have other economists, and therefore should have something interesting to tell us.

But methodologists also suffer from two disadvantages. First, they are not as familiar with what is needed and feasible in the various fields of economics as are those working in these fields. For example, specialists in a particular field may assert that a certain hypothesis should not be rejected, even though the data contradict it, because these data are poor. Methodologists cannot always decide whether that is a valid judgement or a lame excuse. Similarly, methodologists might reject some approach, say instrumentalism, for good epistemological reasons, but in dealing with a particular problem nothing else may be feasible, and yet some answer has to be given.

The second disadvantage of letting methodologists instead of practitioners judge knowledge claims is that methodologists, like other specialists, have their own agenda. They are tempted to seek respect more from fellow-methodologists and philosophers than from practicing economists. Hence, as discussed in the previous chapter, they may pay too much attention to a problem that is likely to lead to serious error in some other science and therefore interests philosophers of science, but is inconsequential in economics.

Making methodology useful to practicing economists
To justify their standing as the primary judges of knowledge claims methodologists should minimize both of these disadvantages by standing at the elbow of the practicing economist instead of sitting far away in a judge's chambers,

disputing fine points of the law with other judges. If they do so, then there are several ways in which they can help practicing economists. They can educate them about methods of assessing claims for progress that have proved useful in other sciences, or in other sub-fields of economics. For example, some economists are critical of the increased emphasis on formalism. It would help to know if there are examples from other sciences where a premature formalization proved damaging. Second, methodologists can bring their training in philosophy of science and the history of economic thought to bear on relevant problems in contemporary economics, such as the debates about causality or about the need to reduce macroeconomics to microeconomics. Third, they can warn economists about potential errors in methods that, while perhaps not unique to economics, are less likely to lead to errors in other sciences, and have therefore not received much discussion. In addition, they could point out the limits to economic analysis, bring to the fore hitherto unnoticed questionable assumptions, and help economists to better understand their relation to other social scientists.

More specifically, they should supplement their traditional work by paying attention to those methodological problems that concern practicing economists, such as the appropriate role of survey methods, the misuse of significance tests (see McCloskey, 1985; Mayer, 1993b, ch.9), the problem of data mining, the need for replication, the legitimacy of the common practice of eliminating variables with insignificant coefficients, and the methodological issues in determining how data should be used to appraise theories, issues that underly the debate of Friedman and Schwartz (1991) versus Hendry and Ericsson (1991). These are day-to-day questions on which practicing economists badly need help. Methodologists could also pay more attention to the appropriate role of formalism in economics with reference to specific problems rather than generalities. In addition, they might develop a typology of biases and errors that affect economics. To do so they could pick some errors from the history of economic thought, and try to explain why they were not quickly corrected. A good example is the interpretation of the Phillips curve in nominal terms, and the resulting claim that there is a long-run trade-off between inflation and unemployment. David Hume already knew that this is not so. Why was this knowledge lost? Another example is the failure to see the danger inherent in our savings and loan system before that danger became obvious.

Admittedly, applying philosophy of science to economics in the way I suggest is difficult. One difficulty is that those who specialize in methodology are not as familiar with other fields of economics as those who specialize in these fields. But it should not take all that much time to acquire an adequate working knowledge of a particular issue in one of these fields and, if necessary, a methodologist could collaborate with a practicing economist. In addition, practicing economists could learn enough methodology to work on problems in applied methodology in their fields. That would usually not require a deep understanding of philosophy of science.

Perhaps a bigger difficulty is avoiding the temptation to gain prestige within one's own speech community by offering technically sophisticated solutions to difficult problems, even though these problems are not relevant for the practicing economists who should be the methodologist's prime clientele. A third difficulty is that many, perhaps most, practicing economists cannot understand complex methodological arguments formulated in philosophical terms. Nor, given the low regard in which they hold methodology, are they inclined to try to work their way through such papers. The solution is, of course, to write some papers addressed to working economists, alongside papers intended for the methodological speech community. Economists in many other fields, such as monetary economics and public finance, write non-technical papers for policymakers, as well as papers addressed to their colleagues.

A good example of the failure of methodologists to interact effectively with practicing economists is their treatment of Friedman's essay on methodology. Most methodologists are highly critical of it, because *as philosophy of science* it is confused and outdated. Yet practicing economists generally treat it as the received view on which they base, or rather claim to base, their methodological decisions. Methodologists may be tempted to ascribe this to the ignorance and thick-headedness of practicing economists who refuse to read what methodologists write. But is this correct? Isn't it possible that the widespread acceptance of Friedman's methodology is due to its resonating in the day-to-day experience of practical economists in the sense of their experience telling them, 'Yes, this is the way to get the job done'? It is, of course, possible that they are as wrong in this as Aristotelean physicists were in insisting that explanations in physics follow their paradigm, but methodologists should not brush aside the views of practicing economists.

If the gap between practicing economists and methodologists is to be bridged, methodologists will have to build most of the spans. In building these spans they must accept, whether they like it or not, that practicing economists do not care much about the niceties of philosophy of science, or even about some matters that are more than mere niceties. That is not surprising. Indeed, there are good (as well as bad) reasons for it.

Bad philosophy, but good economics
One good reason is that something may be questionable as philosophy of science and yet provide a useful methodology for economics in the pragmatic sense that it facilitates the advance of economics. This is so for two reasons. First, different fields have to settle for different degrees of rigour. We would like, but do not expect, the typical paper on economic policy to be as rigorous as a paper in the *Journal of Economic Theory*, and we do not expect papers in

that journal to be as relevant for policy as the typical memorandum written by economists at the Treasury. Similarly, papers in a physics journal are generally not as rigorous as papers in a mathematics journal. Second, a principle may be a useful heuristic despite its not being absolutely valid, because it combats a bias that leads to even greater errors. For example, the maxim 'always express yourself as clearly as possible', is something we may want to teach our students even though, by not balancing marginal benefit against marginal cost, it is inconsistent with rational behaviour. Similarly, there is the precept that one should decide whether a data set is reliable enough for testing one's hypothesis before seeing what results it yields. One can show that this precept is not valid in principle, yet, all the same, adherance to it would, on the whole, advance economics.

A pragmatic approach to methodology – and that is what I am advocating – recognizes that a relatively underdeveloped science like economics may have to use crutches, some of which are inappropriate in a better developed science. Thus, as discussed in the next chapter, positivism, despite its weakness as philosophy of science, furnishes a good heuristic for economics.

Economics is not alone in this. Biology made much progress while using teleological arguments, despite the low status of teleology in philosophy of science. Similarly, John Dewey (1948, p.44) wrote: 'Like many things in philosophy, the [social contract] theory, though worthless as a record of fact, is of great worth as a symptom of the direction of human desire.' Or consider the dictum of journalism that the news columns should give the 'facts', while opinions belong only in the editorial columns. Though naive as philosophy, that dictum probably improves journalism. Other examples of the way something can be 'wrong' and yet appropriate are the uses of Newtonian physics instead of the correct relativity theory, and the physicists' employment of both quantum mechanics and relativity theory, despite their being inconsistent (Hawking, 1990). Notwithstanding the logical error of combining inconsistent statements, it would take a bold methodologist to tell physicists to stop what they are doing. Moreover, quantum mechanics uses a procedure called 'renormalization' that is questionable mathematics. Although for this reason new classical economists presumably do not consider quantum mechanics to be 'serious physics', it is still useful. Paul Feyerabend (1975) has given many examples where practices that violate some textbook rule of good scientific method have led to outstanding science.

To be sure, one should not carry this idea too far, and argue that 'anything goes'. It does not. For every example that Feyerabend gives where bad methods led to good science, there must be a vast number of cases where bad methods led to bad science. Mindless application of philosophical dicta may harm economics, but so would mindless rejection of these dicta. Departures from the rules may be appropriate in particular cases, but they need justification by showing that these departures provide useful heuristics.

Another reason why one may be less than enthusiastic about using the best that philosophy of science has to offer is that the philosophy of science used by practicing scientists is likely to be, not the correct version, but a vulgarized version of a philosophy of science. Since the loss resulting from such vulgarization is not equal for every philosophy of science, a discarded philosophy of science could be more useful as a guide to practice than a better one if its vulgarization does less damage. When you give a stranger directions to your house, he may get there sooner if you describe a longer but simple way instead of a shorter but more complicated one.

Such a pragmatic willingness to settle for an inferior methodology may seem to give up too easily in the quest for knowledge. But knowledge about the economy is hard to obtain, and we may have to make various compromises. As Daniel Hausman, a leading philosopher of economics, has remarked (1992b, p.4) 'one of the most important senses in which methodological norm N may be superior to norm M is if one is more likely to learn something if one follows N than if one follows M.' Besides, at a time when we do not have an agreed upon philosophy of science, even for the natural sciences (see Hollis, 1985, p.132), there is much to be said for such weak-kneed pragmatism.

Placing more emphasis on heuristics should not be thought of as a low-brow rejection of philosophy in favor of 'mere' practicality. Heuristics has an honored place in philosophy of science. As Hands (1992, p.21) pointed out: 'Popper's goal was the more mundane task of characterizing a set of rules (a method) which would allow us to learn from experience.' Similarly, Lakatos referred to a heuristic when he insisted that a scientific research program must explain previously unknown facts.

None of this means that all methodologists should turn to the kind of applied work I am advocating; we need both applied and 'theoretical' methodologists. Nor does it mean that methodologists should ignore current developments in philosophy of science. That would be like saying that mathematical economists should ignore developments in mathematics. But just as good mathematical economics is not merely good mathematics, but also something that economists can use, so good economic methodology that talks to economists, rather than interpreting economics to philosophers, should say things that economists can use. In acting as an importer of philosophical insights the methodologist, like any other importer, must pay due regard to what the customers can use. This does not mean that she can only import those goods the customer is already using – the customer's tastes can sometimes be changed – but, ultimately, the goods must meet some customer's wishes.

Note
1.   Roy Weintraub (1989) has also argued that methodologists who seek to impose rules that come from outside of economics are ineffective. But, as Vivienne Brown (1994) points out, his own examples contradict this conclusion.

3 Positivism and economics

In the previous chapter I argued that a methodology may be inadequate as a philosophical doctrine, and yet provide economists with a useful rule of thumb. In this chapter I demonstrate this with the example of positivism.[1]

Criticisms of positivism

As a philosophy of science, positivism is subject to two major criticisms. The first points out technical problems regarding its logical coherence. For example, consider what to treat as confirming evidence. Positivists tell us that we should increase our confidence in a hypothesis whenever it is tested and not refuted by the test. But there is a problem. Suppose our hypothesis is that all ravens are black. Then the existence of anything, such as a red pencil, that is not black and not a raven is consistent with the hypothesis, and with the hypothesis not having been rejected by this test it gains some confirmation. This is surely not acceptable. By 1977, Suppe (1977, p.632) could write that 'virtually all of the positivistic program for philosophy of science has been repudiated by contemporary philosophy of science'.

But various problems may invalidate positivism for the philosopher without reducing its practical usefulness for the scientist, who at least with respect to epistemology uses more relaxed criteria than a philosopher does. In practice we know intuitively that sighting an additional black raven does help to confirm the hypothesis that all ravens are black, while seeing a red pencil does not, even though we cannot formulate our reasoning rigorously. Indeed, a common reason why a journal rejects a paper is just that: the referee points out that the regression results that the author offers as confirming evidence can also be explained just as plausibly by something else.

As a more extreme example of what is relevant for a philosopher's evaluation of positivism and the usefulness of positivism to a practicing economist, consider the source of our knowledge of the external world. A fundamental tenet of positivism is that all such knowledge is not intuitive, but originates in our experience of the external world, that is ultimately in the sensation that we feel. If that position were decisively refuted, positivism as a philosophical doctrine would come crashing down. But it would not make positivism any less useful as a guide to economists.

The second criticism of positivism is that it is a bad description of what the successful sciences actually do, so that it does not provide any help to other fields that wish to emulate the successful sciences. Outstanding scientific successes were achieved when some scientists, for example Galileo, broke the positivistic rules. Hence, say some critics of positivism, these rules should be discarded, and no other rules should be put in their place – practicing scientists know better than philosophers or methodologists what they should do.

This argument is pertinent for economics. Although many practicing economists claim to follow the positivistic dictum of formulating their hypotheses in refutable terms, and then testing them against the data, their actual practice is not in accordance with positivism because they employ soft rules for testing that protect their hypotheses from disconfirmation. Data mining is an obvious example, and so is the prevalent misuse of significance tests (see Mayer, 1980, 1992, ch.10; McCloskey, 1985). Much econometric testing is what Mark Blaug (1992, p.241) has called 'playing tennis with the net down'. Economists treat positivism as a Sunday religion. Are they right in doing so?

The critics of positivism are correct in claiming that flouting the rules of evidence laid down by positivists has *sometimes* advanced science (see Kuhn, 1970; Feyerabend, 1975). Hence, if positivism is interpreted as stating: 'only by obeying the following rules can scientific progress be achieved', then Kuhn and Feyerabend have invalidated it. But their falsification of this hard version of positivism does not invalidate a softer, probabilistic version, that merely states: 'In most cases obeying the following rules will foster scientific progress.' To negate such a version the critics of positivism would have to show that in a representative sample of cases science progressed faster when the positivistic rules were ignored than when they were obeyed. But they have not even tried to do that. They just show that disreputable methods sometimes help to achieve great paradigmic breakthroughs, but that does not mean that they are helpful in normal scientific work, or even that in paradigm shifts and proposed paradigm shifts these methods are *on balance* helpful.

But does not the very fact that economists often disregard the positivistic rules in their day-to-day work tell us that these rules *should* be disregarded? Doesn't the trained intuition of those who dirty their hands with the actual work put them in a better position than some philosopher or economic methodologist far removed from the grime and dirt of real work, to judge how the work should be done? This stance is the standard justification that economists give for not paying attention to methodology.

But if anyone has a duty to question the attitude of trusting practitioners to do what is right, it is economists. Economics teaches us to focus on the question whether the self-interest of producers coincides with the public interest, or whether the producers have merely convinced themselves that it does (see Klein, 1994). This question is particularly salient when dealing with a field like economics. Academic economists claim to produce knowledge that society wants, but actually are each others' main customers. Producers of knowledge, like producers of other things, are likely to have biased ideas of what is good for society, and to overvalue technical sophistication and the conquest of difficult technical problems. In addition, there are practices that enhance the reputation of economics as a profession. These are likely to be rewarded in the editorial offices of journals, and therefore likely to be followed by researchers. (See Mayer, 1993b, ch.2.) Moreover, anyone who claims that what practicing economists actually do, not what they say, must be the right way to do economics, ignores one of the great teachings of economics: only agents themselves act, so we must look at the incentives faced by the individual agent. Producers of economic research have an incentive to seem like scientists by preaching high standards, while themselves putting shoddy intellectual goods on the market. Thus, at least in this case, what is preached may be a better guide to what should be done than is what is actually done.

More generally, this view is much more tenable for a highly successful science, such as physics, than it is for economics. Perhaps the achievements of physics show that physicists can be trusted to make the right decisions without much guidance from philosophers and methodologists. It is much harder to make this argument for economics. To be sure, economics has its successes. But these are hardly so great that one can say that the methodology that economists follow is necessarily the best one.

McCloskey's critique of positivism

So much for generalities. Turning to specifics it is convenient to look at McCloskey's (1985, pp.7–8) critique of what he calls 'modernism' that he seems to identify with an extreme version of positivism. He lists Ten Commandments of modernism and then proceeds to criticize them. Let us see, not whether these commandments express eternal philosophic truths (they do not), but whether they nudge economics in the right direction.[2]

Although defending these Ten Commandments as useful heuristics, I will not defend their dogmatic application. McCloskey is absolutely right in castigating the narrow-minded extremism with which many economists apply these Commandments. Because it combats such extremism McCloskey's attack on positivism (though itself extreme) has done much good. It was, I believe, Lord Russell who remarked that a half-truth is a good enough stick to beat a dogma with. But an unthinking narrow-mindedness is no more an inherent part of positivism than it is of any other methodological doctrine. Any dominant paradigm is likely to succumb to that disease.

The first Commandment McCloskey lists states that one should treat prediction and control as the purposes of science. Someone who rejects this would presumably want science to be more concerned with explanation and with the development of intellectually satisfying constructs. Fritz Machlup (1978, p.145) expressed this wish for explanation as distinct from mere prediction well when he wrote that an explanation should give one a feeling of 'Ahaness' – the satisfaction of understanding why it is so. But one should be careful about attributing to positivists a narrow philistine wish for mere forecasts, and 'never mind the why'. A major product of positivism is the covering law model. According to this model, only by showing that the case to be explained is an instance of a general law can one provide a general explanation. Positivists do not use the term 'prediction' to mean mere forecasting.[3]

The question is then whether economists should be told to treat such a broad concept of prediction and control as the goal of economics. Suppose, purely for the sake of the argument, that the extreme positivists are wrong, and that an adequate scientific explanation demands much more. Even then, telling economists to focus on prediction and control, while wrong in principle, is useful because it focuses attention more on practical issues and less on formal theory. Not that formal theory is useless. Both it and more empirically orientated economics make valuable contributions. The issue is which is more valuable at the margin. Elsewhere (Mayer, 1993b) I have argued at length that we overemphasize formal theory. Obviously this involves a value judgement, but that is no reason to shy away from the question of what the aims of economics should be. We must either let the public make the underlying value judgement or make it ourselves. In the former case the answer is clear. Surely most voters would prefer to have their taxes spent on subsidizing research that improves their living standard than in research that builds elegant models with little practical application. And the tenor of a report of the American Economic Association's Commission on Graduate Education (Krueger *et al.*, 1991) suggests that professional economists, too, think that we overemphasize formalist economics.

The second Commandment is that only a theory's observable implications matter.[4] This may, or may not, be bad philosophy when intended as a rule for all fields. But for economics it is appropriate, if the word 'only' is replaced by 'mainly'. If one defines the task of economics as explaining or predicting certain characteristics of the economy, how else can one determine the success of the theory, except by looking at its observable implications? To answer that one can instead look at the validity of its assumption is not an adequate response because, as discussed in Chapter 7, those assumptions whose validity determines the validity of the theory can also be treated as the implications of that theory.

To evaluate this Commandment pragmatically one should ask, not whether it embodies an eternal truth, but whether adherance to it improves economic research; in other words, whether it is better or worse than the commandment that would otherwise rule in its place. That alternative commandment is not hard to find. It is to place an even greater emphasis than prevails now on formalism and on the elegance and sophistication by which a model develops the implications of rational utility maximization, rather than by how well it explains and predicts observed behavior. I suspect that McCloskey would agree that such a shift would be not progress, but retrogression.

The third Commandment that McCloskey lists is: rely on objective reproducible experiments, and eschew questionnaires because respondents might lie. This raises several distinct issues. First, if the terms 'objective' and 'reproducible' are meant to denote evidence that can be demonstrated to others, as distinct from, say, the 'evidence' of one's feelings, then surely such interpersonal evidence is more useful than evidence that others cannot see. Paul Feyerabend (1975), a leading anti-positivist, has made the existence of an 'invisible college' that agrees on many points of procedure the touchstone for science. Such a college cannot exist unless its members can exhibit their evidence to each other. To be sure, not all knowledge can be objective and reproducible, but such knowledge is to be preferred, particularly in a field like economics, where it is all too easy to let one's personal biases and interests masquerade an expert judgements.

Another part of the Commandment, that one should rely primarily on experimental evidence, surely does not in the literal sense apply to economics, with its limited role for experiments. Perhaps it should be interpreted as saying that only econometric evidence and the evidence provided by experimental economists, such as Vernon Smith, is acceptable, while evidence from surveys and from the natural experiments that history throws up from time to time is not. But if the Commandment is interpreted in such a restricted way it is not part of positivism. Positivism does not say that econometric evidence is preferable to the evidence from the natural experiments or from surveys. One might therefore interpret the third Commandment much more loosely, as merely saying that one should rely on empirical evidence. Then it is indeed a component of positivism, but one that is hard to criticize if one views economics as an empirical science and not as a formalist science, akin to geometry and logic.

The last component of the third Commandment is that one should eschew questionnaire surveys. I agree with McCloskey that the widespread scorn that economists show for surveys is unwarranted.[5] It appears to be based on three reasons, none of them good. One is that in the 1940s and 1950s economists who studied decision making by firms frequently used questionnaires that were very poorly designed, thus giving questionnaire surveys a bad reputation. Sociologists have developed elaborate and subtle techniques for constructing reliable questionnaires, but many economists seem unaware of this. The second is that these surveys came up with results that contradicted economic theory, and purveyors of bad news are seldom applauded. Third, surveys are a tool of sociologists and certain other social scientists. We disdain to employ the tools of such 'lesser' people, particularly when these tools threaten to compete successfully with our own favorite tool, econometrics.

These reasons seem sufficient to account for the low status of survey research in economics, and there is no need to blame it on positivism – particularly since it is not part of positivism. To assert that surveys are inconsistent with the positivist's injunction to avoid subjective evidence is to confuse two meanings of the word 'subjective'. The subjectivism that positivists reject is a subjectivism that claims to derive knowledge of the external world from inside one's own head. Survey evidence about what *other* people think is no more 'subjective' in that sense than is evidence from time series regressions.

The fourth Commandment that McCloskey cites is that a theory should be considered falsified only if its experimental implications are falsified. If 'experimental' is interpreted broadly enough to denote empirical evidence in general, then this is an important component of positivism, but one that plays only a limited role in economics. We reject many, probably too many, hypotheses, not because the data compel us to, but because these hypotheses are inconsistent with rational profit-maximizing behavior. We do, however, follow this fourth Commandment when we say that the realism of a theory's assumptions is irrelevant as long as its implications are confirmed. As discussed in Chapter 7, when sufficiently nuanced this is a reasonable procedure. In general, would economics be better off if we placed less emphasis on validation by empirical testing, and more emphasis on validation by elegance?

The fifth Commandment is to treasure objectivity and to reject subjective sources of knowledge, such as introspection. As a general maxim this commandment may perhaps rest on weak foundations. But would we produce better economics if we allowed our personal preferences and biases to play a larger role in our work?

The sixth Commandment, to emphasize measurement and to be skeptical of anything that cannot be expressed in numbers, is hard to evaluate. On the one hand, it is harmful because the insistence on measurement, even when sufficiently reliable measurement is not feasible, makes for pseudo-science. It tempts us to lay claim to knowledge and to a degree of certitude that we do not possess. It also leads to a rejection of non-quantifiable knowledge, and that impoverishes economics. It esteems the precisely wrong over the vaguely right. But on the other hand, while the insistence on measurement has thus done much harm to economics, it has also done much good by helping to eliminate theories that lack empirical support, and by directing economists' attention to empirical issues. It is therefore not at all clear whether an admittedly often naive and at times dogmatic insistence on measurement has, on the whole, done more harm than good to economics.

The seventh Commandment is to separate the context of discovery from the context of verification, and to accept that, while 'introspection, metaphysical belief, aesthetics and the like' (McCloskey, 1985, p.8) may well play a role in the context of discovery, these factors are irrelevant to determining the truth of a proposition. McCloskey is right in saying that the rejection of metaphysics, introspection and aesthetics in the context of verification, is naive.[6] But has it done much harm to economics? That is hard to say. If we were less afraid of introspection, then perhaps we would be less rigid in our adherence to the assumption of rational utility maximizing, and accept that our utility function contains more than just our own income. The refusal to explicitly discuss metaphysical considerations has also done damage by concealing a major reason why economists disagree on policy, and thereby inhibiting effective debate (see Mayer, 1994b). But the Commandment's charge to de-emphasize aesthetics is helpful in countering the temptation to chase after the bitch–goddess of rigour, simplicity and elegance.[7]

The eighth Commandment, that methodology should distinguish between scientific and non-scientific statements, and therefore between normative and positive statements, is better seen as a commandment of a certain outdated branch of positivism, logical positivism, than of positivism as a whole.[8] By now few, if any, positivist philosophers maintain that one can draw a sharp line of demarcation between science and non-science. Nor would they draw a sharp line of demarcation between positive and normative statements (cf. Rudner, 1953). Should positivism be blamed because economists hold to a position that sophisticated positivists dropped long ago? Perhaps one should blame the professional self-interest of economists that induces them to claim scientific status with a vehemence and dogmatism that people sometimes show when in their hearts they know that their argument is weak.

That some (most?) economists believe that one can clearly distinguish scientific from non-scientific statements does considerable harm when combined with the belief that we should discuss only 'scientific' questions. Pretending that non-scientific issues are just not there, that it is all a matter of disagreement on the scientific evidence, causes confusion and bewilderment. For example, some economists value equity relatively more, and economic growth relatively less, than do other economists. That leads them to take different positions on policy. But when they come to debate these they tend to focus on points where they disagree about technical economics, rather than about their value judgements. Such failure to trace disagreements to their non-economic roots make an economist wonder how her colleagues can possibly reject the impeccable logic and compelling empirical evidence that she provides for her conclusion, while the public is puzzled by the extent of disagreement among economists. Moreover, claiming a distinction between one's own 'scientific' economics and certain other economists' 'unscientific' economics has become a cheap debating point.

One place in economics where this Commandment plays an explicit role is in interpersonal comparisons of utility. It is certainly legitimate to make statements like 'A dollar of income to A has greater utility than a dollar of income to B' (see Robbins, 1981). But, following Robbins, such statements are often described as 'unscientific'. Given the problematic of delineating what is scientific one might question how appropriate that is. But in any case, a commandment to treat subjective statements as unscientific does no harm as long as we remember that there are some unscientific statements which may deserve just as much or more credence than scientific statements. Don't we all believe more firmly in the non-scientific statement 'It is wrong to boil babies alive and eat them' than in the scientific statement 'The speed of light is 186000 miles a second'? Fortunately, although economists may disparage interpersonal comparisons of utility as unscientific when telling beginning students that economics is a *science*, they are perfectly willing to make such comparisons at other times, such as when engaged in benefit/cost analysis. So not much harm is done.

The ninth Commandment, that scientific explanations *must* bring the phenomenon to be explained under a covering law, is hard to accept – as long as it contains the word 'must'. But, surely, we should do so whenever that can be done without some substantial cost. It satisfies our wish for insight and minimizes the number of separate explanations we must keep in mind. The Commandment creates a problem only when it is interpreted dogmatically and results in an insistence that all economic phenomena can be explained by a specific covering law, such as rational utility maximization or the class struggle.

The final Commandment that McCloskey cites is that, having in accordance with the eighth Commandment distinguished between scientific and non-scientific statements, economists, in their role as scientists, should say nothing about values. This may, or may not be poor philosophy, but it is good advice for economists in one respect. We sell our work, not on the argument that we are more intelligent than others, but on the argument that we have studied the positive aspects of economics in more detail than others have. We can sell a more honest product, and a product the buyer prefers, if we avoid a tie-in sale with value judgements, where we have no great advantage over other producers, such as philosophers and sociologists. This does not mean that we should dismiss the study of values as ideological chit-chat. Values are not 'mere' tastes unworthy of much thought or discussion (see Hausman and McPherson, 1993). And being an economist does not disqualify one from participating in debates about values. Indeed, thinking about values might bring out some hidden value judgements that we make.

There is a down-to-earth reason for separating, to the limited extent that we can do so, value judgements from positive judgements. One can treat value judgements as assumptions that some of one's readers will not share. Hence, it is efficient to present the major part of one's paper, the positive analysis, in such a way that it can be detached from the value judgements, and is therefore interesting even to those who do not share one's assumption about values. When looked at in this practical way, rather than as a fundamental principle of 'scientific method', drawing an admittedly imperfect distinction between positive and normative statements is less open to criticism.

Thus many of the positivist Commandments that McCloskey lists provide useful guidelines for practicing economists. And in several cases those components of the Commandments that are harmful are not part of positivism per se, but only of an extreme version of positivism. Hence, from a pragmatic point of view, economists can disregard that, as McCloskey (1985, p.8) points out: 'No more than a few philosophers now believe as many as half of these commandments. A substantial, respectable, and growing minority believes none of them.'

None of the justifications for moderate positivism given in this chapter is meant to disparage the great value of McCloskey's criticism of the mindless and dogmatic way modernist and positivist methodology is often practiced in economics, of what he calls '3 × 5 card' methodology. His criticism hits home when its target is mindlessness and dogmatism, but not when it is positivism per se.

Bad is better than worse

In an ideal world there would exist a definitive methodology of science that economists could use as a guide. It would be both unproblematic as philosophy and helpful as a book of rules for practicing scientists. At present such a methodology does not exist. But life and work must go on, and we have to use something. So it is not unreasonable to use positivism as a methodological guide, because it works relatively well in day-to-day situations, even though philosophers have found fault with it.[9] Hutchison's (1992) powerful defense of positivism on practical grounds is not damaged by the problematic nature of positivism as philosophy.

Consider what would happen if economists were to abandon their crude version of positivism. Since economists tend to interpret positivism mainly as an injunction to focus on empirical testing, they would drift further toward a deductivism that is primarily concerned with deriving theorems whose implications are not tested empirically from axioms whose relation to reality is not treated as important. Such a change would hardly enhance the usefulness of economics. Nor, judging by the attitude frequently shown by economists with such a deductivist orientation, would it bring us closer to McCloskey's goal of letting a thousand flowers bloom. It is easy to share McCloskey's antipathy for the hidebound and autocratic character of the *ancien régime* of positivism. But if this monarch is deposed he is likely to be succeeded, not by a Jeffersonian democrat, but by a new classical Robespierre.

In a poem by Hilaire Belloc (1918) a little boy is taken to a zoo by his nurse. There he runs away from her, climbs into the lion cage and is promptly eaten by a lion. The last line of the poem is 'And always keep a-hold of nurse, for fear of finding something worse.' On that basis one can readily defend positivism.

Notes

1. I am using the term 'positivism' broadly enough to include falsificationism. To most practicing economists positivism probably *is* falsificationism. Clive Beed (1991) is puzzled that Mark Blaug, after presenting a strong case against positivism, urges economists to strive harder to meet the positivistic canon. The explanation may be that Blaug thinks that positivism provides a good rule of thumb, despite its many problems as philosophy.
2. Such a focus on practicality is not unknown to the philosophy of science. Thus, as Hands (1992) points out, Popper did not present falsificationism as an epistemological doctrine, but as a way of allowing us to learn from experience.
3. Many economists probably attribute the emphasis on the predictive success of a theory to Friedman. But as Hammond (1990) has shown, Friedman does not draw a sharp distinction between predicting and explaining. Nor does he treat McCloskey's Commandments as a valid description of his own position.
4. This statement is not correct in a literal sense. Everyone agrees that simplicity and generality matter too. I assume that McCloskey means with 'only' predominantly.
5. Fortunately, that attitude seems to be changing. With Alan Blinder at Princeton and Robert Shiller at Yale sending out surveys, can John Jones at State University be far behind?
6. Introspection does play a large, though hidden, role in our verifications, by ruling out certain alternative hypotheses to the ones we do test. All scientific statements rest on a metaphysical basis; the very claim that truth exists is metaphysical. Our preference for simplicity and generality is partly aesthetic. For the role that aesthetics plays in the theories of physics, see Ferris (1988).
7. As Hausman (1992a, p.89) points out, the leading advocates of Popperian ideas in economics 'have simply argued for the importance of criticism and empirical testing. In doing so, they have certainly not done the profession any harm. Indeed, in their emphasis on the importance of testing in science, they may have done some significant good.'
8. I am using the term 'positive' in its usual meaning in economics, as the opposite of 'normative', not as something related to positivist doctrine.
9. Perhaps critical rationalism might provide an alternative if it were developed further to make it more specific.

4 How much do microfoundations matter?

In the new classical assault on traditional macroeconomics methodological considerations played a large role (see Mayer, 1993b, chs 7 and 8). They did so in a strange way. The new classicals made a series of methodological claims, more or less disguised as claims about how the economy works, and their opponents seemed reluctant to join battle on the methodological level. I will illustrate this with the debate about microfoundations.

When new classical economists announced with great vehemence that traditional macro theory is invalid because its supply function is inconsistent with any acceptable microfoundations (a charge that could also be levelled at monetarism), Keynesians responded by developing their own microeconomics, that is 'new Keynesian theory'. That Keynesians chose to fight the battle on substantive instead of on methodological grounds may be due to the low tolerance that economists have for methodological arguments. Perhaps it was fortunate because the search for Keynesian microfoundations generated important insights. But some of these insights are problematic (see Romer, 1993) and they were acquired at the cost of much effort that might perhaps have been more productively employed elsewhere.

It is surprising that Keynesians conceded the methodological issue with almost no argument, though Alan Blinder (1987a) and Robert Solow (1986) did point out in passing that other sciences get along without the reductionism that the new classicals insist on. Only in countering the Lucas critique did traditional Keynesians take a methodological position (one that is similar to the position I take here) but they did this without setting it in its appropriate context. New classical economists write as though the case for reductionism is self-evident, without referring to the ongoing discussion about reductionism in philosophy and in many sciences. This is problematic since, as Caldwell (1992) points out, in the physical sciences most of the notable efforts at reduction have failed. In particular, one might question the feasibility of reduction in economics (see Woo, 1990). A philosopher of science, Alan Nelson (1992, p.114), after calling reduction 'one of the most important theoretical activities in science', expressed doubt that at present it is feasible in economics, because microeconomics lacks sufficient empirical confirmation on the level of individual behavior. Moreover, not all aggregate concepts need to have a direct micro counterpart. Maarten Janssen (1993, p.15) gives the example of the natural rate of unemployment, which is meaningful at the macro level, though one cannot say that a particular person is naturally unemployed.

Given the popularity of Friedman's (1953) essay on methodology, with its strong instrumentalist bent, Keynesians might therefore have challenged the new classicals' insistence on reductionism. After all, reduction is only one of several ways of explaining a phenomenon (see Janssen, 1993, p.27). This is not to deny that the reduction of macroeconomics to microeconomics, if it could be done successfully, would provide important practical benefits (discussed below), along with enhanced elegance. But there is a distinction between reduction being desirable and it being both feasible and necessary.

Perhaps the reason the new classicals succeeded in imposing their reductionist standpoint on the profession is a belief that held sway for a long time, and that, despite the influence of Friedman's and Popper's positivistic methodologies, still seems to have much influence. This is that what validates economics is its derivation from self-evident propositions (rational behavior, utility maximization and the law of decreasing returns). If this is so, any hypotheses that are not derived from this microeconomic base lack justification. But that is no longer a tenable position (see Chapter 11).

Indeed one might argue that the insistence on reducing macroeconomics to microeconomics is inappropriate because microeconomics itself lacks adequate foundations. Two basic postulates of microeconomics, that agents are fully rational and entirely self-interested, surely cannot be derived from the more basic science of psychology, but are instrumentalist hypotheses (see Woo, 1990). With microeconomics thus not being reducible to the more basic science of psychology, why should macroeconomics be reducible to microeconomics? To respond that reductionism should rule within each particular science, but not necessarily between sciences, is hardly convincing, both because it is inconsistent with the standard reductionist view and because the boundaries of various sciences are essentially arbitrary.

This chapter therefore discusses whether Keynesians could legitimately have responded to new classical economists by arguing that they do not need additional microfoundations. That requires a brief consideration of what economic analysis is intended to accomplish.

Formalist economics and empirical-science economics
To decide whether macroeconomics needs microfoundations one first has to ask what macroeconomics is trying to accomplish. One possible answer, the answer of those whom I shall call 'formalists', is that economic theory is a formal science that models itself on mathematics and logic. In its pure form it is an analytic discipline that deduces the implications of three postulates, rational profit maximization, decreasing marginal utility and decreasing returns (Hausman, 1992b). While these postulates are intended to reflect reality as determined by introspection or casual empiricism, they are chosen, so to speak, in the antecham-

ber of economics, and economics proper then deduces their implications. These implications may be 'tested' by confronting them with empirical data, but such tests are not all that critical. Non-Euclidean geometry is valid even in a Euclidean world. Instead of goodness of fit to generally noisy data, formalists therefore stress the mathematical criteria of rigour, generality, parsimony and elegance.

They consider a theory that does well on these four criteria preferable to one that gives a better fit to the data, but is less closely related to the basic postulates of economics. In particular, ad hocery is to be avoided, not primarily for the reasons that concerned Popper,[1] but more for its sin against parsimony. Problems for research are chosen in good part for internal reasons, such as the technical 'sweetness' of the feasible solutions, rather than for their salience in explaining observed behavior or for their relevance to policy. A good example of this approach is the new classical response to the argument that long-term wage contracts inhibit wage and price flexibility. They claim that if long-term contracts interfered with the appropriate adjustment of wages these contracts would be indexed. They are not concerned that very few contracts are anywhere near fully indexed, and that it is hard to see how unindexed or only partially indexed contracts would *not* interfere with wage flexibility.[2] The world of formalist economics need not correspond to the observable world.

The alternative answer to the question of what economics is trying to accomplish takes as its model, not mathematics and logic, but the empirical sciences, fields that may employ elaborate analytic machinery, but evaluate hypotheses primarily by their fit to observations. They, too, favor statements that are rigorous, general, elegant and parsimonious, but these criteria do not dominate. I will call this approach 'empirical-science economics', for which the postulate of rational utility maximization is an extremely useful working hypotheses, but not an axiom. If necessary it can be relaxed. This is not just so in papers that appear in institutionalist journals, but can occur even in the *American Economic Review* (see Ausubel, 1991). It treats economic theory, not as an imposing structure hewn from the white marble of indubitable truth, but as a convenient tool. Unlike the formalists, empirical-science economists are willing to abandon parts of the theory if that is necessary to get the prediction to agree with the data.

The distinction between formalist and empirical-science economics is not the distinction between theory and empirical work. Empirical-science economics also contains a heavy element of theory. The difference is in the primary goals set for the theory: on the one hand to show the implications of certain axioms, and on the other to explain a set of observations. To be sure, formalists also want their theories to fit the data, and empirical-science economists do want their theories to be rigorous, general, parsimonious and elegant, but they differ in the relative importance they ascribe to these goals.

The two positions just described are polar positions; most economists are somewhere in-between. Nonetheless, a considerable part of the disagreement among economists can be understood as a debate between those stressing formalist criteria and those stressing empirical-science criteria (Mayer, 1993b, chs 7 and 8). In particular, the contrast between the two sets of criteria is central to the debate about the need for microfoundations.

Formalist economics and microfoundations
The formalist research program is to deduce as much as possible from the basic postulates of rational utility maximizing. It is not clear what role, if any, this leaves for macroeconomics. To the extent that the formalist program succeeds, macroeconomics can be eliminated, since all its valid propositions can be deduced from microeconomics. If macroeconomics is kept at all, it serves merely as a kind of shorthand, a quick way of expressing certain truths deduced by microeconomics. For that role it clearly needs microfoundations. Any macroeconomic statement not translatable into microeconomics has no more validity than an alleged theorem that lacks a proof. No wonder that formalists may find it hard to see how anyone can deny the need for microfoundations.

Can one respond that, as discussed above, microeconomics, just as much as traditional Keynesian theory, itself lacks foundations? No, not within the framework of formalist economics. That is an intellectual discipline within its own right, and can start from any set of propositions that its practitioners want to take as their axioms.

Looking at the demand for microfoundations as a manifestation of formalism helps to explain a peculiarity of this demand. Not just any grounding in some theory or other of the household and the firm will do. Only a grounding in the theory of competitive markets unhindered by any difficulties in trading is acceptable. The reason for insisting on such a simplistic version of microeconomics is surely not a desire for a theory that is easy to learn. Instead, this insistence is due, in part, to the wish for tractability and simplicity. The perfect markets paradigm readily yields a unique solution, while the solution for the imperfect markets paradigm often depends upon the details of the special assumptions made about information and so on. Furthermore, in game-theoretic models of oligopolistic markets multiple solutions may emerge. The reliance on simple competitive markets is also related to the insistence that all mutually profitable trades are carried out, that there are no $5 bills lying on the pavement. That type of microeconomics has the simplest and most direct links to the cherished postulate of rational, utility-maximizing behavior, and avoids such institutional complexities as unenforceable contracts and transactions cost. Moreover, a pavement picked clean of $5 bills has great intuitive appeal to economists, and hence serves as an effective sound-bite.[3]

But, despite its intuitive appeal, the proposition that all feasible trades are carried out is problematic. Is it possible for firms to collude? If so, then competitive theory must be jettisoned. But if collusion is not considered feasible, what else is not feasible? Unless this question is answered, the proposition that all feasible trades are carried out is vacuous and consistent with wage and price stickiness. Thus, while it is understandable that formalists wish to reduce macroeconomics to a clean 'microeconomics' in which all mutually profitable trades take place, macroeconomists do not have to satisfy that wish, even within the context of formalist economics.

The need for microfoundations in empirical-science economics

For empirical-science economics it is not absolutely necessary that macroeconomics have a solid microeconomic foundation. If macroeconomics explains and predicts well, it may be useful even without solid foundations in micro theory, just as microeconomics is useful despite its lack of foundations in psychology. All the same, microeconomic foundations, while not strictly necessary, are desirable. Not only would firm microfoundations help with respect to the Lucas critique, but they would also enhance the predictive success of economics in general, since it seems plausible that the underlying micro relationships are stabler than the observed macro regularities (cf. Janssen, 1993, p.59). Moreover, they can prevent careless errors and deficient analysis.[4]

The theory of the consumption function provides a persuasive example of the way inadequate attention to microfoundations can generate such deficient analysis. Keynes did not provide an adequate microeconomic foundation for his consumption function, though the required micro theory was available (Fisher, 1930). Instead, he relied on nothing more than the following:

> The fundamental psychological law, upon which we are entitled to depend with great confidence both *a priori* from our knowledge of human nature and from the detailed facts of experience, is that men are disposed, as a rule and on the average, to increase their consumption as their income increases, but not by as much as the increase in their income. (Keynes, 1936, p.96)

Had Keynes used instead of this casual empiricism Irving Fisher's (1930) microeconomic theory of saving and consumption, forecasts of postwar unemployment in the United States would not have been so far off the mark. Moreover, much debate about the consumption function would have been avoided. It was not until the 1950s that Modigliani and Brumberg (1955) and Friedman (1957) published widely accepted consumption functions with solid microfoundations, in Friedman's case by explicitly going back to Fisher. The discovery of at least the basic idea of the life cycle hypothesis could have occurred in 1936, had Keynes paid some attention to the microfoundations of his consumption function.

Similarly, had economists shown more concern about its loose microeconomic basis, the early version of the Phillips curve, with its flawed assumption that money wages and not real wages matter, would not have been allowed to persist until 1968. Phillips himself showed awareness of the money-wage/real-wage problem, but the subsequent literature ignored it (see Leeson, 1994, p.616n).

In general, it is useful to see if a macroeconomic proposition either (1) has a sound microfoundation, (2) cannot be related to any microeconomic proposition, or (3) is inconsistent with received micro theory. In the second case (unrelatedness) we might accept the macroeconomic proposition simply as an observed regularity. This entails some risk because previously observed regularities that lack a theoretical basis may suddenly break down, particularly when they are used as policy guides. Goodhart's law (after Charles Goodhart) states that, as soon as any observed regularity is used as a basis for policy, it ceases to hold. The behavior of M-1 velocity in the 1980s is a good example. All the same, in principle, observed but unexplained regularities do not lack scientific status.

How about the third case where an observed macroeconomic relation does contradict microeconomic theory? For example, a macroeconomic model might require the assumption of rapid wage and price flexibility, despite microeconomic evidence that wages and prices are sticky. The principle of methodological individualism may seem to imply that such a model must be abandoned. That is the appropriate response in many cases, but not in all. Aggregates are not always just summations of their individual components, even when the set of lower-level components encompasses 'all there is'. Aggregation problems can be pervasive and serious, and give rise to phenomena such as the Keynesian 'paradox of saving' (see Kirman, 1992; Janssen, 1993). Lower-level theories may omit certain items that are unimportant at that level, but are important at a higher level of aggregation. Assumptions, such as constant relative prices, may be inappropriate at the micro level, where resource allocation is the central problem, and yet be appropriate at the macro level. Reductionism is not always appropriate (see Alan Garfinkel, 1981, ch. 2).

There is nothing inherently 'unscientific' about using conflicting theories at different levels of analysis. For a long time physicists treated light as a wave when dealing with one set of problems, and as particles when dealing with other problems. Not until the development of quantum theory in the 1920s, when physics was much further along than empirical-science economics is now, did they unify their treatment of light. The extent to which it is appropriate to use contradictory theories at different levels is related to the debate about instrumentalism. If the instrumentalists are right that theories are nothing but 'inference tickets', then it is perfectly legitimate to maintain contradictory theories.

All the same, for the reasons discussed above, a contradiction between macroeconomics and microeconomics sends a danger signal. The Lucas critique makes that clear.

The Lucas critique

Within the context of formalist economics the Lucas critique is devastating: using traditional macroeconomics to predict the effects of policies involves a logical contradiction. But for empirical-science economics there is a possible solution. As traditional macroeconomists often point out, most policy changes might have only second-order effects on behavioral parameters. The empirical evidence here is both skimpy and mixed. Nevertheless, it suggests that the Lucas critique is less relevant for labor markets than for financial markets, though even for labor markets there is some evidence of a 'Lucas effect' (see Alogoskoufis and Smith, 1991).

So what should economists do when asked for macroeconomic policy advice? One possibility is to say: 'I don't know.' When Lucas was asked what he would do if he were chairman of the Council of Economic Advisers he replied: 'I would resign' (Klamer, 1984, p.54). For economists to retreat to their studies in this way, and not emerge until they obtain reliable deep parameters might be an acceptable solution if these deep parameters could be estimated, say within 10 or even 20 years. But this seems unlikely. Econometric studies not only suffer from noisy data, but often also lack robustness with respect to minor variations in the specification of the model or changes in the sample period. Moreover, giving policy advice frequently requires estimating not just one relationship but several, and errors in any one of the estimates may be fatal. In addition, there is the problem of standard errors. The standard error of a conclusion based on the estimation of several parameters is a combination of the standard errors of all of these parameters, and that might easily produce a range around the point estimate that is too broad for useful policy advice. This is most evident in a case where the coefficients derived from one equation are then used as point estimates in another equation. Beyond these econometric problems there is also a conceptual problem. As Henry Aaron (1994) points out, if tastes (or one might add, the household production function) are affected by current and past consumption, then microeconomic parameters are also subject to the Lucas critique.

A more practical alternative is to invest only some of our effort in digging for deep parameters, while most macroeconomists continue to give policy advice. They should take the Lucas critique into account, both by warning policymakers about the fallibility of their advice, and by making some rough, common-sense allowance for policy-induced changes in parameters.

Consider, for instance, a paradigmatic case for the Lucas critique, estimating the effect of a temporary tax cut on consumption in an economy in which there had never been such a tax cut. One might make a rough estimate of capital rationing and of irrational behavior, as well as of the proportion of the population that will not believe the government and will think that the tax cut is permanent. The result obtained would only be a rough approximation. But it would not be all that much better if we somehow had estimates of deep parameters of the utility and production functions. We would still have to guess the extent to which the public believes the government, and that means that our answer to the policy-maker's question would still be only a crude approximation. Adding a number that we estimate as somewhere between two and three to another number estimated to five places of decimals does not yield an answer that is reliable to five places. Fortunately, when giving policy advice, precision, though desirable, is usually not necessary. The useful things we have to say are generally broad and vague. Hence, as empirical-science economics, macroeconomics can provide useful information even without knowing deep parameters.

Reduction to what?
If all the same we decide, as we usually should when that is feasible, to provide macroeconomics with microeconomic foundations, what microeconomics should we use? As discussed above, the new classicals have a simple answer: the neo-Walrasian paradigm. This answer follows naturally within the framework of formalist economics because this paradigm is so well developed and tractable. But in empirical-science economics just what microfoundations to use is a much more troubling question. To reduce macroeconomics to microeconomics requires that every valid conclusion of macroeconomics can also be derived from microeconomics (see Garfinkel, 1981, p.30). It is by no means obvious that this is so when microeconomics is interpreted as the neo-Walrasian paradigm and nothing else.

Moreover, as Willem Buiter (1989, pp.10–11) has remarked:

> It is ironic that at the very time that macroeconomic theory was abuzz with exciting new developments (the asymmetric information paradigm, principal agent theories, monopolistic competition, oligopoly and game theoretic approaches to rivalry between firms, etc.) the ... [new classicals] should have opted for a recycling of the conventional pre-Seventies competitive paradigm. ... Macroeconomic modelling should start from the self-evident and crucial facts of (1) incompleteness of markets, (2) non-competitive behavior in most of the markets that do exist and (3) essential heterogeneity among economic agents.

Similarly, Joseph Stiglitz (1992, p.40) calls it 'curious' that the 'perfect markets' model of microeconomics became popular in macroeconomics just when micro-economists started to abandon it because they realized the importance of factors such as imperfect information and the inadequacy of markets for risk.[5]

Moreover, as Janssen (1993) has recently made clear, individual utility max-imization generates rational expectations and the competitive equilibrium solution only under special conditions. With neo-Walrasian economics thus being only a special case of neoclassical economics, the obviously valid principle that 'only individuals act' does not imply that one has to base macroeconomics on neo-Walrasian foundations. To develop useful microfoundations for macro-economics we should study industrial-organization theory, not the Arrow–Debreu model. But once we abandon the Arrow–Debreu model in favor of industrial-organization theory, how can we obtain reliable foundations? Game theory tells us that many outcomes are possible. As Janssen (1993) shows, the Nash solution is just one of several possible solutions. Which of these solutions is the appropriate foundation for macroeconomics? Such issues negate the new classical criticism of the traditional aggregate supply function.

The aggregate supply function: wage stickiness revisited

Much of the microfoundations debate was motivated by the issue of wage and price stickiness, something that the new classicals treated as an unwarranted ad hoc assumption that is inconsistent with micro theory. They brushed aside with disdain Keynes's explanation that workers are concerned with relative wages and that there is no mechanism allowing for a coordinated economy-wide reduction in nominal wages that would keep relative wages constant.

How valid is the Keynesian story? As formalist economics it is unsatisfactory, both because formalists tend to treat the addition of relative income to the utility function as ad hoc, and because it does not allow some mutually beneficial trades to be carried out. But most Keynesians and monetarists are closer to the empirical-science position, and as empirical-science economics the Keynesian argument *may* well be sound; there is much evidence that households are concerned about their relative incomes (see Chapter 13). Coordination failure in nominal wage reductions seems highly plausible, so that the burden of proof is on anyone who seeks to deny such failure. Whether the relative-income effect for nominal wages is strong enough to bear the weight that Keynesian theory puts on it is an empirical problem that cannot be resolved by method-ological proclamations.[6]

A related problem is why unemployed workers do not bid down wages and replace workers who are unwilling to take nominal wage cuts. James Haley (1990, pp.143–4) suggests that workers implicitly agree not to underbid each other, or that firms may be concerned about their reputation in the labor market if they use an increase in the number of unemployed workers to force down wages. Insider–outsider theory suggests that workers may be unwilling to help train new, lower-paid recruits. Still another reason may be that the relative wage that concerns workers is not just their wage relative to other workers, but also their current wage relative to their previous wages. And then there is, of course, efficiency wage theory.

The alternative new classical explanation, that the seemingly involuntarily unemployed workers are not willing to work for lower wages, seems less plausible. Lucas's paradigmatic case of teachers who are 'unemployed' during the summer and therefore work harder during the school year does not seem applicable to workers who have been unemployed for more than a year.

The charge is sometimes made that the Keynesian theory of wage stickiness is 'sociological', because it introduces concerns about relative wages and factors such as an unwillingness of workers to underbid each other. But 'sociological' is not a synonym for reliance on 'irrational behavior'. Having one's relative wage in the utility function is neither irrational nor somehow unnatural (see Frank, 1985). It can be considered a taste as legitimate as any other taste. And so can a reluctance to underbid fellow workers. Since tastes are in large part socially determined, economics must either implicitly or explicitly take account of sociological factors. Keynesians could therefore have stayed with Keynes's original explanation of wage inflexibility, together with the simple notion that workers are reluctant to underbid each other, and would therefore not have had to develop new-Keynesian theory.

Moreover, wage rigidity is not required to obtain the Keynesian aggregate supply curve. Price rigidity can serve instead. Once one takes account of transactions costs and coordination problems, such price stickiness cannot be ruled out. Whether it is strong enough to bear the weight Keynesians may put on it is an empirical issue, and not something to be settled by reference to the implications of the Arrow–Debreu model.

Conclusion

If treated as a contribution to formalist economics, Keynesian economics is defective because of its ad hoc assumption of wage and price stickiness. But Keynesian economics is not intended to be formalist economics. It is empirical-science economics. For that type of economics what matters is whether the empirical evidence supports the Keynesian hypothesis of sticky wages or prices, and not whether it can be deduced from the narrow set of postulates used in formalist economics, a set that does not permit relative wages to be in the utility function. Similarly, the Lucas critique, while devastating in the context of formalist economics is, in the context of empirical-science economics, just one of the many sources of error in our estimates (see Sims, 1982).

Hence, Keynesians could have replied to the new classicals' charge of ad hocery and failure to conform to the heuristics of economics with a methodological defense instead of developing new Keynesian theory. They could have pointed out that new classical theory is just as, if not more, ad hoc than Keynesian theory since it is founded on a particular type of microeconomics that has little empirical support.

Keynesians could also have agreed with the new classicals that macroeconomics does require appropriate microfoundations, and could then have asked the new classicals to demonstrate that their neo-Walrasian microfoundations are the appropriate ones. To some extent that did happen when Keynesians challenged the assumption of rapid market clearing. Alternatively, Keynesians could have argued that the reduction of macroeconomics to microeconomics is infeasible, not because of the inadequacy of macroeconomics, but because of the inadequacy of microeconomics.[7]

The history of the microfoundations debate therefore raises several interesting questions. To what extent did the extreme self-confidence and the strong language of the new classicals discomfort the Keynesians so much that they made an unnecessary concession? To what extent was their decision to reply on the substantive and not the methodological level due to the poor reputation of methodological arguments in economics? And to what extent was it due to the inherent advantages of doing more work on the micro-foundation of the aggregate supply curve, regardless of new classical criticisms.

Notes

1. Popper criticized the addition of ad hoc elements to a theory because they can be used to immunize the theory against disconfirmation. For example, my theory may assert that consumption depends only on permanent and not on measured income. Suppose now that the government cuts taxes by 5 per cent, but announces that taxes will be raised next year by 10 per cent. Consumption rises. By making the ad hoc assumption that the public did not believe that taxes will be raised, I can protect my hypotheses from this disconfirmation.
2. This cannot be justified by an appeal to Friedman's position that the realism of assumptions is irrelevant because indexing can be treated as an implication of the theory. (See Chapter 7.)
3. An additional (or alternative?) explanation is that the assumption that all profitable trades are carried out is useful in establishing the policy-invariance proposition. But that proposition is not central to new classical theory (Mayer, 1993b, pp.80–81).
4. Janssen (1993, p.158) suggest that one reason for the shift to formal modeling in the 1970s was that several informal macro models turned out to be flawed. He cites specifically the fact that some models ignored the government budget constraint. However, in this case formal modeling did not prevent confusion (see Mayer, 1990b, ch. 11).
5. Along the same lines, as Laidler (1992) points out, despite their vaunted microeconomic rigor, real business cycle theorists ignore the conceptual problems of the production functions that generated the Cambridge controversy.
6. Thus James Tobin (1993) believes that concern about relative wages is strong enough to explain wage rigidity. For a discussion of the empirical evidence on concern about relative wages as an explanation of nominal wage stickiness, see James Haley (1990). For data showing that nominal wages are not as inflexible as traditional Keynesians assume, see Kenneth McLaughlin (1990) and Blinder and Choi (1990). In recent years academic salaries have also shown some downward flexibility.
7. In general, one might question the alleged superiority of microeconomics over macroeconomics, if one takes as the task of microeconomics the explanation of relative prices. It is by no means clear that microeconomics can predict and explain relative prices better than macroeconomists can predict and explain GDP and inflation. As Stiglitz (1992, p.45) remarked: 'While much of microeconomics is concerned with abstract questions such as the existence and efficiency of equilibrium, macroeconomics seeks to "explain" certain phenomena.'

5   The debate about Ricardian equivalence

In his survey of the literature on Ricardian equivalence John Seater (1993, pp.143, 182–3) reported that:

> two overall conclusions are now clear. The first appears uncontroversial: it seems almost impossible that Ricardian equivalence holds exactly. The theoretical foundations for any effects of debt on the economy depend on subtle concepts such as the intensity of intergenerational altruism. ... Careful examination of those factors suggests that exact Ricardian equivalence is implausible. The second conclusion is far more controversial: despite its nearly certain invalidity as a literal description of the role of public debt in the economy, Ricardian equivalence holds as a close approximation. Although there is much empirical evidence appearing to reject Ricardian equivalence, a dispassionate reading of the literature leads to the stated conclusion. ... Traditional non-Ricardian views of the effects of government debt ought to be abandoned.

Given the theoretical difficulties that Seater mentions, one would not expect that nearly all economists accept Ricardian equivalence. But, given the empirical evidence that he cites, one would expect a substantial proportion to do so, particularly since some of the theoretical arguments against Ricardian equivalence might be dismissed as valid in principle, but as empirically inconsequential.

Yet surprisingly few economists believe in Ricardian equivalence. In a survey of American economists (Alston, *et al.*, n.d., p.204) only 9 per cent of the respondents disagreed with the statement that 'fiscal policy ... has a significant stimulative impact on a less than fully employed economy'. Among those in the top 10 departments only 5 per cent disagreed.[1] And some of those who doubt the effect of fiscal policy might do so for reasons other than Ricardian equivalence, such as financial crowding out (see Holmes and Smyth, 1972; Mankiw and Summers, 1986). If Seater's reading of the empirical evidence is correct, how can one explain that so few economists accept Ricardian equivalence?[2]

One possibility is that Seater's reading of the evidence is *not* correct. In a previous survey Douglas Bernheim (1987) concluded that the empirical evidence rejects Ricardian equivalence. But Bernheim's paper appeared in 1987, while Seater's paper appeared in 1993, so that Seater covers a substantially larger and more recent literature. Bernheim's bibliography lists 28 items, the latest dated 1986. Seater's lists 206 items, with 41 per cent dated after 1986. This does not necessarily mean that Bernheim is wrong and Seater right, but it does leave one wondering why fewer than 10 per cent of economists agree with Seater's support of Ricardian equivalence.

Another possibility is that Ricardian-equivalence theory applies only under conditions of full employment, while the survey question specified that there is less than full employment. *Perhaps*, if asked whether a rise in the deficit raises nominal GDP, without unemployment being specified, most respondents would have said 'no'. That is possible, but seems to me implausible. It seems likely that a substantial majority of American economists do not believe that the economy is at full employment much of the time. If so, the proviso of less than full employment is not what is governing their answer. Put somewhat differently, if one believes that in many of the years covered by Seater's evidence there was less than full employment, then one must either accept an extreme version of Ricardian equivalence that does not require full employment, or one must reject Seater's evidence. I will therefore assume that the majority of American economists reject Ricardian equivalence despite the evidence that Seater cites for it. This is admittedly a somewhat arbitrary assumption, and one that is crucial for the argument of the rest of this chapter.

What seems a more plausible explanation than the full employment proviso for the divergence between most American economists' view of Ricardian equivalence and the evidence that Seater cites is McCloskey's (1985) analysis of the rhetoric of economics. He argues that we economists do not practice the austere 'scientific' methodology we proclaim, but are greatly influenced by many common-sense considerations that do not meet our avowed criteria for scientific evidence.[3]

Is that legitimate or is it a reprehensible failure of professional nerve? Inconsistency with common sense did not stop physicists from developing quantum mechanics, so should it prevent economists from accepting Ricardian equivalence? Yes it should, because economics is not physics. Physicists developed quantum mechanics because that was the only way to explain certain indubitable experimental results. Our econometric results are not that indubitable. We believe the strange things that physicists tell us because we can see that so much else that physicists have said is correct.

It is therefore not necessarily wrong for economists to be skeptical about the econometric evidence supporting Ricardian equivalence because they think Ricardian equivalence is inconsistent with common sense. What is more questionable, and has done much harm, is the failure to articulate this objection. By and large we know, or should know, that such 'unscientific' thinking affects our own beliefs, and we know that this is so for other people too, but we are afraid to admit it. Long live the well-dressed emperor.

One common-sense argument against Ricardian equivalence is that people do not look far enough ahead to let their current consumption be influenced by relatively small changes in the expected disposable income of their descendants.

It is easy to agree with the permanent income theory that consumption depends on income over several years, or even over one's whole lifetime. But it is something else to agree that consumption depends on the present value of income received both by the current and future generations.[4] This is so particularly when the expected change in income is trivial. Suppose the deficit increases for one year by 2 per cent of disposable personal income, and that the real rate of interest is 3 per cent. The rise in taxes to pay the additional interest lowers the disposable personal income of future generations permanently by 0.06 per cent. Given the uncertainty about the incomes of our progeny we are likely to ignore such a change.

Such a failure to follow the rational maximizing principle all the way to its inexorable conclusion in situations of great uncertainty can readily be justified by Herbert Simon's position that bounded rationality is a better assumption than unbounded rationality. A standard rejoinder to that position is that for most purposes unbounded rationality is a sufficiently close approximation to bounded rationality to permit the use of the more tractable assumption of unbounded rationality. But Ricardian equivalence requires such a strong rationality assumption that the difference between bounded and unbounded rationality becomes much more relevant.

Another common sense argument against Ricardian equivalence is that most people do not pay enough attention to economic events to know how large the deficit is. Economic sophistication is a scarce good. To be sure, in the last decade the idea that deficits impose a burden on future generations was much discussed in the media, but that has not been so for much of the postwar period. Moreover, the media focus much of their attention on the deficit in the President's budget, or in the budget passed by Congress, rather than on the actual deficit. Furthermore, instead of distinguishing between the nominal and the real deficit they scare their audience with stories about the high proportion of government expenditures that goes to pay interest on the debt. A facile response would be to say that, though most agents may err substantially in their beliefs about the size and effect of the deficit, these errors cancel out. But that assumes an implausible symmetry. Many of those who pay little attention to economic events are likely to treat either the size of the deficit or its effects on the economy as though it were zero. The very notion of not paying attention to something implies ignoring changes in it. To be sure, households may save more in the expectation that deficits do occur and impoverish their children, without paying attention to when these deficits occur or to their size at any particular time. But such a permanent increase in the savings ratio would not generate the offsetting decrease in consumption whenever the deficit increases that Ricardian equivalence requires. Fortunately, some data on the public's knowledge of deficits are available. In a survey done at a time when the projected deficit was $400 billion, William Walstad and Max Larsen (1992, p.35) found that the following distribution of the public's estimate:

Billions of dollars	Per cent of respondents
100	5
400	19
700	20
1,000	43
None of these	1
Don't know	12

(Sample size 1005)

What is even worse, they found that almost half the respondents did not know what the deficit is. When confronted with three choices only 51 per cent chose 'government spending is greater than tax revenues', 16 per cent chose 'US imports are greater than US exports', while 26 per cent chose 'the total demand for money is greater than the supply of money'. 'None of these' was chosen by one per cent, while six per cent responded with 'don't know' (Walstad and Larson, 1992, p.33).

That level of information is hardly consistent with the rational expectations assumption underlying Ricardian equivalence. But it is consistent with the limited incentive that the people have to inform themselves about fiscal policy. It should therefore not be all that surprising if many economists are skeptical about the level of information that supporters of Ricardian equivalence attribute to the public.

But it is not just critics of Ricardian equivalence who show some concern about the public's knowledge. Supporters do not ride the rational-expectations and sufficient information train all the way to its terminal either. They include in their consumption functions a measure of the deficit, instead of the more relevant and very different figures that emerge from generational accounting, or from an evaluation of changes in the government's net worth. Presumably they assume that generational accounting data or net worth data are unknown to the public, or that these data are so inaccurate that the public disregards them completely. Either assumption may be consistent with common sense, but it is hard to reconcile with the extreme rationality assumption; even highly inaccurate data provide some information.

But once one abandons the assumption of extreme rationality where should one stop? Those who test Ricardian equivalence by fitting consumption functions sometimes stop far short of the type of rationality that Ricardian equivalence implies because they frequently use nominal instead of real interest payments in their regressions (see Gramlich, 1989, p.29). That households do not adjust the published deficit figures for the difference between nominal and real interest payments may be a highly plausible assumption, but is it consistent with the behavior that Ricardian equivalence attributes to households?

'As-if' and Ricardian equivalence

There is a standard reply to those who complain that a theory makes unrealistic assumptions about people's behavior. This is that all useful theories make unrealistic assumptions (see Seater, 1993, p.149). 'As-if' reasoning is a standard tool of economics, so either you accept Ricardian equivalence or else you must reject most of economics, and indeed most of science.

How valid is this response? That despite its unrealism we generally assume rational utility maximization in microeconomics, and obtain valid results that way, does not require us to accept the strong rationality and utility-maximizing assumptions underlying Ricardian equivalence. In the theory of the household and the theory of the firm we can argue as follows: agents try to maximize utility. Our algebra shows that a particular action leads to maximum utility. We therefore predict that agents will undertake this action. The unrealism of the assumption that the agents know sufficient algebra is irrelevant because their wish to maximize utility will induce them to act as though they solve the equations that we solve. But in the debate about Ricardian equivalence the nature of the utility that agents maximize is not something that is given, but is instead a central issue in the debate. If, as many critics of Ricardian equivalence claim, agents do not try to maximize the present value of a utility stream that extends as far into the future as Ricardians assume, then they will not act 'as if' they tried to maximize such an income stream.[5]

Critics of Ricardian equivalence also challenge the strong rationality assumptions that it requires. Here, too, the argument that 'throughout economics we assume rational behavior,' is not an adequate response. We generally accept the assumption of rational behavior for three reasons. First, it more or less agrees with what we as human beings know about the way people behave. Second, there is the Darwinian argument that those who do not behave rationally will be eliminated. Third, theories that assume rational behavior have predicted well in many uses. None of these justifications apply to the rationality assumption of Ricardian equivalence. Our experience as human beings does not tell us that people are necessarily forward looking enough to treat a tax cut as a mere postponement of taxes that does not raise the present value of the disposable income stream. The Darwinian argument does not apply: households that treat tax cuts as though they raised the present value of the income stream do not die out. That other theories that assume rationality predict well does not mean that the rationality assumption required by Ricardian equivalence theory is innocuous, because Ricardian equivalence requires a higher degree of rationality than most theories.

If hiding behind the back of standard micro theory does not suffice to meet the charge of unrealism, can the charge be rejected on the general principle that the realism of its assumptions is irrelevant to the truth of a theory? This is a more subtle question. The moderate instrumentalism that, along with other philosophical tendencies, underlies Friedman's methodology is now widely (and I think correctly) accepted in economics (cf. Chapter 7). But it is a moderate version of instrumentalism that does not say that only prediction matters. If it did we would be running many more time series analyses and vector auto-regressions than we actually do. It is an instrumentalism that, far from rejecting the need for explanation, takes great pride in the explanations furnished by economic theory. Friedman's own work certainly puts much more emphasis on explanations than on merely finding some regression that predicts well.[6] We want our analysis to tell a story, to show how observed behavior is the outcome of rational utility maximizing. Keynesians were very much on the defensive in the 1970s when they were charged with not having a theory that explains price and wage inflexibility. We call an argument that has a missing link and depends on an observed but unexplained regularity, ad hoc – and that is no term of praise.

More specifically, our standard methodology does not permit us to show that an action flows from a combination of utility maximizing and of information that the agents do *not* possess, unless there is some algorithm that mimics the missing information and induces agents to behave as though they had it. (Cf. Leijonhufvud, 1992.) For instance, managers may be unfamiliar with the general principle that, when marginal cost is above average cost, average cost is rising. But since they know in their particular situation the conditions under which their average cost is rising, the neoclassical theory of the firm is not invalidated. A more subtle example is the response of households to inflation. It is likely that many households do not know that a part of their nominal interest receipts is not income, but just a return of capital. However, at least in an inchoate sense, they know that the real value of their bonds has fallen, perhaps because they evaluate the adequacy of their stocks of wealth in relation to their current nominal incomes, which have been raised by inflation. A consumption function written in real terms that disaggregates income may therefore produce a coefficient on interest income that seems to imply no money illusion, even though households overestimate their true interest incomes. For estimating a consumption function one can therefore assume that interest recipients do not have a money illusion. But that should not be used to argue that interest recipients can distinguish accurately between nominal and real interest rates in other contexts, for example in evaluating the fairness of high nominal interest rates at a time when real rates are low. As Friedman (1953, ch.1) has argued, a theory may be valid if used to answer one question, and invalid if used to answer another.

The question is therefore whether some mechanism exists that induces households to behave as though they had the information set and the degree of rationality that Ricardian equivalence theory attributes to them. If not, and if one does not make extremely strong rationality and information assumptions, then there is a deus ex machina at the heart of the theory, and it cannot be exorcized by pronouncing the formula, 'the realism of assumptions does not matter'. That formula fails to distinguish necessary assumptions, which do matter, from unnecessary ones that do not (see Chapter 7). Unless there is some alternative mechanism that generates the same results as do the extreme rationality and information assumptions of Ricardian equivalence theory, these assumptions are necessary assumptions, and hence their truth matters.

Since the proponents of Ricardian equivalence have not shown that such an alternative mechanism exists, it is not surprising that those economists who find its extreme rationality and information assumptions implausible have a strong prior against the validity of Ricardian equivalence. But a prior is just that, a prior. If the empirical evidence does show what Ricardian equivalence theory predicts, then there are only three choices: (1) abandon the prior, and conclude that despite their surface implausibility the necessary assumptions for Ricardian equivalence are met to a sufficient extent; (2) conclude that some other mechanism exists that generates Ricardian results; or (3) show that the data can also be explained by another, less implausible hypothesis, such as portfolio crowding out.

What do the data show?
In his comprehensive review article Seater (1993, pp.160 and 182) stated:

> When I began working on this review article I was concerned by the riot of conflicting empirical results; it really did seem, as is often asserted, that macro-econometric evidence can verify anything or nothing ... However, as I worked through the literature patterns and coherence emerged. ... I think it is reasonable to conclude that Ricardian equivalence is strongly supported by the data.

Seater does not arrive at this conclusion just by counting the number of positive and negative studies. Instead, he finds that those meeting the criteria of good econometric practice tend to be the ones that support Ricardian equivalence. This evidence, while impressive, is not entirely compelling because these studies were done before we had sufficient data on the great natural experiment of the 1980s, when deficits reached unprecedented peacetime levels. Many economists have argued that the concurrent *decline* in the savings ratio buries Ricardian equivalence. Seater countered that such a casual argument is unconvincing. It does not control for the effect of other variables, it ignores serious measurement issues and it provides only 10 sample points. Moreover, it ignores the fact that interest rates in the 1980s did not show a positive correlation with deficits, as they should have if Ricardian equivalence did not hold. We should therefore delay expressing a definitive opinion on whether the data support Ricardian equivalence until we see the results of tests that both meet Seater's criteria for good econometric practice and include the 1980s.

Suppose that the results of subsequent studies that include the 1980s and 1990s are consistent with Ricardian equivalence. One *might* still reject Ricardian equivalence by arguing that there is some other hypothesis that is also consistent with these data, and does not require the implausible assumptions of Ricardian equivalence theory. But what could this hypothesis be? To argue that deficits crowd out consumption either by a movement along the LM curve (Hicksian crowding out) or by shifting the LM and IS curves (portfolio crowding out) is no answer, because that implies a rise in interest rates, while the data show a negative effect of deficits on interest rates (Seater, 1993).

But someone with strong priors against Ricardian equivalence could seize on that perverse behavior of interest rates and argue that it shows that some as yet unknown factor is at work, that Ricardian equivalence gives a good fit merely because it is a proxy for that factor. Such an ad hoc argument is hardly satisfactory. However, that does not necessarily mean that it must be rejected and Ricardian equivalence must be accepted. As I have tried to show, the Ricardian position is also unsatisfactory. Hence if further data are consistent with Ricardian equivalence we seem to face a Hobson's choice. But there is a way out, though hardly an agreeable one. This is to admit our ignorance, or at least to avoid taking a strong position until we learn more.

The lesson
Advocates of Ricardian equivalence have done oustanding econometric work – but have converted only a small minority of American economists. This is not surprising because, as Summers (1991) showed, despite what we say, sophisticated econometrics has little effect on what we think when it has to struggle against common sense reasoning. Even an audience that has been socialized into the professional ethos by years of graduate training is reluctant to abandon what common sense tells it. It will yield to the temptation to hide behind those studies that reach results consistent with common sense.

At least in this case that is not necessarily bad. If a *necessary* assumption for Ricardian equivalence is that the public has a certain information set, and if it can be shown that the public does not have it, then Ricardian equivalence is invalidated. Testing by the realism of assumptions is not *always* wrong.

Advocates of Ricardian equivalence should therefore have dealt head-on with arguments such as that the public does not know the size of the deficit accurately enough. One possibility would have been to design surveys that determine just what the public knows about deficits and believes about their effects. The bad reputation that survey evidence has among economists is largely undeserved. It might also be possible to develop econometric tests. For example, one might compare the fit of regressions that use the book value of the debt with the fit of regressions that use the current market value. Since it is most implausible that the public knows the change in market value better than the change in the book value, Ricardian equivalence predicts that the regressions using book values should fit better. Similarly, one might compare the fits of regressions that use the published figures on the deficits with those that use the more refined estimates that almost nobody but economists know about.

On a more general level, the debate about Ricardian equivalence shows that refusing to engage in a serious discussion of methodology is bad. Unqualified claims about the naivety of testing theories by the realism of their assumptions have not only masked a basic weakness in the theory of Ricardian equivalence but have also driven opposition to the theory underground, where reasoned argument cannot reach it. Repression is bad for a profession's psyche as well as for an individual's.

Notes

1. However, 31 per cent of all respondents, and 33 per cent of respondents from the top 10 departments agreed with the statement cited in the text only with a proviso.
2. Seater (1993, pp.183–4) argues that political ideology affects the acceptance of Ricardian equivalence; that it is not coincidental that those on the political right tend to accept it, and those on the left to reject it. But there is some contradictory evidence. Only 2 per cent of the business economists polled by Alston *et al.* (n.d.) believe that fiscal policy is ineffective in a less than fully employed economy, in contrast to 9 per cent of government economists and 5 per cent of economists in the top 10 departments.
3. In a more cynical vein, he cites what he calls Mankiw's maxim that: 'No issue in economics has ever been decided on the basis of the facts' – and 'Nihilistic Corollary I: no issue has ever been decided on the basis of theory, either' (McCloskey, 1985, p.31). That may be going somewhat too far since the data have succeeded in settling some issues (see Mayer, 1994a).
4. Paul Evans (1991) has shown that Ricardian equivalence is a good approximation even if only relatively few households pay attention to the welfare of their offsprings. But to do so he has to assume that households rationally allocate consumption over their entire lifetime in accordance with the life cycle hypothesis.
5. As Seater (1993) points out, there is an alternative position that produces something close to full Ricardian equivalence even if agents care little about the utility of their heirs, because with a high discount rate the present value of the utility of their heirs is low for all but elderly households. But if the household's discount rate is high, while the (marginal) interest rate on government debt is not, then the whole basis of Ricardian equivalence is endangered, since a tax cut then raises the present value of the household's lifetime income stream (see Pesek and Saving, 1967, pp.257–61).
6. Friedman, after all, is the author of a price theory text that tries to explain many characteristics of our economy by using economic theory. He has been accused by some, such as Kaldor (1970), of basing his monetary theory on 'mere correlations'. But this is wrong. Friedman does far more than chase high R^2s. He (Friedman and Schwartz, 1963b) agrees that quantity theorists have to answer the 'how' question. Hence Friedman and Schwartz sketch a transmission mechanism, and Friedman embedded the quantity theory in the general theory of demand for durable goods. (See Friedman and Schwartz, 1963b, 1982; Friedman, 1956). That Friedman devoted so much effort to showing a correlation between money and income is easily explained. When he started his work it was widely believed that money had little, if any, effect on income. The best way to break through this conventional wisdom was to show that money and income are highly correlated. For an explicit statement by Friedman on the importance of explanation, see the letter cited in Hammond (1990).

6　The hidden persuaders

> I once again observe the importance of catchy and preferably somewhat mysterious labels in attracting attention in our profession. ... for many years I and others have argued that prolonged actual unemployment will become 'natural' ... but no one paid heed until the label 'hysteresis effect' came into vogue. (James Tobin, letter to Rod Cross, cited in Rod Cross, 1991, p.300)

When Don McCloskey urges economists to abandon the abstractions and abstruseness of an outdated philosophy of science he shows how rhetoric can sweep away unnecessary constraints on valid ways of thinking and arguing. In this chapter I follow McCloskey in singing the praises of rhetoric, but to a very different tune. He treats rhetoric as a liberator from the dictates of the narrow-minded schoolmarm he calls positivism. I, too, will treat rhetoric as a schoolmarm, but as one who raps knuckles that deserve to be rapped. As McCloskey points out, rhetoric does not say 'anything goes', nor does it say 'if everyone does it, it must be OK'. It, too, imposes rules.

One set of rules of rhetoric deals with semantics, that is the correct and incorrect use of words. I do not mean just grammatically incorrect, nor do I mean the use of words in a way inconsistent with their previously established meaning, such as the nowadays chronic use of 'methodology' (which strictly speaking means the *study* of method) in place of 'method', or 'masterful' (which means domineering) instead of 'masterly'. That sort of thing is inelegant, but since our audiences know what we mean, it does not retard understanding. What I do mean is the use of words in a way that hides sloppy thinking, or that tries to arouse inappropriate feelings in the reader. Emotive language, mislabeled words, words that confound several ideas and deceptive metaphors are my targets. Some of these errors are widely recognized and form a staple of Econ. 1 courses. The confusion of large firms with monopolies, high prices with rising prices, and money with income are some examples. Less readily recognized is that advocates of formalism (or what McCloskey calls 'modernism') have been particularly adept at promoting their methodological views by the use of emotive language.

Such a semantic critique of economics is not new. Its grand master was the late Fritz Machlup (see Machlup, 1991). To illustrate, after World War II many economists, who should have known better, argued that, regardless of any reasonable policies that various countries might adopt, there would be a permanent excess demand for dollars. The law of comparative advantage, they said, no longer applies. Machlup (1950) carefully classified the three distinct meanings that the term 'dollar shortage' had in these arguments. By doing so he showed that the dollar shortage was a chimera. His aim in these writings is well illustrated by the title of one of his essays, 'Structural and Structural Change: Weaselwords and Jargon'.

While following Machlup's lead I certainly do not claim to offer a complete list of abused terms. You, gentle reader, will probably be able to think of several other examples. Indeed, my purpose is as much to generate an awareness of a source of error as it is to pillory particular examples of the error. I start with and spend most time on some semantic confusions that appear in discussions of economic methodology, and then turn to some substantive economic issues, and conclude with some examples from the political arena.

Science

If an economist disagrees with a colleague she might tell him that his work is wrong, which will upset him. But what will upset him even more is if she tells him that his work is 'unscientific'. This would be understandable if there were a perfect correlation between being scientific and being right, and if we had a criterion by which we could tell whether something is scientific. As a general rule, neither condition holds. I am much less certain about the truth of the scientific statement that the universe is between 10 and 20 billion years old than I am about the non-scientific statement that sadism is bad. I do not deny that science provides the best procedure yet developed for obtaining knowledge of the external world, but only that the distinction between scientific and unscientific statements, even if it were unequivocal, would not provide a sure way of distinguishing truth from error. The history of what we call science is full of ideas that were once accepted and are now known to be erroneous.

Moreover, the distinction between scientific and unscientific statements or procedures is problematic. When considering strong cases it is easy to say in an intuitive way that one statement or procedure is scientific and the other is not. But strong examples do not a workable distinction make. Philosophers of science have spent much effort searching for a criterion that distinguishes 'science' from 'non-science'. That search has so far proved fruitless. Even a philosopher who is fairly sympathetic to positivism, Philip Kitcher (1993, p.195), recently remarked '... one of the great morals of the demise of logical positivism was the difficulty – or to put it bluntly, apparent impossibility – of articulating a criterion for distinguishing genuine science'.[1]

What then do economists mean when they call economics a science, or call a certain argument 'unscientific'? Have they discovered that Holy Grail of philosophy of science, a demarcation criterion? Of course not. It is likely that many economists do not even know that the definition of science is problematic. They believe that they know science when they see it. And how do they decide? In the same way as we so often decide about people we do not know; that is by their clothes and manner of speaking. Someone wearing elegant and costly clothes, and speaking in a certain way, has high status. An analysis formulated in elaborate mathematics, and expressed in a ponderous language that shows that the author takes himself most seriously, has scientific status. Modeling, that is setting out the assumptions (or more correctly some of the assumptions) in the beginning, and then expressing certain relations by equality signs, pluses and minuses, and by using abbreviations for the variables, makes an argument more 'scientific' than it would be if the assumptions were introduced throughout the argument, if words were used in place of the mathematical symbols and if the names of the variables were written out rather than abbreviated. If the author is lucky the reader may fail to notice if no mathematical operations other than simple addition or subtractions are taking place, and the paper will still seem 'scientific'. To economists science is whatever is high-tech, while simple, common sense analysis is not science.

To see how the tendency to confound high-tech with science leads to confusion, compare two papers. One paper simulates various monetary policies in a large econometric model, a task that requires some technical competence. The other paper is more modest. Its author has come across a puzzling set of data, and presents them without claiming to have any explanation, and hence does not use any sophisticated techniques.[2] Most economists would consider the first paper to be the more scientific. Indeed, a good journal is unlikely to publish the second paper, unless the data contradict some theory, so that it shows some theory-relatedness.

Yet the second paper is more 'scientific', in the sense of following a procedure that leads to enhanced knowledge of the world. Despite its paraphernalia of statistics and so on, the first paper lacks one of the attributes that have made scientific work so successful: an acknowledgment of its limitations. Since in simulating monetary policies different econometric models generate wildly different results (see Mayer, 1989), the paper's results are probably highly model-dependent. And, since there is usually no way of determining whether one model is superior to the others, its policy simulation is not persuasive evidence. This does not mean that it is worthless; it provides *some*, though precarious, evidence on the effect of monetary policy. Moreover, one can look upon such a study as only the first step in a larger research program. If subsequent studies using other models reach similar results, then one can treat the hypothesis as confirmed. Hence, if the author were to present his results in that modest way, the paper would increase our understanding of monetary policy. But authors of such papers often do not warn their readers that they should interpret the results in so limited a way.[3] Yet a skeptical attitude towards one's results and a willingness to warn readers is a principle that scientists should adhere to. One might respond that the readers obviously know that the results depend upon the particular model used. That is true. But do they also know how greatly the results of monetary policy simulations differ for various models? Some do, but I suspect that many do not, so a warning is needed.

By contrast, the second paper, which presents the puzzling data set, does provide scientific information. This information does not, by itself, enhance our understanding because, as yet, we lack an explanation of what the data show. But science is a social and cumulative endeavor. Someone else may develop an explanation for the puzzling data, and they may even lead to the development of a new theory. Or, if they are not just inexplicable, but inconsistent with some theory, they may eventually lead to the abandonment of that theory. In the natural sciences anomalies are prized because they are seen as part of a step-by-step process that enhances our understanding. Apparently, economists disdain such slow advances.

The confusion of science with high-tech has many disadvantages. Elsewhere (Mayer, 1993b) I have used many examples of the way it induces economists to allocate much greater effort than is appropriate to those parts of their analyses that are more amenable to formalization, while detracting attention from other parts of the analysis that need the effort more. Economists act as though the strength of an argument were equal to the strength of its *strongest* link. Another disadvantage is that, since the gathering of data usually does not require sophisticated techniques, those who gather data are considered less scientific than those who develop abstract models, so that economists have little incentive to collect data. Yet science is an activity not entirely unrelated to data. A further disadvantage is that, as McCloskey (1994, ch.5) has shown, any evidence that does not fit the stilted view of what is science is sometimes brushed aside as inconsequential.

Scientific economics or applied economics?
Paul Jones is a development economist. He goes into South American slums and surveys its inhabitants to see whether they prefer an improvement in their water supply to an improvement in their electricity supply. His wife, Jane, is also an economist. She works on existence proofs of general equilibrium theory. Many, probably most, economists would say that Paul's work may be the more useful, but that Jane's work is the more scientific. Why? That people in a certain slum prefer clean water to a better electricity supply is an empirical generalization, and if Paul follows correct scientific procedures, for example if he avoids biasing his samples, his work is, at least loosely speaking, scientific. So is Jane's, and her work may sooner or later, like his, have some practical use.

Can one say which is more scientific? An obvious problem with any such statement is that we lack a demarcation criterion for science. But suppose one brushes this problem aside by relying on some vague, intuitive notion of science. Those who say that Jane's work is the more scientific probably do so because they think of mathematics as the paradigmatic science. But that is a misuse of the term 'science'. This term is used more generally to denote the empirical sciences than to denote mathematics. And what is more important, when we say: 'look at the great progress that science has made, and at the benefits it has brought', we are more apt to think of physics, chemistry, engineering and medicine, than of mathematics.[4] To be sure, science, like all serious thinking, or even casual observing, requires abstraction, and mathematics is our prime abstracter. But is there any reason to think that, beyond a certain low level of abstraction, the more abstract, the more scientific?

Maybe there is. Thus one might argue that the function of science is to explain the external world and, since abstract theories have a greater reach, they explain more. But that argument is defective, for three reasons. First, it refers to the *usefulness* of theories, but what is at issue here is not whether more abstract theories are more useful, but whether they are more scientific. Second, it evaluates theories by only one criterion, their generality, while ignoring such other criteria as truthfulness. Third, it is not necessarily correct that a highly abstract theory tells us more than a less abstract theory does. It refers to a broader range of phenomena, but may tell us less about each of them than does a less abstract theory.[5]

All in all, it seems preferable to reject the conflicting claims of both economic theorists and of institutionalists that *their* work is the more scientific. If we want to say that one piece of research is more scientific than another, we have two choices, neither of them satisfactory. One is to do so on the basis of the inputs, such as the objectivity, care, knowledge, ingenuity and effort that went into the work. The other is to use some criterion that is supposed to distinguish scientific work by its output, such as potential falsifiability. The problem with the input measure is that what it provides tends to be a gauge of the general quality of the work, not of the extent to which it is scientific. Besides, it is hard to specify the input criteria for science, or for that matter for good work, in a clear and practicable way. It is easy to list some salient characteristics of good scientific work, but what are the weights by which they should be combined? The output measure also fails since philosophers of science cannot provide us with an agreed upon set of criteria.

Fortunately, it is not important that we cannot satisfactorily evaluate economic research by the extent to which it is 'scientific', as that term is generally used in economics. We do, of course, need to classify work by whether it reaches the correct conclusion. But that distinction does not map into the distinction between theoretical and therefore 'scientific' work and applied work. What does map into the distinction between so-called 'scientific' and applied work is something else. It is a distinction bequeathed to us by an older, aristocratic culture: that is, the distinction between 'noble knowledge', such as mathematics, literature and philosophy, on the one hand, and useful and thus 'base knowledge', such as technology and agronomy, on the other.

Theory

The confusion between high-tech and science is mirrored in the tendency to confine the term 'theory' to high-tech work, so that 'theorist' becomes an honorific that is bestowed only on those whose work contains complex mathematics (cf. Strassmann, 1994). As (McCloskey 1991, p.14) has observed: 'The leading middle-aged economists laugh when Gary Becker is described as a theorist ... and the leading young economists do not even think it funny.' Yet Becker's work is surely theoretical, as that term is used in the natural sciences and in philosophy of science. His theory of household behavior contains law-like generalizations that are empirically testable and that are, in turn, derived from the higher-level generalizations of standard economic theory.

The dictum, 'if no advanced mathematics, then no theory', confuses a frequent condition with a necessary condition. Since theory usually involves a relatively high level of abstraction, and since mathematics is a language specially designed for the manipulation of abstractions, theoretical work frequently uses mathematics. But the use of mathematics is not a necessary characteristic of theory. Darwin developed a revolutionary and very general theory without it. To be sure, mathematics has been used in the subsequent development of Darwinian theory, but Darwin's own work certainly deserves to be called theory. Moreover, a theory, even an elegant theory, that uses mathematics may use only simple mathematics. One example is Baumol's (1952) classic paper on the transactions demand for money. Its mathematics is no more advanced than setting first derivatives at zero.

More generally, one should distinguish between the way the term 'theory' is used in mathematics and in the empirical sciences. Mathematicians use it for a related set of highly abstract propositions. (There is the story of the mathematician who, after reading the *General Theory*, asked: 'but where is the theory?') By contrast, natural scientists use the term 'theory' for a generalization that explains the data and usually subsumes them under a higher-level hypothesis. According to this usage, applied industrial organization is a field with a high theoretical content. By contrast, whether general equilibrium theory, which many economists treat as the prime exemplar of theory in economics, should also be called 'theory' is a much disputed issue because of its tenuous relation to observable data.

This confusion of theory with mathematical economics distorts graduate training. Students are required to take a heavy dose of mathematical economics under the name of 'theory', on the argument that they have to know theory to do good work in the applied fields. But much of the theory that is used in the applied fields is developed in these field courses themselves, and is not the theory taught in the formal theory courses. To be sure, it is related to the theories of the theory courses, and therefore – ceteris paribus – the more theory courses students take the better they will do in the applied fields. But ceteris are not paribus. There is a budget constraint: the more formal theory students learn, the less time they have to learn the scientific theory pertaining to their applied fields.

Vagueness or precision?

'Her work thus replaces vague talk with a precise theorem.' Words like these are typical of the way a formalist might praise the work of another formalist. And it may well be entirely appropriate. To see whether it is or not, one has to pay close attention to the meaning of the word 'replaces'. If the rigorous theorem replaces – in the strict sense of the term – vague talk, then it surely deserves acclaim. But to do that it has to start from the same or weaker axioms as the vague talk and provide conclusions that are at least as strong as those of the vague talk. Otherwise, it supplements, but does not 'replace', the vague talk in the sense of making it worthless. In a sociological sense it may replace it because economists may now talk about that theorem instead of talking about the earlier work. But even so, the vague talk still retains value since it tells us something that the theorem does not.

The debate about fixed rules versus discretion for monetary policy provides a good example. A substantial part of the case against discretionary policy consists of vague talk about the way in which political pressures and the central bank's self-interest seriously distort discretionary monetary policy (see, for instance, Brunner, 1981; Modigliani and Friedman, 1977, p.18). In recent years this vague talk has been largely replaced (in the sociological sense) by models of time inconsistency. These models assume that the central bank's utility function contains only two arguments, output (or employment) and the inflation rate. But the vague talk allowed the central bank a richer utility function than that. Hence, if the time-inconsistency models were to show that within their confines discretionary policy is appropriate, that would not be an effective response to the vague talk's arguments against it.

Moreover, the time-inconsistency models are highly sensitive to small changes in their assumptions, and these are assumptions that cannot be reliably tested. So what would happen if an economist who eschews vague talk were asked by a policymaker whether to impose a monetary rule on the central bank? If he were forthright he would either say 'I don't know', or else would say something like: 'If you make the following assumptions policy X is appropriate, but not if you make the opposite assumptions. And I cannot tell you which set of assumptions is right.' Because the policymaker does not know which set of assumptions is right either, such an answer would be useless. Since the economist knows this, he would usually avoid such an answer, but would instead pick one set of assumptions and answer the question accordingly. But how would he know which set to pick? Wouldn't it be on the basis of 'vague talk'?

When this procedure of setting out a rigorous model based on assumptions that are selected more or less arbitrarily is challenged there is a standard answer: by setting out those steps of an argument that are not controversial, a model allows us to isolate and focus discussion on those steps in the argument that are controversial. But that is not the way it usually works. Because of the prestige that accrues to formal modeling, and because of the fear of appearing vague, the development of a new model is more likely to stimulate work on new variants or refinements of the model than on the appropriateness of its assumptions or the correctness of its predictions. Thus vagueness is not eliminated, but just kept out of sight.

The market for economics, or 'If they'll buy it, I'll make it'

Criticisms such as the ones just presented are often met with the reply that the type of research currently being done, and the type of training given to graduate students, must be appropriate because that is what the market rewards. This reply fails, on two grounds. One is that, since the very purpose of the criticism is to change the market's tastes, it cannot be answered by treating the market's current tastes as given. The second is that this reply uses the term 'market' in a questionable way. One can think of the market as constituted by those who do the actual purchasing, or else by those who are the ultimate beneficiaries of these purchases. Principal/agent theory tells us that the two may have divergent preferences. We would not be greatly impressed if someone tried to defend wasteful government expenditures by saying that these expenditures must be good because Congress has approved them.

There are four markets for economists: business, government, non-profit institutions and academia. In all four the interests of those who do the hiring diverge, at least to some extent, from their principals' interests, but in the business market the difference is probably least. Hence, if there were a large and growing demand for business economists with strong formalist training, it would support the argument that economics is on the right track. But there is no reason to think that businesses prefer economists who have extensive training in formalism (see Hershey, 1993; Zevin, 1992).

The government market for economists also gives us little ground for self-congratulation. Here the principal/agent problem may well be fairly large and, in any case, that market does not favor economists who specialize in formal theory either (see Woolf, 1992). The same is probably true for non-profit organizations.

Thus someone who argues that a market test vindicates our emphasis on formalist theory has to point to the academic market. But it is just here that the principal/agent problem is particularly severe. The high regard in which academia holds formalist training surely does not reflect a clamor for it by donors to universities or by taxpayers. (See Hutchison, 1988, pp.194ff.) Nor does such training meet the needs of undergraduate teachers (see Woos, 1992; Acker *et al.*, 1993). Thus there is no reason to think that it reflects the interests of society at large, for which university officials in their more poetically inspired moments claim to be working. Graduate students may demand it, but they do so mainly because they think it will help them land a good job, not because they think it inherently valuable. (See Klamer and Colander, 1990.)

To be sure, it would be going too far to claim that economics clearly fails the market test, and that it should therefore change. One might well question the efficacy of a market test for academic research even if one could be devised. Market solutions will generally be optimal only if market participants are adequately informed. But it is not obvious that donors to universities, students and those who represent taxpayers are better informed about the value of various types of research than are the researchers themselves. They *may* be, since their judgement is not warped by the researcher's insider bias and 'group-think', but there is no way of telling whether this advantage offsets their lack of technical knowledge. What one can tell is that the argument that we *must* be on the right track because the market says so falls apart once one looks at what we mean by 'the market'.

Risk aversion

The issues discussed so far pertain to methodology. But semantic problems arise also in discussions of substantive issues. One example is the meaning of risk aversion and of the coefficient of risk aversion that supposedly measures it. When John Pratt (1964) developed this coefficient he gave it a narrow meaning by making it a function of the declining marginal utility of income. Defined that way, risk aversion is not an adequate measure of the dislike of risk-taking. Suppose I am offered a gamble that is mathematically fair in terms of *utility*; that is, a gamble in which the mathematical value of the dollar gains exceeds the value of the dollar losses by just enough to compensate for the declining marginal utility of income. I might still refuse this gamble because I dislike risk. As Richard Thaler (1991) has shown, there is evidence for the existence of such risk aversion. Or I might be a risk lover, and jump at the chance to take this gamble.

Such responses to risk are matters of taste, and are therefore not readily amenable to economic analysis. Hence we are tempted to brush them aside. If we had two different terms, say 'declining-utility risk aversion' and 'taste risk aversion' it would not be so easy to forget that there are two sources of risk aversion. But since we have only one term and use it to mean only 'declining-utility risk aversion', it is easy to forget that we are dealing with only one of the two reasons for avoiding risk. Then, when we look at the data showing the reluctance of people to take risk, and use these data to measure the coefficient of risk aversion, we are sometimes surprised by how implausibly fast the marginal utility of income seems to be declining.

Utility or income?

There is no proposition in economics more basic than the idea that agents maximize utility. Given the assumption that man is a striving animal, along with a broad enough definition of utility, the utility maximization hypothesis follows tautologically. So far so good. But a broad definition of utility does not allow one to rule out enough types of behavior to generate interesting and testable hypotheses. When we get down to work we therefore replace the immeasurable maximand, utility, with a measurable one, income or profit. We usually do so implicitly, and thus without warning the reader, as though utility and income were synonymous. They are not. Income maximizing rules out important classes of behavior, such as altruistic voting (and even voting per se), that utility maximizing permits. When one considers how much income we spend on goods primarily intended to secure us the respect of others and our own self-respect, and how important for many people's self-respect is a feeling that they are morally commendable, it is hardly surprising that income maximizing cannot explain all behavior.[6]

The Walrasian research program

Some economists use the term 'neo-Walrasian research program' to denote the research strategy of contemporary neoclassical economics. Roy Weintraub (1985, p.109) has described its Lakatosian hard core as follows:

HC1. There exist economic agents.
HC2. Agents have preferences over outcomes.
HC3. Agents independently optimize subject to constraints.
HC4. Choices are made in interrelated markets.
HC5. Agents have full relevant knowledge.
HC6. Observable economic outcomes are coordinated, so that they must be discussed with reference to equilibrium states.

This may be a good way to describe most neoclassical theoretical work, though proposition HC4 is sometimes relaxed. But why call it Walrasian? One might also consider it a description of the much less formal part of neoclassical economics that is rooted in Marshallian partial equilibrium, such as the work of the Chicago school, if one interprets HC4 (interrelated markets) in a loose way. (Cf. Backhouse, 1991, who, however, describes the heuristics somewhat differently.) Marshallians do not deny that markets are interrelated. They just believe that most problems can be more fruitfully discussed by leaving this inter-relation aside.

Labeling most neoclassical theorizing as Walrasian, with its strong implication of general equilibrium analysis, ascribes undue importance to general equilibrium theory, and therefore to questions of existence, uniqueness and stability. These questions are then seen as the central issues in neoclassical theory, even though nearly all day-to-day neoclassical research pays no attention to them. The neo-Walrasian research program rests on the Cartesian claim that we must settle these fundamental issues before we can get on with the rest of economic analysis, or at least that we cannot feel comfortable in our research until we do.[7] Much of neoclassical economics does not worship at this Cartesian shrine.

Macroeconomics

Another semantic problem, one more common some time ago than now, is to contrast 'monetarists' with 'fiscalists'. The former believe that changes in the nominal money supply are the major determinant of changes in nominal income, while fiscalists are said to believe that fiscal policy is the dominant influence, or at least that fiscal policy can have a significant effect on nominal income (see Fand, 1970). This terminology grew out of discussions of the St. Louis model (Anderson and Jordan, 1968) which, until the early 1980s, seemed to show that monetary policy has a powerful effect on nominal income, while the effect of fiscal policy soon disappears. It is therefore not surprising that monetarists used these results as a club to beat Keynesians with. That is a dubious tactic. In the Keynesian model fiscal policy (along with monetary policy) is only one of several factors that determine income. Fiscal policy might for some reason have little effect on income, and yet some other Keynesian factor, such as shifts in the marginal efficiency of investment, might have a strong effect on income. By using the term 'fiscalist' as a synonym for 'Keynesian', some monetarists defined Keynesian theory in a way that made it an easy target – a standard procedure in politics, but hardly an example of good scientific practice.

The minimum sustainable rate of unemployment – given the prevailing labor-market institutions – is often called the 'natural rate of unemploy-ment'.[8] Those who are familiar with the social science literature usually know that one should be extremely careful about reading a normative meaning into the term 'natural' (cf. Gordon, 1987). But those economists whose training is primarily mathematical may be tempted by the word 'natural' to treat that particular unemployment rate as though it were inevitable, and not something that could be reduced by changing the institutions of the labor market.

Some other semantic problems

In an extraordinarily influential paper, Paul Samuelson (1958) analysed inter-generational trade by using a single durable good, that for some reason he called 'money'. A whole sub-literature grew from that paper, and its overlapping generations models have been a cutting edge of economics for many years. But what is being cut at this edge? Overlapping generations models are generally presented as monetary theory. But it is a peculiar monetary theory because it ignores the salient characteristic of money, liquidity, and treats money purely as a store of wealth – in fact, as the only store of wealth. It is therefore not surprising that some results obtained by these models seem alien to traditional monetary theory. Had Samuelson called his durable, say, 'sewing machines' much confusion in monetary theory would have been avoided. Words do matter.

Donald McCloskey (1985, ch.9) has argued persuasively that economists usually misinterpret significance tests. That a coefficient has a high t value tells us that its difference from zero is unlikely to be merely the result of sampling error, but it does not tell us that it has an economically significant effect on the dependent variable: an obvious point, but one ignored by many economists. Why? While one cannot be certain, it is likely that the word 'significant' has played a large role in the confusion. If the term associated with the t coefficient were, not 'significance' but, say, 'sample-error robustness', it is likely that there would be less confusion about what the t statistic measures.

The simple word 'may' is also a great sower of confusion. Both in writing and in reading it is easy to confuse the statement: 'X may lead to Y' with the very different statement: 'X leads to Y'. The latter tells us what will happen, while the former expresses only a possibility, perhaps only one of many plausible possibilities. If I am told that something will cause me to die today I will be alarmed, but I am not alarmed that being struck by lightning *may* cause me to die today. At one stage of her argument someone may write that X 'may' cause Y instead of 'will', because she is not certain about the indicated relationship. Yet, later in her argument, she may unconsciously act as though she had previously shown that X does cause Y, and then, having shown that Y causes Z, conclude that X eventually causes Z.

Inapplicable metaphors, too, can lead to confusion. Thus some environmentalists talk about 'spaceship earth' to emphasize that the world's resources are limited. But the earth is not a spaceship. To save weight a spaceship carries only as much of any item as is likely to be needed, plus some allowance for contingencies. By contrast, the earth has a much greater supply of some items, a fact brought out in a delightful *New Yorker* spoof of the limits-to-growth argument. It pointed with alarm to the fact that the world's per capita supply of granite is falling.

Political and popular discussions
The prime nature reserve for semantic confusion is, of course, not economics, but politics. An important example is the use of the term 'democratic' to describe two different things. One is a particular system of choosing a government, along with rules that allow the opposition an appropriate opportunity to replace the government. The other is the antonym of 'elitist'. This confounding of two distinct ideas gives an unwarranted legitimacy to egalitarian policies. Anyone who disapproves of 'democratic' institutions in the first of these senses puts himself beyond the pale. Egalitarian policies, on the other hand, at least those that go beyond the prevailing degree of egalitarianism, do not enjoy anywhere

near that support. But egalitarians can make an efficacious argument for such egalitarian policies by calling them 'democratic' and thus removing them from the sphere of ideas that well-meaning people may criticize.

Another weasel-word that is causing much confusion and serves to legitimize questionable policies is the elastic term 'middle class'. When some group advocates a program that will benefit it, it calls itself 'middle class' and conjures up the picture of a hard-working blue-collar couple, struggling against substantial odds to make ends meet. But in the United States few people call themselves, or are called, upper-class. So once the program is agreed to, even fairly well-to-do people can lay claim to the benefits it is supposed to provide to the hard-pressed middle class.

Our current way of describing business fluctuations by two stages, expansion and contraction, instead of by the older four-stage classification of expansion, boom, recession and slump, confuses the public, particularly during slow expansions, such as the US expansion commencing in 1991. If economists are right in saying that the recession is over, why is unemployment so high?

The term 'social conscience' is a peculiar one, at least to someone trained in economics. A standard problem in economics is that authors unconsciously slip value judgements into what purports to be a positive analysis. The term 'social conscience' functions in the opposite way. A combination of value judgements and (often questionable) positive judgements is presented as though it were entirely a moral issue, so that support for, say, a higher minimum wage is presented as a matter of social conscience, that is as a matter of morality.

Another example is the description of fascists as 'right-wing extremists', as though all political attitudes could be lined up on a linear scale. More attention to the meaning of words is no panacea, but its benefit/cost ratio is high.

Notes

1. As McCloskey (1994) points out, the use of the word 'science' to denote primarily the natural sciences is a peculiarity of English. In other languages the corresponding term, such as the German 'Wissenschaft' denotes what we might call a 'discipline', and thus includes history, literary criticism and so on. One should not, however, make too much of this linguistic peculiarity. Logical positivism with its insistence on distinguishing between scientific and unscientific statements developed in Austria, not in an Anglophone country.

2. For example, a chart in a Bureau of Labor Statistics consumer expenditure survey in the 1930s showed that at each income level white-collar workers saved less than blue-collar workers. Until the development of the relative and permanent income theories in the postwar period that finding lacked an explanation. Had it been widely known, rather than buried in a fairly obscure publication, these theories might have been developed earlier.

3. But admitting that a paper rests on a narrow model need not be a manifestation of modesty (see Milberg, 1994).

4. To be sure, physics and chemistry make use of mathematics, but they also use ordinary language, and that does not make us call ordinary language a science.

5. A more sophisticated argument for the greater explanatory power, and hence scientific value, of abstract theories is the following. Researchers distribute themselves across various fields and problems of economics in a way that equates their marginal productivities in each field.

Assume that their utility function contains two arguments, financial support for research and the scientific value of their work. Since financial support is more readily available for applied work, in equilibrium the scientific value of applied work must be less. But this argument, too, is unconvincing because of the limitation of the utility function that it assumes. Abstract work has more prestige than applied work, at least among academics, and once prestige is included in the researcher's utility function, there is no reason to assume that at the margin the explanatory power, and hence scientificity of applied work is less than that of abstract work.

6. The reason people do not spend more on altruistic goods to enhance their self-respect may well be that a little goes a long way; with no great effort one can persuade oneself that even a trivial contribution to charities means that one is generous.

7. Nobody can deny that solving the problems of existence, uniqueness and stability would enhance the coherence of our theories at least somewhat. The relevant issue is by how much it would do so, given all the other potential sources of error in our analyses. Developing more certain foundations for mathematics would, in principle, help too, but would surely not significantly raise our capacity to explain economic behavior.

8. Milton Friedman (1968) coined this term as an analog to Wicksell's natural rate of interest in a paper in which he discussed both unemployment and interest rates.

7   On the realism of assumptions

> The firmest line that can be drawn upon the smoothest paper still has jagged edges if seen through a microscope. This does not matter until important deductions are made on the supposition that there are no jagged edges. (Samuel Butler, 1912, p.298)

Whether the assumptions of economic theory should be realistic – and whether they are sufficiently realistic – is surely one of the oldest issues in the methodology of economics, and still one of the liveliest. Not only do institutionalists and post-Keynesians reject mainstream economics as based on unrealistic assumptions, but even within the mainstream the legitimacy of such 'unrealistic' assumptions as rational expectations and wage flexibility are points of sharp disagreement. Unease about the realism of assumptions is probably more frequent, and accounts for more disagreement, than appears on the surface since complaints about unrealism are often considered antiquated, and are therefore not expressed. Didn't Friedman (1953) show that the demand for realistic assumptions is naive? But patting doubters on the head, and with a superior smile sending them off to read Friedman's essay, is not an adequate response. Friedman did not draw as sharp a distinction between assumptions and implications as many of his readers read into his essay (see Mayer, 1993a). Moreover, his essay has been strongly criticized by methodologists and philosophers of science.

A re-examination of this hoary subject is therefore in order. There is an extensive and complex debate among philosophers of science about whether scientific concepts refer to anything in reality and scientific laws are literally true, as the realists claim, or are all merely instruments of thought, as the instrumentalists believe. If the latter are right, then there is no reason to argue about the realism of assumptions. To avoid entanglement in this debate I shall simply assume that the realists are right, and offer a realist critique of testing by the validity of assumptions within the context of what is useful for economics. Such an avoidance of the philosophical issue is legitimate because the debate in economics about the realism of assumptions uses the term 'realism' in a very different way than it is used in philosophy.[1]

Three issues need to be addressed. First, are questions about the realism of assumptions meaningful? Second, if so, do unrealistic assumptions invalidate a theory? Third, if they do not, do they enhance or reduce the usefulness of the theory? Answers to these questions are relevant to the day-to-day work of economists. If testing by the realism of assumptions is appropriate, then there is less justification for the common practice of relying almost solely on time series tests of the main implication of the theory.

Formal and informal theories

The appropriate response to the first issue, whether questions about the realism of assumptions are meaningful, depends on the type of theory that is erected on the assumptions. One type, which I shall call formal theory, merely develops the implications of certain axioms (assumptions). Such a theory is necessarily correct if there are no contradictions in the axioms, and if there are no errors in the logical chain connecting the axioms and the conclusions. Unrealistic assumptions cannot invalidate such a theory because it does not make any assumptions in the sense of claiming that certain conditions actually occur. Being merely a set of 'if – then' propositions, its truth does not depend upon whether the 'if' ever occurs.

The other type of theory, which I shall call empirical theory, adds the proposition that a specific set of statements, that is 'assumptions', describes actual occurrences with sufficient accuracy for the theory's predictions and explanations to be useful. A good example of the distinction between formal theory and empirical theory in this respect is the distinction between the equation of exchange, $MV = PT$, which is an identity, and the quantity *theory* of money. The equation of exchange merely tells us that, if M increases, either V must decrease or PT must increase. Unlike the quantity theory it makes no claims or assumptions about what will happen or what causes what.

The debate about the realism of assumptions is therefore meaningless with respect to formal theory, so that I need only discuss empirical theory. I shall argue that much of the dispute about the need for realistic assumptions for that type of theory evaporates once one specifies carefully what one means by 'assumptions'.

Two types of assumptions

One type of assumption is a necessary assumption. That type of assumption predominates in formal theory with its focus on elegance, parsimony and rigor. These criteria compel theorists not only to minimize the number of assumptions, but also to use assumptions that have as little content as possible. The ideal is axiomization, and the narrower the scope of the axioms, the more elegant is an axiomization. Occam's razor rules.

Empirical theory, on the other hand, puts less emphasis on parsimony and elegance, and therefore is more forgiving about excess content in the assumptions. Not only may empirical theorists include more assumptions than are strictly needed, but these assumptions may also be worded in a way that gives them broader coverage than is strictly necessary, so that they have excess content. For example, one might state one assumption of the quantity theory as: 'all prices are flexible in the long run'. But all that is needed for the quantity theory to hold is that a large proportion of prices, not all prices, are flexible. Similarly, a theory might state as one of its assumptions that the firm faces a horizontal demand curve, when all that is strictly needed is the less stringent condition that the demand curve is sufficiently elastic for the firm to act as though the quantity it supplies has no significant effect on price. I will call such assumptions with excess content 'fat assumptions'.

Fat assumptions contain a necessary component unless they are entirely excess assumptions, but necessary assumptions do not contain a fat component. Put differently, fat assumptions assert more restrictive conditions than necessary assumptions do in the sense that the real world may correspond to the conditions required by a necessary assumption, but not to the additional conditions required by the fat assumption.

If theorists made only necessary assumptions the question whether assumptions have to be realistic would be easy to answer: if an assumption that must hold *fully* for the theory to be valid, that is, a necessary assumption, does not hold, that is, is unrealistic, then the theory is false. Hence, to argue that some assumptions need not be realistic, one must first argue that some theories do and should have assumptions that are fat because the advantage of using fat assumptions sometimes outweighs their disadvantages.

Advantages of fat assumptions
One benefit of not bothering to pare assumptions down to their strictly necessary content, which might require axiomization, is that this saves time, thus leaving the researcher more time for empirical testing. It also saves the readers' time, because fat assumptions often make a theory easier to understand. Consider, for example, an analysis of the effect of foreign import restrictions on US employment under freely floating exchange rates. Suppose someone develops a theory showing that the unfavorable employment effects of the foreign import restrictions are fully, or more than fully, offset by the favorable effect on employment that occurs as falling exports lower the exchange rate of the dollar. To avoid getting entangled in the issue of the relative employment content of US exports and import substitutes it may be convenient to assume that the US employment content is the same for both. That assumption can be stated in a few words, and is easy to grasp. But it is a fat assumption because the theory holds also if the US employment content of exports is less than that of import substitutes, or even if the employment content of US exports is greater, but not by more than is required to balance the net employment-creating effects of the other variables that the theory puts aside as second-order effects.

Indeed, in part to facilitate communication, many assumptions are formulated as standardized idealizations, and are therefore not confined just to what is needed for the particular theory. Thus we usually assume that agents are rational and that firms maximize profits, even though we know that these statements are not literally true for every agent and every firm, and that our theory does not require them to be. It requires only that they be adequate approximations. Assumptions such as perfect competition or rational expectations therefore differ from statements such as, 'all swans are white', statements that can be refuted by a single exception. Such idealizations are easily understood by readers because much of an economist's training consists of learning to think in these terms.

Disadvantages of fat assumptions
One obvious disadvantage of fat assumptions is that such assumptions make the theory inelegant. But there are also two more practical disadvantages. One is that fat assumptions make it unclear exactly what a theory asserts. Someone might therefore treat the fat part of an assumption as an inherent part of the theory, and mistakenly believe that confirmation of the theory's implication provides some weak, prima facie evidence for the entire assumption, and not just its necessary part.[2]

Second, it is not clear exactly what evidence relating to the assumptions would falsify the theory. Readers should not have to do the often extensive work required to decide whether a particular assumption is a necessary assumption. Here is a concrete example. In a recent paper Alan Viard (1993) argues that issuing indexed government bonds would improve welfare only slightly. Among his assumptions are that there is a zero net supply of bonds, and that agents can readily sell capital and bonds short. Are these purely expository assumptions, whose validity does not matter, or does Viard's conclusion rest on their validity? His paper is complex, and it is unlikely that many readers take the trouble to answer that question for themselves. But if they do not, how can they know whether, under the conditions prevailing in the US economy, indexed bonds would have only a slight effect on welfare? I suspect that most readers simply take a guess, perhaps implicitly by simply ignoring problems created by the assumption. That is unfortunate because Viard's paper provides a painstaking, rigorous analysis, so that it should leave the reader with more than a mere guess.

Comparing advantages and disadvantages
In some cases the benefits from fat assumptions outweigh their costs, in some they do not. Four examples may be helpful.

One case where the unrealism of a fat assumption does not matter is the textbook story that firms estimate marginal cost and marginal revenue, and then set a price that equates the two. The fat assumption that firms estimate something they call 'marginal cost' and 'marginal revenue' is harmless. We know that this assumption is just made for expository convenience, and we can tell what the corresponding necessary assumption is. Another example of a harmless fat assumption occurs in a quantity-theory model of inflation that assumes that relative prices are fixed, and then shows that in hyperinflation prices rise faster than the quantity of money since the cost of holding money, and hence velocity, rise. Our trained intuition tells us that changes in relative prices will have only negligible effects on the price level. As discussed in the appendix to this chapter, Alan Musgrave calls such assumptions 'negligibility assumptions'.

For an example of a fat assumption that is troublesome, consider the Ricardian equivalence theory discussed in Chapter 5. Here the assumption is that, on average, agents estimate the change in the burden of the national debt with sufficient accuracy. Unlike the assumption about managers who set price to equate marginal revenue and marginal cost, it is not clear what is the necessary part, and what is the fat part, of this assumption. Is it that *at any one time*, though some agents overestimate and others underestimate the burden of the debt, their (weighted) average estimate is correct? Or is it that agents estimate the burden correctly only when averaged over long (how long?) stretches of time? Moreover, in estimating the burden of the debt, do agents make an allowance for the build-up of government capital, and therefore consider only the net burden, or do they look just at the outstanding volume of government securities? That is an important question when considering the effect of government expenditure for infrastructure. Hence, until they clarify their assumption about the public's expectations, supporters of Ricardian equivalence proffer a seriously incomplete theory. To argue that none of this matters because we can let the data decide is an invitation to data mining.

Another example of a harmful fat assumption occurs in the time-inconsistency theory of monetary policy. As usually stated, the theory, in its original variant, asserts that central bankers want to generate a moderate inflation that causes workers to overestimate their real wages by enough to offset the disincentive effect of income taxes (and income-related subsidies) on the labor supply. This is a fat assumption because the theory's results also hold if, instead of being concerned with the effect of taxes on the labor supply, central bankers attempt to operate the economy at an unemployment rate below the natural rate. That is fortunate for the theory because, as discussed in Chapter 8, the assumption that central bankers worry about the effect of taxes on the labor supply can readily be rejected.

But this change in assumptions is more than a verbal change that leaves the theory unaffected. When stated the second way, it tells us something about the period for which such a policy might succeed, and suggests that this period is related to other factors that make agents sensitive to indications of inflation. Moreover, the first assumption, unlike the alternative assumption, implies that the central bank should pay attention to the progressivity of the income tax.

The first two examples in which the unrealism of fat assumptions is harmless are cases in which the unrealism is merely a problem of wording or of omitting a second-order effect. The two other examples, in which the unrealism of fat assumptions creates serious problems, are cases where the nature of the necessary assumption contained within the fat assumption is not clear, or where the replacement of an unrealistic fat assumption by a more realistic fat assumption changes the theory significantly.

It should generally not be too difficult to distinguish between those cases in which unrealistic assumptions are harmless, and those in which they are not. In any case, since fat assumptions are helpful in *some* situations, one cannot dismiss the argument for unrealistic assumptions out of hand. The question now is whether they, like necessary assumptions, need to be, or should be, realistic.

Do theories require true assumptions?

Both Alexander Rosenberg (1972, pp.158ff) and Daniel Hausman (1992b, p.164) have criticized Friedman's classic defense of unrealistic assumption by pointing out that one can invert a theory, so that what initially were assumptions are now implications. Previously, Friedman (1953) himself had pointed this out, and Louis de Alessi (1971) has provided a detailed analysis of this topic. For example, take the theory that if it rains I will carry an umbrella. This theory assumes that I own or can obtain an umbrella. It can be restated as saying that, if I am seen carrying an umbrella when it rains, this implies that I own or can obtain an umbrella. Similarly, the theory that an increase in labor costs makes a country less competitive in world markets can be said to have the *assumption* that there are no fully offsetting changes in the exchange rate. Or it can be said to *imply* that the exchange rate does not adjust fully for the change in labor costs. Since a theory can be tested by the truth of its implications, Rosenberg and Hausman argue that one can therefore also test it by the truth of its assumptions.

They are right with respect to necessary assumptions. What we mean by calling an assumption 'necessary' is precisely that its falsity dooms the theory as an adequate explanation, though we may still employ it as a practical forecasting device or an otherwise useful heuristic. But they miss the point of Friedman's argument, because they tend to treat economic theory as a more formal theory than Friedman does. Friedman was talking about empirical theory with its fat assumptions rather than strictly necessary assumptions. To show that such a theory is false because its assumptions are false, one has to demonstrate that the error occurs in a necessary assumption or in the necessary part of a fat assumption. To illustrate this, modify the previous example by changing the assumption that I own, *or can obtain* an umbrella to the more restrictive assumption that I *own* an umbrella. It is then no longer a necessary assumption, and the theory about my carrying an umbrella does not depend on its truth.

A similar argument applies to Hausman's (1992b, pp.166–7) criticism of Friedman's position. He uses the example of someone buying a used car who wants to test the theory that a car she intends to buy will run reliably. The direct test of the theory that the car runs well is a road test. But to obtain an additional test she can also make use of the following theory: on the assumption that the cylinders, the carburetor and so on are in good condition, the car will run well. Hence she should look under the bonnet before committing herself, even though this amounts to testing a hypothesis by the realism of its assumptions. She should do this because:

> a road test only provides a small sample of ... [the car's] performance. Thus a mechanic who examines the engine can provide relevant and useful information. The mechanic's input is particularly important when one wants to use the car under new circumstances and when the car breaks down. ... Given Friedman's view of the goal of science, there would be no point in examining the assumptions of a theory if it were possible to do a 'total' assessment of its performance with respect to the phenomena it was designed to explain. But one cannot make such an assessment. Indeed, the whole point of a theory is to guide us in circumstances where we do not already know whether the predictions are correct. There is thus much to be learned by examining the components (assumptions) of a theory and its 'irrelevant' predictions. Such consideration of the 'realism' of assumptions is particularly important when extending the theory to new circumstances, or when revising it in the face of predictive failure. (Hausman, 1992a, pp.72–3)

Hausman's example does not distinguish between necessary and fat assumptions. Thus suppose the mechanic points out that the carburetor has a leak, and that a leaky carburetor will cause a car to stall. If he is right, then the statement 'the carburetor does not leak' is an implication of the theory that the car will run well, and nobody objects to testing a theory by its implications. By contrast, suppose that the upholstery is torn, and someone tells the potential buyer that the car is therefore not in 'good shape'. The assumption that only those cars that are in good shape run well is a fat assumption, and hence its unrealism when applied to this particular car does not matter.[3]

Distinguishing between necessary and fat assumptions

Fortunately, it is frequently easy to distinguish necessary assumptions from fat assumptions by seeing if one can invert the theory's assumptions and implications. Necessary assumptions can be restated as implications, fat assumptions cannot. That I carry an umbrella when it rains does not necessarily imply that I own that umbrella; so the assumption that I own an umbrella is a fat assumption that makes a greater than necessary demand on reality. Here are two other examples. One is the assumption that agents try to maximize their own utility, not other people's. That some people work as volunteers shows that as a universal proposition this assumption is false. But the theories we build on this 'false' assumption do not have the implication that no volunteer work ever takes place, and therefore the falsity of this assumption does not matter. Another example is the theory that wages are paid because work has disutility. As so stated, the fat assumption that work has disutility is not valid since in very small doses certain types of work may not have disutility for all people. But the *necessary* assumption required to explain why wages are paid is not that all work has disutility, but only that it has disutility at the margin. That becomes apparent when one states the disutility of work as an *implication* of the theory that wages are paid.

The reason why restating an assumption as an implication brings out the difference between necessary and fat assumptions is that we have been taught to be careful, when drawing implications, to draw only those that strictly follow. By contrast, we have not been trained to nearly the same extent to state our assumptions in a form that makes them strictly necessary.

Reformulating assumptions as implications takes care of the point (see Friedman, 1953, pp.27–8) that what is an adequate assumption for the purpose of one theory may not be an adequate assumption for another theory. For example, engineers constructing a bridge can treat the Newtonian laws as valid assumptions/implications; engineers planning a planetary probe cannot. Since the Straits of Marmara that connect the Black Sea with the Mediterranean are very narrow, an ecologist concerned about pollution of the Black Sea can consider it an enclosed body of water. But someone looking for the cheapest way to ship goods from Rome to Odessa cannot. Similarly, the assumption that all relative prices are constant during an inflation may be an adequate assumption for the quantity theory, but not for a theory that tries to explain how stock prices respond to inflation.

If a theory based on a particular assumption predicts well and is otherwise satisfactory, then one can treat that assumption as an adequate approximation *for the purpose of that theory*, and thus as 'true' in that sense. Hence, with respect to empirical theory, instead of saying that the validity of its assumptions determines the truth of a theory, one might just as well say that the truth of the theory determines whether its assumptions are sufficiently valid.

Uncertainty about the nature of assumptions

Sometimes we cannot decide with sufficient certainty what we should treat as a necessary and what as a fat assumption. Suppose that what is necessary for the theory is either a particular narrow assumption, A_N, together with a certain auxiliary assumption, A_A, or alternatively the broad assumption, A_B. Since we have good reason to believe that A_A holds, we say that A_N is the assumption whose truth is critical for the theory, while A_B is a fat assumption, whose falsity would not disconfirm the theory. But even good reasons may turn out to be incorrect, and A_A may be false. We should therefore give the theory more credence if the fat assumption, A_B, is valid than if only the narrow assumption, A_N is.

Realism of assumptions and generality

A major criterion in selecting among theories is their generality. Generality is useful not only because it reduces the number of theories we need to explain what we observe, and thereby enhances the elegance of our analysis, but also because the more general a theory the more opportunities there are to test it. That is a salient consideration in a field like economics where there are so few opportunities for compelling tests. The more numerous and varied the types of observations that a theory predicts correctly, the greater is the probability that it also predicts correctly the particular observations for which we want to use it. Having assumptions that are accurate enough for the theory to be tested with respect to more than just the particular phenomena we are interested in makes it more likely that we will reach the correct conclusion about the validity of the theory for the particular phenomena for which we want to use it. This proposition must, however, be used with care; we do not necessarily want to replace a simple and tractable theory designed to explain a gross characteristic of a phenomenon with a complex and less tractable theory that can also explain details in which we have little interest. There are trade-offs, and judgement is needed. The life cycle hypothesis is an extremely useful theory, even though it does not explain well a particular household's saving ratio in any one year.

The generality of theories is related to the realism of their assumptions. Suppose that an assumption, A_1, is an accurate enough approximation with respect to theory T_1 that explains S_1, but is not accurate enough to explain S_2. By contrast, assumption A_2 is accurate enough to allow a theory, T_2, which is based on it, to explain both S_1 and S_2. Ceteris paribus, we would then use T_2 instead of T_1 because it is more general. One can therefore say that the accuracy of the assumption determines which theory we should use. It is true that the explicit criterion by which we select theory T_2 is its generality, so that one might argue that it is that criterion, and not the accuracy of the assumption, that matters. But generality here is the result of accurate assumptions (cf. Hausman, 1992b, p.167).

This seems contrary to Friedman's frequently cited claim that unrealistic assumptions can at times be desirable, because such assumptions can expand the domain of a theory: 'Truly important and significant hypotheses will be found to have "assumptions" that are wildly inaccurate descriptive representations of reality, and, in general, the more significant the theory, the more inaccurate the assumptions (in this sense)' (Friedman, 1953, p.14).[4] The validity of Friedman's argument depends upon how one interprets the term 'inaccurate ... assumptions'. If it merely means assumptions that abstract from certain characteristics that are irrelevant for the issue at hand, then Friedman is surely right; 'descriptive realism' limits the domain of a theory. A theory of gravitation that deals only with falling objects that are hollow and green is less general than a theory that deals with all falling objects.

On the other hand, if one means by 'inaccurate ... assumptions', assumptions that are counterfactual, then Friedman is wrong. But the last three words of the above citation, '(in this sense)' strongly suggest that Friedman meant, by inaccurate assumptions, assumptions that abstract, rather than assumptions that are counterfactual. The context in which Friedman wrote his essay, and what he was trying to accomplish with it, support this interpretation (cf. Bear and Orr, 1967; Mayer, 1993a).

Many critics of Friedman's methodology have castigated his claim that general theories have false assumptions. If the above interpretation of Friedman's statement is valid, then their criticisms miss the point.

Realistic assumptions versus theoretical coherence

Ronald Coase (1982), among others, has argued that Friedman's focus on prediction is mistaken, that theories are not just tools for prediction, but should explain: 'A theory also serves as a base for thinking. ... Faced with a choice between a theory which predicts well but gives us little insight into how the system works and one which gives us this insight but predicts badly I would choose the latter' (Coase, 1982, p.6). Coase is right in thinking that a theory based on unrealistic and therefore implausible assumptions will sometimes predict well, and yet in some cases be uninformative about the underlying process.[5]

But by no means in all cases will it be so uninformative. In economics unrealistic assumptions are usually not arbitrary assumptions. They tend to be assumptions that are made to relate the observed phenomenon to the main body of economic theory, and thus to enhance the explanatory status of economic theory. Theorists are proud, and rightly so, if they can show that economic theory can explain some phenomenon that at first glance seems inexplicable; for example, if they can show that giving discounts to the elderly is consistent with profit maximization because the price elasticity of elderly consumers is higher. And it is not just a matter of pride in workmanship. A single, general theory is more satisfying than a welter of special theories. Moreover, if an assumption has been used in a wide-ranging theory that predicts well, that, *other things being equal*, makes it more likely that it will yield a good prediction in other applications too.

But other things are not always equal. When a theory is first developed it is applied to a particular set of phenomena for which its assumptions may be a sufficient approximation to reality. Subsequently, an ambitious theorist may apply it to additional cases, and there its assumptions may no longer be applicable. Thus the assumption of profit maximizing is useful in explaining the behavior of firms, but it may be less useful in explaining the behavior of people in casual interactions. When someone stops me on the street and asks directions, I do not demand payment in return.[6]

If unrealistic assumptions are to be justified by their being part of standard economic theory, one must make one or both of the following arguments. One is that these assumptions are at least as likely to be applicable in the specific case under consideration as they are in other cases in which they have proved successful. The other is that, even though they increase the chance of error, or reduce the likely accuracy of the prediction, the loss is not great enough to offset the benefit of having just a single theory. Hence, while one can urge in defense of some seemingly unrealistic assumption that 'this is what we generally assume in economic theory', this defense is not compelling, and should not be invoked heedlessly.

Conclusions

The three questions posed at the beginning of this chapter can therefore be answered as follows. First, questions about the realism of assumptions are meaningful when asked about empirical theories, but not about formal, if-then theories. Second, the unrealism of an assumption invalidates an empirical theory only if that assumption is a necessary assumption, but not if, as is frequently true in economics, it is a fat assumption. Often one can readily distinguish between necessary and fat assumptions by seeing whether one can reformulate the assumption as an implication of the theory. Third, realism is often a useful characteristic of even fat assumptions. It can provide circumstantial, though not conclusive, evidence on a theory's truth, and frequently enhances a theory's generality. Moreover, realistic assumptions save the reader's time, because when confronted with an unrealistic fat assumption the reader has to decide whether the unrealism pertains to the necessary or the fat part of the assumption.

Thus, although it is naive to insist on the realism of assumptions in the sense that the assumptions should be descriptive and minimize abstraction, and Friedman was right to combat it, there is also a more sophisticated sense in which the realism of even fat assumptions can be useful. The issue is not whether logical correctness requires that assumptions be realistic, but to what extent and in what ways realism of assumptions helps in developing and communicating results. When choosing between two theories that predict equally well, and are equally simple and fruitful, there is much to be said for choosing the one with the more realistic assumptions (see Nooteboom, 1993).

Appendix: Musgrave's formulation of the problem

In his critique of Friedman's methodological essay, a philosopher of science, Alan Musgrave (1981), carves up assumptions in a different way than I have done, a way that does not directly distinguish between necessary and fat assumptions. Instead, he distinguishes mainly between three types of assumptions. First, there are 'negligibility assumptions', which say that some particular factor has a negligible effect on the variable that the theory predicts; for example, that air pressure can safely be ignored when predicting the speed of a falling ball.[7] Second, domain assumptions set out the necessary conditions for the theory's applicability. For example, the theory that increases in the money supply will raise output is applicable on the assumption that in the economy that is being studied wages and prices are not completely flexible. Third, there are the heuristic assumptions, which are used in the development of a theory to facilitate a 'process of successive approximations'. Although they may lead to inaccurate predictions, they are still appropriate because they are simplifying devices needed at this particular stage in the theory's development.

What does looking at assumptions in this way tell us about the advisability of testing theories by the validity of their assumptions? As Mäki (1994a) points out, the validity of a negligibility assumption does support a theory. For domain assumptions the usual issue is whether the theory applies to the particular phenomena under investigation, and the best solution is to see how well it predicts. The larger its domain, the better, so that here, too, the more realistic in the sense of general the better. However, the crucial test is predictive power.

The story becomes complex if the theory predicts correctly when the domain assumption is obviously invalid. Suppose laboratory experiments were to show that the theory of rational expectations predicts correctly the behavior of even the most primitive animals.[8] One might then say that the theory, though counter-intuitive, is confirmed, and that is that. One *might*, but one need not. A more reasonable response would be to see if there is another theory that can account for the observed fact without making the implausible domain assumption. Consider Friedman's widely cited example of the leaves growing on the sunny side of the tree. Instead of claiming that the domain assumption of rational agents extends to trees, we might ask a botanist for an alternative explanation. To be sure, if a thorough search for an alternative explanation comes up empty-handed, eventually we would have to accept even some highly implausible domain assumptions.

Heuristic assumptions present a different problem. Neither they, nor the predictions made with the theory they support, are intended to be precisely true. They are intended merely as successive approximations in the development of a theory. Here the appropriate question is whether the theory with its assumptions advances us on the path to the truth. It may do so by predicting better than the theory it is intended to replace. It may also do so by replacing an ad hoc assumption with an assumption that is not ad hoc, thus anchoring the theory more securely in the accepted corpus of knowledge. While Musgrave suggests that the more realistic the heuristic assumption the better, Mäki (1994a) questions this, pointing out that Musgrave does not defend this claim. In any case, one might say that if a heuristic assumption is a necessary assumption, then it can also be called an implication and tested as such, and if it is a fat assumption, then it cannot be used to test the theory.

In summary, negligibility assumptions are better tested by their implications than by their realism. The same is true for domain assumptions. For heuristic assumptions the appropriate criterion is again the theory's predictive capability, that is its implications.

Notes

1. Mäki (1994b and forthcoming) suggests that what economists mean when they talk of the 'realism' of assumptions should be called 'realisticness'. Mäki (forthcoming) also provides an excellent discussion of the realisticness of assumptions in a broader context, pointing out that the fundamental issue is not whether a scientific theory abstracts, and hence has unrealistic assumptions (all do), but in what way its assumptions are unrealistic.

2. The validity of a theory can, of course, never *prove* the validity of an assumption used to derive it. But the more often theories that use this assumption are validated, the more plausible the assumption becomes.

3. Moreover, Hausman's advocacy of indirect tests is not a valid criticism of Friedman's position, because such reliance on indirect tests is entirely consistent with Friedman's methodology when one reads his methodological essay in a 'soft' way (see Mayer, 1993a), and also when one looks, as Hirsch and de Marchi (1990) have done, at his substantive work and not just at his essay on methodology. His *A Theory of the Consumption Function* (1957) is filled with indirect tests, and Friedman placed more emphasis on them than on his time series test of regressing consumption on permanent income. As he pointed out, on that test his hypothesis was not superior to Duesenberry's relative income theory.

4. But Friedman did not say unrealistic assumptions are always desirable; they do not ensure that a theory is significant.

5. As Mäki (forthcoming) points out, in the 16th century the Ptolemaic geocentric theory predicted better than the rival Copernican theory. Friedman has recently indicated that he does not draw a sharp distinction between prediction and explanation (see Hammond, 1990), so that Coase's criticism is not applicable to him.

6. Neva Goodwin (1991, ch.11) has made the interesting point that inaccurate assumptions are likely to generate false conclusions when two conditions obtain. One is that the assumption is a limit-case idealization (such as perfect competition) and there is a discontinuity between the limit case and actually existing cases (such as the discontinuity between infinity and a variable approaching infinity). The other condition is that the argument is coherent only if the idealization is carried to its limit.

7. As Mäki (1994a) shows, Musgrave confounds cases in which an effect is so small that it can be ignored with cases in which it cannot be detected. For other criticisms of Musgrave, see also Mäki (1993b).

8. Kagel *et al.* (1975) have successfully tested demand theory using animals as subjects.

8 The monetarist debate and the new methodology*

The quality gets lost in the panic for technique. (Virginia Johnson, 1994, principal dancer, Dance Theatre of Harlem)

Despite the disdain with which most American and British economists view methodology, many economists would agree that the most important development in economics over the last generation has been methodological: the shift of economics from an informal field, mainly using a natural language and relatively simple techniques, to a more formal field that converses much of the time in the language of mathematics, and puts great stress on the use of the latest techniques. One would have expected methodologists to have much to say about such a fundamental shift. But while all along many institutionalists with an interest in methodology have deplored this shift, as have an increasing number of leading practicing mainstream economists, mainstream methodologists have had surprisingly little to say about it. A plausible explanation is that an appraisal of formalization is not something that fits comfortably into their research agenda of applying philosophy of science to economics. Here the teachings of Popper, Kuhn, Lakatos and others provide little guidance. So, because they are technique-bound themselves, methodologists have, by and large, not examined sufficiently the transformation of economics into a technique-driven formalistic field.

But this transformation surely deserved appraisal. Elsewhere (Mayer, 1993b), I have undertaken such an appraisal mainly in general terms, focusing on the preoccupation with formalism. In this chapter I look at the preoccupation with formalism and with technique in the context of a case study of its efficacy. Specifically, I ask whether it has helped to resolve one particular highly contentious issue, the Keynesian–monetarist debate.[1]

To anticipate, except in the unlikely event that real business-cycle theory is the correct explanation of many economic fluctuations, the new methodology has made no contributions to this debate, while new econometric techniques have made some. This conclusion is subject to two qualifications. First, the criterion I use is the substantive improvement in the answers that economists can give to the questions posed by the general public that pays their salaries,

* This chapter is a revised version of a paper presented at the Second Seminar on Monetary Theory and Policy at the University of Trento in 1990, hence the informal style. I am indebted for comments to my discussants, Joseph Bisignanio and Patrick Minford.

and not the elegance and intellectual satisfaction that these answers provide to other economists. Yet a *l'art pour l'art* criterion is by no means entirely inappropriate in evaluating research, even though the proponents of the new techniques claim to be doing more than meeting just that criterion. As Patrick Minford (1991, p.262) has remarked: 'there are horses for courses. The New Classical methodology is a powerful new tool kit for attacking theoretical issues. ... It has created a new industry and industry standard. ... What NC methodology is not (yet at least) is an alternative to normal applied economic analysis.' To some extent what I am doing is therefore like criticizing a sports car for not being an efficient furniture van. Second, my evaluation is necessarily backward-looking, and does not take into account that the investment in modern techniques may pay off in the future.

The new methodology and new econometric techniques have influenced the monetarist debate both by the contributions they have made to the specific issues that comprise this debate and, what is more important, by reducing the role of this debate within the corpus of macroeconomics. I will first discuss the latter. But before doing so it is necessary to describe what I mean by 'the new methodology'. The meaning of 'new econometrics' is straightforward; it consists of certain techniques, such as Granger tests and error-correction models, that have been developed in recent years.

The new methodology and its contribution to the debate

I have discussed elsewhere (Mayer, 1990b, ch.4) how the rise of monetarism was fostered by the spread of the then new positivistic methodology among economists. This methodology combined the insistence of traditional theory on the rational behavior of maximizing agents with the insistence of institutionalists, such as Wesley C. Mitchell, on explaining observed phenomena. It was largely, but by no means entirely, the work of Milton Friedman. It provided the framework for the monetarist–Keynesian debate and justified the supposition of this debate that whichever theory could predict nominal GDP more accurately was the better theory.

But in the 1970s and 1980s the methodological preferences of economists shifted. Skill at deriving subtle implications of rational utility maximization became the measure of an economist's proficiency. The new methodology not only insists that all statements about the behavior of agents be consistent with utility or profit maximization, but also requires that this consistency be spelled out explicitly in mathematized models. Formalism is praised and 'intuitive' is a term of derogation. Ad hocery is now the most serious of sins. Theory is a device for relating 'assumptions' to implications, and economists now pay increased attention to the rigorous elucidation of this relationship, and less attention to the consistency of the theory's implications with the observed data, or to the realism of the assumptions. Short-cuts that facilitate empirical work, such as the Marshallian partial equilibrium, are avoided in favor of more formal general equilibrium.

At the same time, the mathematical and econometric sophistication of economists improved greatly, and the emphasis that is placed on using the most recent techniques has increased substantially. In addition, though this would be much harder to document, it seems to me that, at least in the United States, quite apart from their much better training in mathematics, the generation that received its PhDs after the mid-1960s is just more able than the older generation.

In talking about a 'new methodology' I do not mean that most of these tendencies are new, in the sense of never having existed before. They can clearly be found in the work of earlier economists. But the 'new methodology' is new in the sense that what had previously been the methodological preferences of a few economists now became the dominant methodology, at least in the 'right circles'. To be sure, work at the 'cutting edge' is not just formal modeling; empirical tests still play a role. The typical paper estimates the model and evaluates the restrictions it imposes on the coefficients, but such empirical testing is no longer central to the papers that are typical of this new methodology. Moreover, with the ready availability of massive computing power one can often run enough variants until the usually highly collinear time series serve up the asked-for conclusions. And, as discussed in Chapter 10, the task of meeting the restrictions imposed by a model is greatly eased by the convention that failure to reject a restriction at the 5 per cent level somehow implies that this restriction is accepted. With empirical testing thus being toothless rather than ruthless, it is not surprising that formalizations are given more status than is empirical work.

The empirical evidence that is considered persuasive also changed in two other ways. It seems that there is now more of a tendency to rely on a single test, usually consisting of time series regressions, rather than on a wide array of less formal evidence covering many periods and many countries. Second, theorizing had previously been constrained, at least informally, by having to be more or less consistent with common sense and casual observation; for example, the occurrence of involuntary unemployment was not to be denied. But now that economists have acquired advanced mathematical tools, they feel sufficient confidence to do what physicists do, that is to develop certain theories that appear totally irreconcilable with what we observe around us.

Moreover, the emphasis has shifted away from the pragmatic search for the correct answer to an emphasis on an answer derived by using the most complex and sophisticated tools. It does not, of course, do so explicitly. Nobody asserts that a pedagogically simple and accurate hypothesis is inferior to a complex and less accurate one. But economists started to act more as though it were (see Hoover, 1989).

Such a methodological value system is not kind to monetarism, and to the whole tenor of the monetarist debate. The monetarists' slogan, 'Just look at these facts and you will see that the money supply determines nominal GNP', now gathers few young recruits. The war-cry of the new classicals, 'Look at my sophisticated techniques', is more exciting to those who have been trained in these techniques.

Some implications of the new methodology

The conflict between the new methodology and the methodology that underlies monetarism is well illustrated by Frank Hahn's (1971) review of Friedman's *The Optimum Quantity of Money*.[2] He states, 'Friedman neither has, nor claims to have a monetary theory. His strong and influential views are not founded on an understanding of "how money works", but on what his empirical studies have led him to believe to have been the course of monetary history' (p. 61). If success in 'explaining the course of monetary history' is not, as I think it should be, the criterion by which monetary theories are to be evaluated, then indeed monetarism has little to offer. It does not rely on a painstaking derivation of its hypotheses from the maximizing behavior of agents (see Brunner, 1989) or on a single 'crucial experiment'. Instead it relies on the circumstantial evidence provided by a wide variety of different data sets, such as time series for many countries, and cross-country studies. None of these pieces of evidence may be compelling by itself, but their cumulative weight mounts up, even though it leaves someone who demands formal proof unimpressed.

As Abraham Hirsch and Neil de Marchi (1990) have shown, such a reliance on a mass of suggestive evidence is typical of Friedman's work. This is not to say that monetarists never work in the new mode. Karl Brunner, Allan Meltzer and Alex Cukierman have developed persuasive rational expectations models, but these models are so detached from the main lines of the monetarist paradigm that they are not likely to turn readers into monetarists.

Keynesian methodology is more or less similar to monetarist methodology. There is somewhat more emphasis on formal modeling, and also on 'commonsense' observations and introspection, but these differences are not great. Hence, when the new methodology became popular, Keynesians were in the same boat as monetarists. It is therefore not surprising that the Keynesian–monetarist debate now sounds old-fashioned to many economists, and that so many young macroeconomists show little interest in it. It is no longer the arena in which to establish one's reputation, or an area that catches the interests of newly trained economists as it once did.

Apart from the direct effect that this shift in methodological preferences had on the role that the monetarist debate plays in economics, it also had a perhaps more important indirect effect. This is its role in the development and popularity of new classical theory, a theory that has made the disagreement between the

Keynesian and monetarist theories look like a mere family squabble.[3] While the discovery, or rather rediscovery, of one of the components of new classical theory, the vertical Phillips curve, can readily be related to what was going on in the economy at the time, new classical theory itself grew out of the new methodology rather than being imposed on economists by the force of actual developments in the real world.

The rise of the new methodology and the development of new classical theory are certainly not the only causes of the declining prominence of the monetarist debate. Other causes are the acceptance by Keynesians of a considerable part of monetarism, the failure of monetarism to provide a workable money demand function, the decline of inflation, and perhaps also an unfortunate choice of research projects (see Mayer, 1990b, ch.4). But surely the development of new classical theory was a major cause.

The validity of new classical theory

If new classical theory is correct, then the new methodology has made an overwhelmingly important contribution to the monetarist debate by showing that both the Keynesians and the monetarists are wrong. But is new classical theory right? Is the evidence that the new classicals present convincing to most economists? One segment of the profession whose opinion should be given much weight when the value of so much human capital is involved is a group that has relatively little vested interest in the outcome of the debate: that is, graduate students.

I have no data on European students, but I suspect that a substantial majority would vote against new classical theory. For the United States there exists a little bit of empirical evidence. In 1985, Arjo Klamer and David Colander (1987) surveyed the views of graduate students at the following universities: Chicago, Columbia, Harvard, MIT, Stanford and Yale. They did not ask directly about new classical theory, but they did ask whether fiscal policy can be an effective stabilization tool. The overwhelming majority, 84 per cent, chose either the 'yes' or the 'yes, but' option, with only 11 per cent replying 'no'. Admittedly, this response was affected by the choice of the sample; at that bastion of new classical theory, the University of Minnesota the result would presumably have been quite different.[4] But all the same, the new classical revolution can hardly be said to have generated much support where it counts, among the young. Paul Samuelson (1947, p.145), in describing how the Keynesian revolution excited graduate students at the time, quotes Wordsworth's lines

> Bliss was it in that dawn to be alive,
> But to be young was very heaven!

Classical theory does not get such a response very often. Indeed, surveys of US economists show that new classical theory is far from sweeping the field. In a survey of American economists, 12 per cent generally agreed with the proposition that 'the major source of macroeconomic disturbances is supply shocks', 28 per cent agreed with qualifications and 55 per cent generally disagreed (Alston, Kearl and Vaughn, 1992, p.205). Surveys of economists in Austria, France, Germany and Switzerland also suggest that new classical theory does not have widespread support among professional economists in Europe (Frey *et al.*, 1984). To be sure, matters of truth are not settled by public opinion polls, but careful surveys of the evidence also suggest that a healthy skepticism about real business cycles is warranted. Thus Steven Sheffrin (1989, pp.79–80) in a survey of real business cycle theory concludes that there are:

> several deep issues with models of real business cycles that have been developed to date. First, it is difficult to detect movements in technical change. Existing attempts ... would give inconsistent results in the presence of monopoly power. Second, the statistical literature on trends and cycles does not ... provide complete support for real business cycles. Conventional monetary models can generate near nonstationary time series which are difficult to distinguish from nonstationary models. Models that do not feature a natural rate ... could also account for the time series properties that are observed. ... Third, the behavior of consumption ... suggests that insurance against economic fluctuations is far from complete. Without full insurance, however, the economy is likely to behave quite differently from the manner predicted by real business cycle theory... Finally, real business cycle theory allows no role for monetary factors. Yet ... evidence on changes in monetary regimes suggests that real variables are significantly affected by regime shifts.

A symposium on real business cycles in the *Journal of Economic Perspectives* contained two papers, one by an advocate, and the other by a critic of real business cycles. The critic, Gregory Mankiw, argued:

> Both its reliance on large technological disturbances as the primary source of economic fluctuations and its reliance on the intertemporal substitution of leisure to explain changes in employment are fundamental weaknesses. ... The choice between alternative theories of the business cycle – in particular between real business cycle theory and new Keynesian theory – is partly a choice between internal and external consistency. ... My own forecast is that real business cycle advocates will not manage to produce convincing evidence that there are substantial shocks to technology and that leisure is highly substitutable over time. Without such evidence their theories will be judged not persuasive. (Mankiw, 1989, pp.79, 89).

The proponent of real business cycles, Charles Plosser, concluded:

> Real business cycle theory is still in its infancy and thus remains an incomplete theory of the business cycle. Yet the progress to date has had a significant impact on research in macroeconomics. In particular, simple real business cycle models have

demonstrated that equilibrium models are not necessarily inconsistent with many characteristics attributed to the business cycle. ... These models have changed the standard by which macroeconomic theories are judged and provided the foundations for an understanding of business cycles that is based on the powerful choice theoretic analysis at the core of economic reasoning. [Their] appeal ... is the apparent power of some simple economic principles to generate dynamic behavior that was heretofore thought to be incompatible with any notion of equilibrium. While the promise is great, much work remains before economists have a real understanding of business cycles. (Charles Plosser, 1989, p.71)

Plosser's support for real business cycles as a promising line of research can hardly be considered a claim of victory. And his emphasis on how well real business cycle theory is integrated into general economic theory will not suffice to persuade those who are more concerned with how well a hypothesis is integrated with the observations that it is intended to explain (see Chapters 11 and 13).

New classical theory, and real business cycle theory specifically are based on the intellectually satisfying assumption of rational expectations, but also require the much more questionable assumption of rapid market clearing. Moreover, while new classical theory is not directed to the question of whether financial markets are efficient, evidence of inefficient behavior in financial markets would throw doubt on new classical theory. If the standard rational maximizing model cannot adequately explain behavior in auction markets dominated by professionals, why would one expect it to explain behavior in the labor market? And, as discussed in Chapter 13, in his survey of the literature on efficient capital markets Stephen LeRoy (1989) concluded that there are some serious discrepancies between this theory and the observed behavior of capital markets.

A firm believer in new classical theory will find none of these arguments convincing. But they do suggest that real business cycle theory, instead of being the wave of the future, is just a bubble. This is not to deny that it may have made some contribution. It is quite possible that real fluctuations will play a larger role than before in our thinking, thus reducing the importance of the demand-side fluctuations that are the focus of the monetarist debate. And rational expectations theory is likely to be an important step in the development of an adequate treatment of expectations. All the same, whatever the benefits of new classical theory in forcing us to re-examine our thinking on micro foundations (see Chapter 4), its contribution to the monetarist debate has been at most modest.

Specific aspects of the monetarist debate
Even though the new methodology, in its manifestation of new classical theory, could not sweep the monetarist debate away, it could still have transformed this debate by contributing to the solution of some specific issues. Moreover, it is

in the resolution of specific issues that one would expect the new econometric techniques to be useful. I will first consider the problem of the stability of velocity and of money demand functions. Then I take up three specific modern techniques, vector autogressions, Granger tests and Kalman filters. Finally, I take up the Lucas critique and time-inconsistency theory.

I will not deal with formal models that have presented a more rigorous analysis of monetary theory. Developing such models can certainly be justified by the wish to make our theory more elegant, but that has little to do with the monetarist debate. Long ago Don Patinkin (1956, 1965) presented a model of the quantity theory showing that monetarism is not 'black box' economics. That is all that is needed, and subsequent refinements, such as Niehans (1978), while certainly valuable for many other purposes, did not add much to the basics of the monetarist debate.

The stability of velocity

The great failing of monetarism in the United States has been its inability to provide a manageable demand function that predicts with sufficient accuracy. With hindsight this failure is not surprising. With the payments of explicit interest on deposits the nature of M-1 changed, and with the elimination of the ceiling on time-deposit interest rates the demand for time deposits changed. When the attributes of a commodity change, one would hardly expect its demand function or income elasticity to remain unchanged.

But the problem goes deeper. There was not just a once-for-all shift in the demand function for money but, in addition, velocity has become less stable. This too, is unsurprising. The traditional argument for the stability of velocity was that, though transactions balances are somewhat responsive to the forgone yield on money, they are a stable proportion of expenditures, because both the payments technology and habits change only slowly. Hence, now that a larger part of M-1 is held as savings rather than as transactions balances, it is hardly surprising that the ratio of M-1 to income has become less stable. Similarly, with the interest rate on time deposits being closer to other interest rates on savings, a larger proportion of time deposits now consists of interest-sensitive deposits. In principle, such an increase in the interest elasticity does not make the demand function for money less stable. But it does mean that the failure to include some relevant interest rates, such as the yield on bond mutual funds, is more damaging. Moreover, it makes the demand for money more responsive to innovations that create new financial instruments.

It seemed for a time as though modern econometrics, in the form of the Hendry error-correction technique, would solve the problem. Using this technique in their 'P*' model, Hallman *et al.* (1989) were able to explain very well the equilibrium price level from a knowledge of M-2, and also to explain the inflation rate tolerably well. But in recent years the predictions of this model have degenerated substantially. Perhaps this is only a temporary blip, but perhaps not. Moreover, even if it did predict accurately, the P* model is consistent with causation running from prices to money (see Hall and Milne, 1994) and hence may not provide a lever for controlling prices. In any case, although this model uses a modern econometric technique, it is not in the spirit of the modern methodology. Just the opposite, it breaks the central heuristic rule of this methodology, which is that ad hoc assumptions must be avoided, because its assumption that long-run velocity is constant is not grounded in any behavioral explanation. This is not necessarily a serious failing of this model. Presumably it was developed to serve as a practical tool, and not as a deep explanation of economic behavior. Hence, if eventually this model turns out to be successful, this should be considered a credit to the Hendry error-correction technique, but not as a contribution of the new methodology.

Base velocity, unlike the velocities of M-1 and M-2, has remained stable, and that may seem to offer a way out. But most of the base consists of currency, and the correlation of currency and GDP may be due primarily to income 'causing' currency (see Benjamin Friedman, 1988).

Hendry and Ericsson v. Friedman and Schwartz

Another example of the use of modern statistical tools in the discussion of M-2 velocity is the Hendry–Ericsson (1983, 1991) critique of Friedman and Schwartz's (1982) *Monetary Trends in the United States and the United Kingdom*. That monumental book had used only simple and traditional statistical tools, perhaps because it was written over many years, perhaps because the authors chose to allocate their time to acquiring a thorough familiarity with the data rather than to employing the latest tools, or perhaps because they were skeptical about the value of these tools.[5] Hendry and Ericsson (who confine their analysis to Friedman and Schwartz's data for the UK) criticize Friedman and Schwartz for using low-brow econometric techniques, and describe their critique as 'not an "anti-monetarist" polemic; ... [but as] a pro-econometrics tract which highlights the practical dangers of seeking to analyze complex stochastic processes while eschewing modern econometric methods' (1983, p.48). Hence, if they have succeeded in showing that Friedman and Schwartz's results are defective, then they have also shown that modern econometrics has made a valuable contribution to the monetarist debate.

Among Hendry and Ericsson's criticism of the informal nature of Friedman and Schwartz's evidence are that: 'exogeneity is nowhere defined and despite assertions as to its existence or otherwise for certain variables, such claims are not tested. ...'Stability' – in the sense of parameter constancy – is asserted for several relationships but again not tested' (1983, p.48). More generally, Friedman and Schwartz's failure to undertake some necessary tests 'removes the *credibility* from their claims' (1983, p.50, italics in original). Hendry and Ericsson also object to Friedman and Schwartz's averaging of the data by using cycle phases as their unit of observation instead of using the underlying annual observations, as they, themselves, do. But even when working with Friedman and Schwartz's phase averages they reach conclusions that differ sharply from Friedman and Schwartz's: 'at a surprisingly large number of points, where FS see a silk purse, we see a sow's ear (1983, p.65).

More specifically, Hendry and Ericsson point out that even when using phase averages one cannot reject the hypothesis that velocity is a random walk. They also show that Friedman and Schwartz's money demand function does not pass a Chow stability test. Using annual data they fit a simple first-order autoregression (with the same dummy variables that Friedman and Schwartz had used) to money demand. This naive equation dominates the Friedman–Schwartz equation. Moreover, when they fit their error-correction model it has an error variance of less than one-tenth the error variance of the Friedman–Schwartz model. Among their other criticisms are that the money supply should not be treated as exogenous, that the disturbances to the Friedman–Schwartz equation are not normally distributed and that, if a trend term is added to this equation, it turns out to be significant.

How valid are these criticisms? I have neither the space nor the expertise to discuss all the important issues raised by Hendry and Ericsson, and hence will discuss only some of them.[6] While Friedman and Schwartz did perhaps make the right choice in allocating their efforts primarily to the data rather than the techniques, this does not invalidate Hendry and Ericsson's criticism of their techniques. However, Hendry and Ericsson's criticism is not as telling as it might seem because they are evaluating Friedman and Schwartz's work by econometric criteria that are not quite appropriate to the task that Friedman and Schwartz had set themselves. Friedman and Schwartz are not econometricians who tried to obtain the best prediction, or rather retrodiction, of GNP and prices. Instead, they are applying the quantity theory to the British economy, both to explain the behavior of GNP and prices, and to test the theory against these data. They therefore have to impose the structure of the quantity theory on the data. They are trying to test a theory, and not to find the best representation of the data.

Ideally, one would like to have a hypothesis that is well-integrated with a higher-level theory and explains the data in each of a large number of countries over many periods better than does any rival theory or equation, even if this rival theory is specific to just one of these countries or periods. In practice one may have to settle for less. One possibility is to focus on goodness of fit and produce a regression equation that gives the best prediction (or retrodiction) for a particular country. This could well be an autoregressive equation that does not explain anything. The other is to apply to each particular country a regression equation that is closely integrated with a theory which has performed well for other countries. That is what Friedman and Schwartz do. What Hendry and

Ericsson do is quite different; as Patrick Minford (1991, p.263) points out, they do not have a theory of money demand.

Suppose that the theory-related equation does not fit as well as an equation derived by an almost atheoretic search of the data set. This does not necessarily mean that the former should be discarded. One can advocate the quantity theory even if its equation fits worse for every single country than does an equation specific to that country, as long as no single one of the country-specific equations does better than the quantity theory in the other countries as well. To be sure, this principle has to be used with caution. Quantity theorists cannot, whenever confronted with unfavorable evidence, brush it aside with a claim that their theory predicts better in other situations without specifying these situations.

One way of illustrating the difference between economic and econometric criteria is to consider the Chow test. Suppose a Chow test shows instability. While this implies that one may want to look for a better fitting equation if one's task is prediction, it does not necessarily mean that one should reject the hypothesis one is testing. Compare two cases. In the first the standard error of the equation is extremely low, so that even a small degree of instability causes a rejection by the Chow test. In the second the standard error is high throughout, so that the Chow test does not bite. Thus performance on a Chow test is not always a good criterion by which to select hypotheses.

Moreover, the quantity theory does not assert that the demand for money is stable in the sense that all the observations come from the same universe, but only that it is stable enough for one to be able to explain observed changes in income primarily by changes in the supply of money, or else by changes in the independent variables of the money demand function. More generally, whether a function is stable enough to be of use depends, not only on how stable it is in an absolute sense, but also on whether there exists a usable rival function that predicts better, and on whether its prediction is accurate enough to help solve the questions for which it was developed. If I want to know whether to carry an umbrella, I only need to know whether it will rain, and not the rainfall to the nearest millimeter. Statistical and economic stability are not the same thing.

Friedman and Schwartz's reply to Hendry and Ericsson brings out this distinction between economic and econometric evaluations. They describe Hendry and Ericsson's approach as follows: 'start with a collection of numerical data bearing on the question under study, subject them to sophisticated econometric techniques, place great reliance on tests of significance, and end with a single hypothesis (equation), however complex, supposedly "encompassing" ... all subhypotheses' (Friedman and Schwartz, 1991, p.39). By contrast, their own method is:

> to examine a wide variety of evidence, quantitative and nonquantitative, ... test results from one body of evidence on other bodies, using econometric techniques as one tool

in this process, and build up a collection of simple hypotheses that may or may not be readily viewed as components of a broader all-embracing hypothesis; and, finally test hypotheses on bodies of data other than those from which they were derived. (Friedman and Schwartz, 1991, p.39)

Friedman and Schwartz also argue that Hendry and Ericsson picked on just one regression among the numerous ones they had offered. Moreover, Hendry and Ericsson are wrong in claiming that this regression is variance-dominated by theirs, because these regressions measure different things; in the Hendry–Ericsson regression the dependent variable is the first difference, while it is the log of the level of money in the Friedman–Schwartz equation. Other points that Friedman and Schwartz make are that, since they, unlike Hendry and Ericsson, were concerned with longer-run relationships that abstract from cycles, they were justified in using phase averages. They also point out that many of Hendry and Ericsson's parameter estimates are similar to those that they had found. Moreover, Hendry and Ericsson, despite their great emphasis on econometric analysis, made no allowance for regression bias.

Because their paper was a reply only to Hendry and Ericcson's 1991 paper, Friedman and Schwartz did not discuss Hendry and Ericsson's earlier (1983) result that velocity is a random walk, a result that, at first glance, may seem extremely destructive of the quantity theory. But actually it is not. Consider a simple money demand function that contains only a constant term and income. Any money demand function is intended to be just an approximation to reality, and not a photograph of it. Hence changes in the constant term – if they are small and occasional – do not necessarily invalidate the money demand function. The question is whether these shifts are important enough for the demand function to give forecasts that are either inferior to rival forecasts or are so far off the mark that they are altogether useless. Moreover, we all agree that a money demand function should include the interest rate. If the interest rate follows a random walk, then this may cause velocity to be a random walk too. In addition, as Bordo (1984) notes, Hendry and Ericsson's evidence for a random walk relates only to the short run, and could therefore be due to erratic changes in the money supply, since the dependent variable we use in a money demand function is actually a measure of the money supply. Moreover, there is a basic issue in interpreting the evidence for random walks: inability to reject the claim that a series is a random walk is hardly firm evidence that it actually is a random walk.

But none of this warrants outright rejection of Hendry and Ericsson's criticisms. After reading their paper I am less impressed by Friedman and Schwartz's evidence than I was before. Their paper does make a contribution to the monetarist debate, though it has hardly slain the quantity theory. The quantity theory is not based on a single piece of evidence, but is founded on a whole body of evidence from a wide array of circumstances, none of which is conclusive individually, but which jointly add up to a strong case.

Vector autoregressions, Granger tests and Kalman filters

VARs have now become a common way of estimating the role that various shocks play in determining income. Sims (1980) found that, when interest rates are entered in a VAR along with money, monetary shocks have only trivial effects on industrial production and wholesale prices. One response to this finding has been to challenge its robustness. (See, for instance, Spencer, 1989.) But Todd (1990), using a wide variety of alternative formulations, has shown that Sims's finding with respect to the role of money is remarkably robust.

Monetarists can, however, object that both Sims's and Todd's test are biased against the quantity theory. One reason is that the quantity theory, when applied, as it is in these tests, to relatively short periods, tries to explain changes in nominal income, rather than in either industrial production or in wholesale prices. Second, the quantity theory has its comparative advantage in explaining longer-run movements in nominal income and in the price level, rather than the monthly and quarterly changes that Todd deals with. This makes the quantity theory particularly vulnerable to rejection by a VAR. By including lagged terms of the dependent variable, a monthly or quarterly VAR requires the independent variables to explain only monthly or quarterly movements in the dependent variable, and gives the independent variables little credit for explaining the more persistent movements in the dependent variables that are the forte of the quantity theory. Third, and more fundamentally, there are the basis methodological criticisms that have been raised against VAR methods. (See Hoover, 1988, ch.8, and the literature cited therein.)

The extent to which causation runs from income to money, rather than from money to income, is one of the most contentious issues in the monetarist debate. One way to deal with this problem is to use Granger causality tests. Is this appropriate? Quite apart from the much-discussed problems of interpreting the results of Granger tests in general (see Hoover, 1994, and the literature cited there), Granger tests are not applicable to the question at hand. This is because both monetarists and Keynesians agree that much of the time money is endogenous. Indeed, monetarists spend considerable energy denouncing the Fed, often vehemently so, for following an accommodative policy that makes the monetary growth rate behave procyclically. Monetarists then add that at certain times the Fed steps sharply on the brakes and thereby generates a recession. Then, during the recession, the Fed becomes too expansionary, thus setting the stage for the next cycle. In this story the money supply is exogenous before upper turning points, but endogenous much of the time.

Hence monetarists have no quarrel with any econometric results that, on the average, show money to be endogenous. If Granger tests showed instead that money is exogenous, this too would be consistent with monetarism, since monetarists do not claim that the Fed follows an accommodative policy that has a stable coefficient relating money to income, and it is only stable coefficients that are registered by correlation tests, such as the Granger test. At the same time, either money 'causing' income, or income 'causing' money is also consistent with Keynesian theory. Thus Granger tests have little to add to the monetarist debate.

Monetarists have long argued that shocks to the money supply precede cyclical turning points, and this provides at least a presumption that money causes income rather than the reverse. Their techniques have consisted of a simple comparison of cyclical turning points with turning points in the growth rate of a monetary aggregate (Friedman and Schwartz, 1963b) or with deviations of the growth rate of money from its trend (Poole, 1975). Allan Meltzer (1986) introduced a more modern and superior technique by using a Kalman filter to separate unusual fluctuations in the growth rate of the monetary base from more usual ones. He found that 'shocks to the monetary base led the shock to output at seven of the nine turning points, but two of the leads are relatively weak' (p.176). The importance of this finding is, however, reduced by Tobin's (1970) demonstration that in at least one Keynesian model (though a rather implausible one) in which money is just accommodative, turning points in the monetary growth rate also precede turning points in income.

The Lucas critique
What has made a much more substantial contribution to the monetarist debate is the Lucas critique. Before it appeared, a cutting edge of macroeconomic research was to develop feedback rules (or as they were then called, 'semi-rules') for stabilization policy. The Lucas critique took the sharp edge off this work, and it declined for a time. In recent years it has made a comeback, mainly in the form that is derived more from a quantity-theory framework than from a Keynesian framework (see Meltzer, 1987; McCallum, 1987, 1988; Mayer, 1987; Thornton, 1993). Intuitively, feedback rules that have the central bank adjust monetary growth only on the basis of past changes in velocity and the growth rate of GDP seem less damaged by the Lucas critique than are rules based on a Keynesian structural model, particularly if McCallum (1987) is correct in suggesting that the Lucas critique is more important for equations linking nominal and real magnitudes than for other equations. These rules require only that changes in the trend of velocity and the autocorrelation of GDP growth rates show sufficient persistence. And it seems more or less plausible that the trends of velocity growth and GDP growth are at least somewhat more policy-invariant than are the coefficients of a structural model. Admittedly, this is much more

of a guess than the result of rigorous analysis, and one study (Dotsey and Otrok, 1994) found that the Lucas critique is significant for at least one feedback rule. But, in any case, quite apart from the Lucas critique there is a question about how well feedback rules work. Their good performance on various tests could be due to the endogeneity of the currency component of the base, which is the monetary variable mostly used (see Benjamin Friedman, 1988; Modigliani, 1988).

All in all, while there is still much dispute about the practical importance of the Lucas critique it should be considered a substantial contribution to the monetarist debate, for two reasons. First, it has reduced the importance of the feedback rules literature. Second, it also reduced the appeal of Keynesian theory. One of the advantages of Keynesian theory is that it enables one to build econometric models with which to gauge the effect of various policy proposals. In a Lucasian world that is at present an idle exercise. To be sure, the evidence for the empirical significance of the Lucas critique is mixed (see Mayer, 1993b, appendix to ch.7), but 'mixed' does not mean 'unimportant'.

Time-inconsistency and monetary policy
Many recent theoretical discussions of central bank policy have dealt with the time-inconsistency problem. This literature, with its claim to rigour, its use of complex game theory and its emphasis on making behavioral assumptions explicit, is a typical example of modern methodology. Not surprisingly, it has received much attention, and time-inconsistency appears to have become the most popular justification for imposing a rule on the central bank. (See, for instance, Papell, 1989.) My focus in this discussion is on a narrowly defined version of this theory that stresses the central bank's attempt to raise output above the level desired by agents, not on a looser version that relies on the different slopes of short-run and long-run Phillips curves. Such a looser version is much more plausible, but it is a direct implication of traditional monetarist theory, and hence not a contribution of the new methodology. All the new methodology has added to it is a translation of a verbal argument into the mathematical language of game theory.

Despite its popularity it is doubtful for three reasons that the time-inconsistency literature has made much of a contribution to the monetarist debate, at least for the United States. First, the results reached by this literature are not helpful. Small differences in the assumptions of various models – assumptions not readily amenable to empirical tests – result in radically different conclusions.

Second, the argument for monetary policy being time-inconsistent cannot be sustained by observing the record of the Fed's thinking.[7] Instead, it is founded on the 'as-if' methodology that tells us that we do not have to observe agents to know how they behave, that we can simply assume that they act to maximize their welfare. But 'as-if' reasoning is much more hazardous in this case than when it is used to explain the actions of private agents. For private agents the assumption that they act as though they want to maximize income is a reasonable and highly useful working hypothesis. But what is it that central bankers try to maximize? Is it the welfare of the politicians who appointed them, the prestige of the central bank, their personal prestige, or a feeling of having done a good job? Without knowing what is being maximized, little is gained by assuming that people act as though they are maximizing that unknown something.[8]

Third, time-inconsistency theory is intended to explain why central banks, specifically the Fed, *generally*, and not just occasionally, have an inflationary bias. At least for the United States, it is far from clear that this is so. Fed policy was not inflationary from the end of World War I inflation to the 1930s. It was then, on the whole, deflationary in the 1930s. Following the inflation associated with World War II it was again essentially not inflationary until the mid-1960s, with the exception of the Korean War period.[9]

A tempting response is that time-inconsistency results in a tendency towards inflation, but that most of the time this tendency was suppressed or offset by other factors. But such a response would, at most, allow one to say that the historical data do not necessarily reject the hypothesis, not that there is evidence for the existence of a systematic inflationary bias that time-inconsistency theory can explain. One possible factor that one might invoke to explain the lack of a consistent inflationary bias is the constraints imposed at times by fixed exchange rates. But, as discussed in the appendix to this chapter, such an argument receives no support from the historical record.

Suppose, then, that for these reasons one uses time-inconsistency as an explanation only of the great American inflation of the late 1960s and 1970s rather than of Federal Reserve behavior in general. This would require the ad hoc assumption that some unknown factor made time-inconsistency theory more applicable in that period than at other times, and hence could be rejected for this reason. And even if it were not, the proponents of time-inconsistency theory would still have to show that their theory can explain this inflation better than do rival theories. A plausible rival is that policymakers underestimated the natural rate of unemployment. Estimates of the natural rate diverge substantially (see Weiner, 1986) and it may have taken policymakers many years to learn that the natural rate was higher than they thought. Whether or not this is the main explanation of the great inflation is not the issue. What is important is that those who try to explain this inflation by time-inconsistency have not even tried to show that their explanation is superior to its rivals.

Hence, despite the brilliance with which it has been developed, time-inconsistency theory has not made a major contribution to the understanding of monetary policy. This is not to deny that it has made *some* contribution, but only that this contribution has been large enough to justify the great effort devoted to this topic.[10]

Conclusion

This chapter has appraised seven potential substantive contributions of the new methodology and modern econometrics to the monetarist debate. One, real business cycle theory, if valid, would essentially eliminate this debate as a serious issue. But it does not seem valid. The work of Hendry and Ericsson has damaged a major monetarist contribution that is based on the older econometric techniques to a limited extent. And the error-correction technique *may* turn out to be a major contribution to rescuing the quantity theory from its current troubles, although it has not done so to date. Meltzer's application of a Kalman filter is also a useful contribution, though it does not protect a timing test from the objection raised by Tobin. But in other instances the new methodology and modern econometric techniques have added virtually nothing useful.

Given the vast amount of labor and ingenuity expended, this is a disappointing result. It would be foolish to argue from this single example that the new methodology and techniques have in general not paid their way. But their disappointing performance in this case makes it worth seeing if they have also been unsuccessful in other fields of economics. By carrying out such appraisals, and by drawing conclusions from them, methodologists could make a substantial contribution.

Appendix: international constraints and inflationary policies
In the 1920s the US gold stock was large and increasing in most years, so US monetary policy was not constrained by the gold standard. The influence of the gold standard in the early 1930s is more controversial. Then there occurred a massive gold inflow. Prices rose rapidly after 1933, but given the extensive unemployment at the time this inflation can hardly be attributed to the Fed's wish to induce agents to supply more labor than they intended at the prevailing real wage.

In the postwar period the size of the US gold stock and the position of the dollar as the reserve currency left the Fed more or less unconstrained by balance of payments considerations until the late 1960s. It was only after the start of the great inflation that such considerations had the potential of being a serious constraint on an inflationary policy. Yet that was just the time when the Fed was following such a policy. After the collapse of the Bretton Woods system removed the balance of payment constraint, the Fed continued on an inflationary policy for about six years before adopting a sharp deflationary policy. All in all, this is hardly the picture of a central bank whose inflationary proclivities were constrained by fears about the balance of payments. Someone unfamiliar with economics who is just told the times at which the United States faced balance of payments problems and the times at which it followed inflationary policies would hardly guess that balance of payments considerations are supposed to restrain inflationary policies.

Notes
1. For a discussion of monetarism stressing methodological aspects, see Mayer (1994a).
2. Although Hahn is certainly not a new classical, his emphasis on abstract and polished theory is similar to that of the new classicals.
3. More than 20 years ago Don Patinkin (1971) already argued that what Friedman called the 'quantity theory' is closer to Keynesian theory than to the traditional quantity theory as taught at Chicago in the 1930s. Not surprisingly, Friedman (1972) disagrees. The dispute is due to Patinkin classifying theories by the techniques they use, such as analysing stocks and not flows, while Friedman classifies theories by the results they reach, for example, by what variables they consider important in explaining changes in income. There is a somewhat similar dispute about the quantity-theory credentials of Brunner and Meltzer. (See Stein, 1976, ch.2.)
4. As Klamer and Colander point out, economics graduate students at different universities have divergent views.
5. Thus Friedman's skepticism about the Cochrane–Orcut adjustment (Milton Friedman, 1988) may explain why he and Schwartz did not adjust for serial correlation, but perhaps they should then have used other procedures.
6. Much of the following discussion is based on Bordo's (1984) insightful comment on Hendry and Ericcson's paper, where he draws the useful distinction between applying econometrics and economic analysis to an empirical problem.
7. Almost verbatim transcripts of Federal Open Market Committee (FOMC) meetings are currently available until the more recent years, for which substantially less detailed summaries have been published. These records do not show time-inconsistency, at least in the sense defined here. Instead they show that the FOMC operates at a surprisingly low level of economic sophistication, a level so low that it is most implausible that it is aware of agents' optimal output level being below the socially optimal level. Subtle ideas such as this do not enter FOMC discussions. (For examples of the crudity of FOMC thinking, see Lombra and Moran, 1980; Mayer

1990b, chs 7 and 8.) This is not due to a lack of ability of FOMC members. Instead, Robert Hetzel (1990) attributes it to the FOMC's perceived need to bow to political pressures. Giving in to such pressures is less embarrassing when one operates at the level of casual reasoning, where many things are easy to justify, than if one uses serious economic analysis, analysis that may show that the politically required policy is clearly wrong. Elsewhere (Mayer, 1990a), I attribute the FOMC's casual way of thinking to its wish to avoid feelings of regret when it turns out that its previous policy was mistaken. One might, of course, respond that the FOMC's thinking is not relevant, that monetary policy is largely made by the White House (see Woolley, 1986; Havrilesky, 1993, and the literature cited therein) and the White House has often pressured the Fed to be more expansionary. But there is no evidence that it did this largely, or to any significant extent, for the reasons discussed by time-inconsistency theory. Quite apart from inducing agents to work more, expansionary policies have more obvious short-run benefits for the President by temporarily lowering interest rates and the unemployment rate. To be sure, one might refer to the political system's tendency to overemphasize the short-run benefits of inflation as 'time-inconsistency', but if time-inconsistency theory is interpreted this broadly, it adds little that is new to the monetarist's case against discretionary policy.

8. Moreover, for private agents a Darwinian argument provides some, though only weak, support for an 'as-if' reasoning (see Chapter 13). But the Darwinian argument does not apply to central banks.

9. From the first quarter of 1954 to the first quarter of 1965, the mean inflation rate was 2.1 per cent if measured by the GNP deflator and 1.4 per cent if measured by the consumers' price index. The following 15 years of high inflation unconnected with a major war are unique in American history. (The Vietnam war, whatever its terrible consequences, was not a major war as far as US military expenditures are concerned. In no year did they exceed 9 per cent of GNP.) Whether since then the Fed has been too inflationary, or has tried to reduce the inflation rate too fast, is a debated issue. Such a record hardly supports a hypothesis that implies a systemic bias towards inflation.

10. Some of the time-inconsistency literature concludes that the central bank will not be inflationary because it is concerned with its reputation. This is consistent with the empirical evidence. But where is the evidence that the game-theoretic considerations of time-inconsistency theory play any role in the Fed's avoidance of inflation at certain times? Moreover, if the time-inconsistency literature is interpreted merely as saying that central banks try to avoid inflation out of concern about their reputation, then it tells us little that is not obvious. As Alan Blinder (1987b, p.410) has put it, 'The conclusion of this latest round of the rules-versus-discretion debate, it seems to me, amounts to saying that it is better to have farsighted decision-makers than shortsighted ones. Stated in this way, the conclusion is (a) obvious and (b) strikingly similar to the earlier monetarist distrust of politicians.'

9 What do economists think of their econometrics?

Do econometric studies convince economists? Presumably their authors think so. But by no means all economists agree. Thus Edward Leamer (1978, p.13, 1983, pp.36–7) wrote:

> There is a growing cynicism among economists towards empirical work. Regression equations are regarded by many as mere stylistic devices, not unlike footnotes referencing obscure scholarly papers. ... The econometric art ... involves fitting many, perhaps thousands, of statistical models. One or several that the researcher finds pleasing are selected for reporting purpose. ... The concepts of unbiasedness, consistency, efficiency, maximum-likelihood estimation, in fact all the concepts of traditional theory, utterly lose their meaning by the time an applied researcher pulls from the bramble of computer output the one thorn of a model he likes best, the one he has chosen to portray as a rose. *The consuming public is hardly fooled by this chicanery.* (Italics added)

Similarly, Thomas Cooley and Stephen LeRoy (1981, p.826) argued:

> particularly in macroeconomics, therefore, we often have what is very nearly a zero-communication information equilibrium. The researcher has the motive and opportunity to present his results selectively, and the reader, knowing this, imputes a low or zero signal-to-noise ratio to the reported results.

This chapter reports the results of a survey on whether economists are as cynical about econometric results as Leamer and Cooley and LeRoy claim. Such a survey may seem redundant. Isn't the widespread use of regressions better evidence that economists take their regressions seriously than anything they say in response to a survey? No, it is not. They may be skeptical about regressions and yet include regression results in their papers. Suppose that one-third of all economists believe regression results and two-thirds do not. Since it is irrational to ignore the tastes of one-third of the potential referees and readers, all economists have an incentive to festoon their papers with regression output. Hence in this case asking questions is a better method of ascertaining beliefs than is observing behavior, particularly since the question at issue here is not how economists behave, but what they believe.

I sent 278 questionnaires to a sample of mainly American academic economists, asking them about the extent to which the likelihood of data mining, which Steven Caudill (1990, p.251) calls the 'dominant research strategy' of economists, reduces the credence they give to econometric results.[1] (Appendix A to this chapter shows the questionnaire, and Appendix B discusses some issues in processing the responses.) Some 66 per cent responded with usable answers to at least one of the questions.

The issue explored in the survey is the opinion of economists on a problem on which they have little incentive to develop firm and definitive views. Hence, while most have probably given the issue some thought, one cannot expect them to articulate precise views. Accordingly, the questions had to probe for a general disposition, and therefore could not be sharply worded and precise. When the information requested is itself vague, vague questions are appropriate.[2]

Table 9.1 shows the replies to the three basic questions asked, the frequency of data mining, the effect of such data mining on the credibility of the results, and on the respondent's willingness to abandon prior beliefs in response to contrary econometric results. These replies contradict the previously cited strong statements of Leamer and Cooley and LeRoy.[3] They do, however, support the weaker statement that economists consider data mining to be a serious problem. Only 9 per cent of the sample think that data mining is infrequent, while 17 per cent believe that it occurs in nearly all cases. Fewer than 10 per cent call data mining only a minor problem, and it makes almost 30 per cent either 'quite skeptical' or distrustful of most or all econometric results. About one-sixth are reluctant to abandon conclusions for which they have strong theoretical priors merely because of contrary evidence in a particular econometric study. But many more accept contrary results that are confirmed by several such studies. This response may, of course, be biased. Few people want to admit that they are dogmatic and ignore evidence that contradicts their views. However, such a bias is not likely to be large, because in the context of this questionnaire failure to take contradictory evidence seriously can readily be rationalized as a concern about data mining.

Of the respondents, 30 provided free-ranging comments. Almost half of them pointed out that some data mining results from editorial practice; journals do not welcome negative results. It is not clear to what extent they think that this biases researchers themselves and not just editorial selection.

The questionnaire asked about certain characteristics of the respondents to see if concern about data mining is correlated with whether an economist teaches in a department that offers a doctoral degree, is a recent PhD, received that degree from an elite school, teaches in an economics department, does primarily empirical or theoretical research, and specializes in microeconomics or macroeconomics.[4]

These characteristics fail to explain economists' beliefs about the prevalence of data mining. The responses to this question can be scaled with only a small loss of accuracy, and then used as the dependent variable in an ordinary least squares (OLS) regression. The resulting R^2 is only 0.04.[5] The other two questions provide choices that cannot be scaled cardinally, so that I had to use logit regressions for which no reliable measure of fit is readily available. Table 9.2

Table 9.1   Response to questions about reporting bias

I. Frequency with which only favorable results are reported, and equally well-grounded unfavorable results are ignored:

		Per cent excluding	including	Number of cases
		non-response		
1.	Only infrequently	9.3	6.5	12
2.	In about a quarter of the cases	24.0	16.8	31
3.	In about half the cases	25.6	17.9	33
4.	In about three-quarters of the cases	24.0	16.8	31
5.	In nearly all cases	17.1	12.0	22
6.	Cannot say	—	29.9	55
	Total	100.0	100.0	184

II. The possibility of selective reporting has the following effect on the credence I give to empirical results in the journals:

1.	Almost no effect since it is a minor problem	8.4	8.2	15
2.	Almost no effect since I distrust econometric results in any case	6.7	6.5	12
3.	It makes me somewhat, but no more than somewhat, skeptical	55.6	53.8	99
4.	It makes me quite skeptical	27.0	26.1	48
5.	It makes me distrust most or all econometric tests	2.2	2.2	4
6.	Non-response	—	3.2	6
	Total	100.0	100.0	184

III. The possibility of selective reporting influences my response to econometric results as follows:

1.	It makes me reluctant to abandon results with a strong theoretical basis	17.8	14.1	26
2.	Even if I have no strong theoretical priors I take seriously only those results that show up in several papers by different authors	32.8	26.1	48
3.	If I have strong priors I take contrary econometric results seriously only if they appear in several papers by different authors	49.3	39.1	72
4.	Non-response	—	20.7	38
	Total	100.0	100.0	184

shows the results for the effect of data mining on the credibility of econometric results for those variables that are significant at the 10 per cent level. To have a sufficiently large sample this table combines four of the alternatives into two categories.[6] It shows that those who teach in a PhD-granting department, and those who hold a more recent degree, are more concerned about data mining, while those who teach in an economics department, do primarily empirical research and received their PhD from an elite department are less concerned. On the whole, these responses do not show a pronounced and consistent tendency for 'elite' economists to differ from others.

The variables just listed play a lesser role in economists' decision whether to abandon their priors in response to disconfirming econometric results. Here, none of them is significant at the 10 per cent level in a multiple regression.[7] All in all, considerable, but not extreme, concern about data mining predominates.

Table 9.2   Coefficients significant at the 10 per cent level

	OLS coefficients
Question 1 (extent of bias in reporting favorable but not unfavorable results[a]):	
Highest degree given by respondent's department:	
PhD	−41.4*
MA	−37.9
BA	−43.6*
PhD from elite school	−12.1

Question 2 (credibility of econometric results[b]):

	Logit coefficients[c]	
	A	B
	Little	Much
	skepticism	
Respondent's department offers PhD	−1.41*	1.33*
Year received PhD	−0.04	0.07*
Teaching in economics department	2.01*	−1.80*
Focus of research is empirical[b]	0.56	−0.72*
PhD from elite school	1.17*	−1.51*

Notes
* Significant at 5 per cent level, two-tailed test.
[a] Responses were graded from 10 (data mining occurs only infrequently) to 90 (data mining occurs in nearly all cases.)
[b] Responses to the question about the focus of research were classified as follows: mainly theory = 1, mainly empirical = 3, some of each = 2.
[c] 'A' denotes the agreement with either one of the following: (1) data mining has almost no effect since it is a minor problem; (2) it makes me somewhat, but no more than somewhat, skeptical. 'B' denotes agreement with either of the following: (1) it makes me quite skeptical; (2) it makes me distrust most or all econometric tests.

Appendix A: questionnaire on beliefs about reporting bias in econometric tests

1. Some economists believe that authors of empirical papers in the journals often report only favorable results and not unfavorable results, even when the unfavorable ones are as well-grounded in theory and econometrics as the favorable results. Granted that one can only guess about how often this happens, do you think this occurs:

(1) only infrequently (__)
(2) in about a quarter of the cases (__)
(3) in about half the cases (__)
(4) in about three-quarters of the cases (__)
(5) in nearly all cases (__)
(6) I cannot even venture a guess (__)

2. To indicate how the possibility of selective reporting affects the credence you give to the empirical results you read in the journals, please read through the following statements and check the one that corresponds best to your position. None of them may represent it precisely, but please choose the closest one. In addition to checking one of the statements 1–5 you may also want to check one of the statements A–C.

(1) It has almost no effect because I think it is a minor problem (__)
(2) It has almost no effect since I distrust econometric results in any case for other reasons (__)
(3) It makes me somewhat, but no more than somewhat, skeptical (__)
(4) It makes me quite skeptical (__)
(5) It makes me distrust most or all econometric tests (__)
(A) It makes me reluctant to abandon any results that have a strong theoretical basis despite what a specific econometric test may show (__)
(B) If I have strong priors I take contrary econometric results seriously only if they show up in several papers by different authors (__)
(C) Even if I have no strong priors I take seriously only those results that show up in several papers by different authors (__)

To analyse the results I would appreciate some information about you. But if you prefer not to provide it please ignore the following questions.

3. I hold an academic job, or am retired from teaching: yes (__), no (__) The highest degree given in my department is a: PhD (__), other doctoral degree (__), LLB (__), MA (__), BA (__), other (please specify):_____.
I received my doctorate in 19__ from_____Univ.
I am working on my doctorate from_____Univ.
I neither hold, nor am working on, a doctorate (__)
I teach mainly in an economics department (__), a____department.
My research is: mainly theory (__), mainly empirical (__), some of each (__)

My main fields of interest are: macro (__), micro (__). More specifically they are:_____

4. If you have no objection to giving me your name and address, please do so. I will keep it confidential.

_____   _____
          (name)   (address)

5. Please provide on the back of this form any comments you care to make: To receive a copy of the results, please check here:__

Appendix B: notes on procedures

A.   Treatment of replies to substantive questions

The responses to question 2 were made binary, with the first two alternatives being combined into one group, and the fourth and fifth into the other. The replies to question 3 were also made binary by treating each response as a separate dummy variable. In question 2 the responses were made binary by combining 1 and 3 into one group and 4 and 5 into the other.

B.   Treatment of replies to questions about respondents' background

The information on the highest degree given by the department was used in two ways. In one set of regressions each alternative was used as a separate dummy variable. In another set the responses were combined into a single dummy variable for whether the department gives a PhD. The replies to the question about type of research were scaled 1, 2, 3 with 'bit of each' given a 2.

C.   Excluded variables

Since all but a few respondents hold a PhD and very few currently hold non-academic jobs, these variables were not used in the regressions.

Notes

1.   The sample comes from the 1989 AEA Directory. I intended to include only academic economists and graduate students, but at the time they received the questionnaire a few respondents no longer had an academic connection. They were kept in the sample. Foreign economists were undersampled. The figure of 278 questionnaires excludes questionnaires that were returned because of faulty addresses, the addressee having died, or the addressees not filling them in because they had retired, and so on. Completed questionnaires from retired persons were included in the tabulation. The questionnaires were sent out in Spring 1991.

2.   Such questions are likely to seem unclear to some respondents because they are not formulated in terms in which they themselves think. Formulations that accord with one person's thinking may well sound alien to another person.

3.   This does not necessarily mean that Leamer and Cooley and LeRoy are wrong in believing that data mining *does* invalidate most econometric results. That is another question.

4.   Among the schools represented in the sample, the following were classified as elite: California (Berkeley), Chicago, Columbia, Harvard, Johns Hopkins, Michigan, Minnesota, MIT, Northwestern, Pennsylvania, Princeton, Stanford, UCLA, Wisconsin (Madison) and Yale. The questionnaire also asked about some other characteristics of the respondents. For these there were insufficient cases for analysis.

5.   Nonetheless two variables were significant, or close to it. Whether the respondent received the PhD from an elite school barely missed significance at the 5 per cent level, with a coefficient indicating that those who attended an elite school believe that data mining is less common than other respondents do. The highest degree given by the respondent's department is significant at the 5 per cent level, but the sign of the coefficient is hard to interpret since both those who responded 'PhD' and those who responded 'BA' consider data mining to be less prevalent than other respondents do.

6.   In combining the five alternatives for question 2, I ignored the second alternative (that data mining does not matter since econometric work is unreliable anyhow), a response that very few respondents chose.

7.   In a bivariate regression whether the respondent's department offers a PhD is significant at the 5 per cent level for the second alternative, but since this is one of 14 simple regressions that I tried (seven variables for each of the two alternatives 1 and 2), that could well be due to data mining.

10 Insignificant coefficients

This chapter makes a very simple point, something that we all know, but tend to forget about as we sit at our PCs. It is the limited significance of significance tests. Significance tests are not unproblematic (see Morrison and Henkel, 1970). They are intended to tell us one thing, and one thing only: whether there is a more than, say, 5 per cent probability that the non-zero value of a particular coefficient is due to sampling error (see McCloskey, 1985, ch.8).

As we all learned in elementary statistics, if a regressor is statistically insignificant, that does not necessarily mean that it has little or no effect on the dependent variable. Whether a variable has a significant coefficient obviously depends, among other things, on the size of the sample. If the sample is small enough the price variable in a highly elastic demand function will be insignificant, while in a very large sample nearly all coefficients will be significant. Second, if a change in X has a strong effect on Y, the coefficient of X may still be insignificant even in a reasonably large sample, if the variance of X is low, or if the variance of its effects on the dependent variable is high.

Neither a low variance of X nor a high variance in its effect on Y can be ruled out as implausible. Variables that have a low variance most of the time may still matter.[1] In a regression that explains the US housing stock a variable measuring the number and magnitude of earthquakes may have an insignificant coefficient, but, as I sit here in California, I nonetheless worry about the major earthquake that geologists say will come sooner or later.

Moreover, high variances in the effect of X on Y are not so improbable. For example, a sharp rise in interest rates may have a much greater effect on GDP when debt ratios are high than when they are low, or when it generates expectations of further increases. High variances can also result from variable lags. In other words, linear regressions and their t statistics at most tell us about stable effects of X on Y, but effects do not have to be stable to matter.[2]

So suppose that my theory requires that X generates changes in Y, but my PC tells me that the coefficient of X is insignificant. Should I panic and either bury my theory or go down into the data mine? Neither, because economic theory can only tell us the sign that a coefficient should have, and occasionally something about its size, but it does not demand that the coefficient of a linear regression be statistically significant in a sample that may be fairly small by standards that statisticians often use in fields other than economics. Yet I suspect that in most cases in which an economist finds that his central variable is not significant he does don his miner's clothes, if only for fear of what the referee will say.

Similarly, it seems to be frequent practice, if any of the control variables are insignificant, to rerun regressions without them, and to treat this second regression as the appropriate one. Often the suppression of the first regression will not even be reported.[3] Can one justify this and, if so, how? That depends on whether the purpose of the regression analysis is forecasting, explaining the behavior of the dependent variable or testing hypotheses.

Forecasting

For forecasting what matters is accuracy, not elegance. So why drop a variable that makes any contribution, however small, to the fit of the regression equation? One reason may be that dropping a variable with a t value of less than 2 will generally raise R^2. But maximizing the sample period R^2 does not necessarily improve the forecast. Another reason is to attain the benefit of simplicity in the pedestrian, not the philosophical, sense of the term. The more separate regressors are used, the more variables must be predicted, and that may be time consuming. Eliminating variables may also ease the problem of multicollinearity. These problems may justify dropping variables that make only a small contribution to the accuracy of the forecast relative to the costs they impose on the forecaster. But variables that make a small contribution are not necessarily the variables with a low t value. The F test and out-of-sample diagnostics, not t values, are the relevant tests.

Moreover, as McCloskey (1985) has pointed out, the decision about what critical t value to use in eliminating variables should take into account the loss functions for Type I and Type II errors. Even if there is only a 1 per cent probability that the inclusion of a certain variable will improve the forecast by enough to save me $1000, I will include that variable if the cost of doing so is less than one dollar.

Another reason for eliminating insignificant variables is that, if a variable has a t value of, say 0.1, it may still improve the fit of the regression in the sample period slightly, but there is little reason to think that its inclusion will improve the fit during the forecast period. However, that does not justify dropping all variables not significant at the 5 per cent level. To do that is to use significance tests the wrong way round. Even if a variable is significant only at the 20 per cent level, there is likely to be a substantial chance that it is not just sampling error that accounts for its non-zero coefficient during the sample period, so that its inclusion is likely to improve the forecast. Hence, in the context of forecasting, it is reasonable to drop variables that do not improve the forecast by enough to justify the trouble of keeping them, but it is not the t test that identifies these variables.

Explaining

In most cases we do not want to forecast just in the sense of responding to the demand: 'give me a number'. We want to *explain*, that is to answer questions, such as 'what caused the change in Y?' Strictly speaking, regressions should not be used as explanations. They just give us filtered summaries of the data that may help in developing an explanation. But in many papers they are used as though they themselves provide an explanation, and that is not likely to change. Hence, despite the fundamental objection that can be raised about these 'explanatory regressions', it is worth seeing if the elimination of insignificant variables creates an additional problem.

When using regressions for explaining rather than forecasting, different criteria apply. Everything depends on everything else, but we do not respond to a question about why Y changed by citing thousands of factors. Parsimony tells us to eliminate unimportant variables, but what does 'unimportant' mean in this context? There are three alternative meanings. One is that X is unimportant if a one unit change in X has only a small effect on Y. The regression coefficient provides that information. A second is that during the sample period only a small proportion of the observed changes in Y is due to changes in X. That is measured (in a relative sense) by the beta coefficient and by the partial correlation coefficient.[4] The third meaning of 'unimportant' is that the seeming effect of X on Y has too high a probability of being merely the product of sampling errors. That is what the *t* value measures.

All three of these meanings of 'important' provide legitimate criteria for formulating an explanation. Someone who asks what explains changes in Y because he needs to know if he can change Y by varying X, for example a central banker who wants to change nominal income by changing the money supply, needs an explanation that provides information on the size of the regression coefficient and its standard error. He is not concerned with the extent to which previous changes in GDP are attributable to changes in the money supply, because that depends, in part, on the extent to which the money supply varied during the sampling period. By contrast, an economic historian who studies whether monetary policy contributed substantially to fluctuations in nominal income in the 1970s needs to know, not just the regression coefficient of money on income, but also the magnitude of variations in the money supply in this period. In addition, both the central banker and the economic historian need to know the reliability of the information that they are given, and therefore the *t* value of the coefficients.

Hence the limited number of variables that constitute an adequate but sufficiently parsimonious explanation must be selected with one eye on the magnitude of the regressor's effect on the dependent variable (the regression coefficient in the case of the central banker, and the partial R^2 or beta coefficient for the economic historian) and with the other eye on the *t* value of the variable. As

McCloskey (1985, ch.9) has pointed out, this simple point is often ignored, and we tend to cite as the explanation of the dependent variable all the significant variables in the regression, however weak their effect, while excluding variables with strong effects if they are statistically insignificant. We thus offer an explanation that says, in effect, here are those explanatory variables for which we are highly (95 per cent) confident that their non-zero coefficients are not just the product of sampling error, even though they may have very little effect on the dependent variable, and may perhaps explain little of its past fluctuations.

There are three problems with this type of explanation. First, our audience usually wants to be told about all the important variables that are likely to explain the behaviour of Y, and not just about those variables that have at least a 95 per cent probability of doing so. Second, if there is substantial multicollinearity – hardly an uncommon occurrence – then the exclusion of one variable may change the coefficients of the other variables. The policymaker may therefore be told that the elasticity of Y with respect to X_1 is 2.5. But had X_2 been kept in the regression, then she would have been told that the elasticity is only 0.1. Suppose that X_2 is significant at the 30 per cent level. Then, if the loss function gives equal weight to Type I and Type II errors, there is a reasonable chance that she should probably have been told that the best estimate we have of the elasticity is 0.1 and not 2.5. In addition, not only the elasticity, but also the significance of other variables, is affected when some variable is eliminated, so that there is a problem somewhat similar to the one that arises when one decides on the sequence of variables in a VAR.

Third, if all insignificant variables are omitted the proffered explanation is likely to omit those variables whose effects on the dependent variable have a high variance, as well as variables that themselves had a low variance during the sample period, even if they are important. This is so particularly if the sample is small. This can have serious consequences. Suppose, for example, that the minimum wage has a strong effect on teenage unemployment, but that the variance of this effect is high. A policymaker who asks about the determinants of teenage unemployment may then be offered an explanation that does not mention the minimum wage, and thus be misinformed.

More generally, when someone is told, 'here is an explanation', she has a right to expect that she is told about *all* the relevant and important variables that we know about. When sampling error makes us uncertain about whether a variable matters, we should say so, and not omit this variable, particularly if we do not say that this is what we are doing.

The simplest assumption to make is that our clients attach equal importance to Type I and Type II errors. That suggests that we use a significance level much higher than 5 per cent when our purpose is explanation. The conventional 5 per cent level has its rationale in the context of hypotheses testing, but is much harder to defend in the context of explanation. To say that parsimony urges us to be hard-nosed about how many variables we include in the explanation is not a persuasive answer. To be sure, parsimony may tell us to include no more than, say, five variables. We should then choose these five variables in part on the basis of the size of their effect on the dependent variable, in part on the basis of the loss function, and in part – but not entirely – on the likelihood that their coefficients are not just an artifact of sampling error.

Testing hypotheses
In hypotheses testing significance tests are used in two ways. One is to reject the hypothesis 'X_1 causes Y' if the regression coefficient of X_1 is insignificant. That is part of the scientific convention that any new hypothesis be considered guilty until proved innocent. This convention is justified because otherwise too many hypotheses would clutter the landscape. The other use is to eliminate certain control variables because their coefficients are insignificant. That use raises a problem.

This problem is that the standard 5 per cent significance level is hard to justify, while no other significance level is clearly indicated. Far from being a conservative procedure that guards against accepting doubtful hypotheses, using a 5 per cent level is – in some cases – an extraordinarily lax procedure. Often some of the regressors are multicollinear, so that if one eliminates one, some of the remaining regressors become more significant, and some others less significant. In some cases the maintained hypotheses benefits, in some it loses. Suppose that the maintained hypothesis is that X_1 has a positive effect on Y, and that in the regression X_1 is significant at the 5 per cent level only if X_2 is eliminated. Suppose further that X_2 has a t value of only 1.0, so that there is a one-third chance (on a two-tailed test in a large sample) that its true coefficient is zero. That leaves what may well be a substantial chance that the effect of X_2 is *not* an artifact of sample error, so that X_2 should be kept in the regression. Hence, if one can conclude anything here, it is that the maintained hypothesis is not confirmed, and not that it is confirmed, as one is led to conclude if X_2 is eliminated.

A suitably conservative procedure in this situation would be to accept the hypothesis only if X_1 is significant, both when X_2 is kept in the regression, and also when it is eliminated. This approach has been formalized by Edward Leamer (1978), but his specification search technique is used only infrequently. Perhaps this is because of questions that, rightly or wrongly, have been raised about its validity. But it *may* also be due to what usually happens when it is used – in most cases the maintained hypothesis is rejected at the 5 per cent level. If this is the problem then, instead of rejecting the technique, it may perhaps be better to loosen the criteria for acceptance by adopting a, say, 10 per cent or even higher significance level.

In a field like economics, where truth is so much harder to come by than in the physical and biological sciences, a 5 per cent level *may* be a counsel of perfection. Given the various difficulties we encounter, such as identification problems, the probability that a particular econometric result is correct is likely to be much less than 95 per cent, even if the relevant coefficient is significant at the 5 per cent level. Perhaps we are so stringent about sampling errors for no better reason than that these errors, unlike other errors, are easy to quantify. If econometric papers really did demonstrate their results with the 95 per cent probability that the *t* tests seem to claim, then there would be much less disagreement in economics than there is now. On the other side, one might argue that, since various other difficulties, such as identification problems, already reduce the credibility of econometric results, we do not want to reduce credibility even further by allowing a greater opportunity for sampling errors to generate misleading results.

But regardless of whether or not one uses a 5 per cent level, a variable should usually not be considered significant if it becomes significant only when a theoretically plausible, but statistically insignificant, variable is dropped from the regression.[5] This does not invalidate Hendry's proposal for general to specific modelling, but merely suggests caution in interpreting its results. In any case, Hendry's procedure is better suited for ascertaining what process generated a data set, than for testing hypotheses (Mayer, 1993b, pp.15–16).

Conclusion

It is therefore hard to justify the common practice of more or less automatically eliminating regressors that are insignificant at the 5 per cent level. Presumably it originated in the context of hypothesis testing, and was transferred more or less automatically to the contexts of explanation and forecasting. And even for hypothesis testing it is reasonable only with respect to those regressors that the maintained hypothesis requires to be significant, and not with respect to those used just as control variables. When used to eliminate control variables it will sometimes give unwarranted plausibility to the maintained hypotheses.

In contexts other than hypothesis testing, statistical significance is certainly a valid consideration in deciding whether to eliminate a regressor, but it is only one of several. The size of the coefficient relative to the size of other coefficients, the partial R^2 or beta value of the coefficient, and the regressor's theoretical justification may all be as important or more important than the *t* value of the coefficient. For forecasting the cost of obtaining the relevant data also matters. Thus there is no unique *t* value that tells us whether a variable should be eliminated. And even if there were, it would almost certainly not be the standard 5 per cent level.

When to eliminate a variable is a matter of judgement. That may alarm those who insist that, since economics is a *science*, it must, like geometry, rely on unequivocal demonstrations and avoid personal judgement. That is a naive view of science. As the late Richard Rudner (1953, p.6), a philosopher of science, pointed out: 'the slightly juvenile conception of the coldblooded, emotionless, impersonal, passive scientist mirroring the world perfectly in the highly polished lenses of his steel rimmed glasses' is not adequate.

But although some subjective judgement cannot be avoided, there is one rule that can be established: if the confirmation of the maintained hypothesis depends on whether a variable in the initial regression is, or is not, eliminated then this should be reported.[6]

Notes

1. The very purpose of the analysis may be to evaluate a policy that will try to affect Y by making X more variable than it has been in the past.
2. Variable coefficient regressions may provide a solution, but only if one can specify the determinants of the variation in the strength of X_2. If the magnitude of the effect of X on Y is a function of the change in X, non-linear regression may also be an appropriate procedure.
3. There is no way of knowing how often this occurs because many authors probably eliminate insignificant regressors without reporting it.
4. The beta coefficient is the regression coefficient times the ratio of standard deviation of X to the standard deviation of Y (Goldberger, 1964, pp.197–8).
5. Whether X_1 should be considered significant depends on the joint probability distributions of its significance when X_2 is included, and when X_2 is excluded, as well as on the significance level of X_2.
6. This is just a very weak version of the specification search that Leamer (1978) advocates.

11 Seeing ourselves as others see us: Rosenberg's view of economics

We should pay attention when Alexander Rosenberg, a philosopher of science who has written extensively on economics, publishes a book (Rosenberg, 1992) critical of the way in which many, probably most, economists perceive their subject. That this book has won the Lakatos prize given in philosophy of science makes it all the more worthwhile paying attention. This does not mean, of course, that we need to accept his message. On the contrary, I will argue that it is mistaken.

Rosenberg's critique of economics

Rosenberg is not, like most critics of economics, an institutionalist, who rejects economic theory as too abstract. On the contrary, those who applaud the formalist turn that economics has taken in recent decades can cite Rosenberg in support. He believes that economics, at least as currently practiced, is not an empirical science, but is better viewed as applied mathematics. This is why the book is so important at this time when the formalist turn is being widely criticized. I will argue that Rosenberg is mistaken, that most, though not all, of economics should be viewed as an empirical science. In doing so I will draw on his earlier writings, as well as on his recent book.

Like Rosenberg, I do not claim to offer a demarcation criterion for science, and will call economics a science merely as a matter of convenience. My interest is not in whether economics is a science or non-science, but in whether it is an empirical or mathematical science/non-science. But first, two preliminaries to clarify the question Rosenberg is asking.

Saying that economics is X can mean that all of it is X, or that just the major part of it is X. Rosenberg appears to consider most, or almost all, economics to be a mathematical science. Beyond this, when someone says that 'economics *is* X' he may mean that economists try to do (or claim to do) X. Alternatively, he may mean that, regardless of what economists try to do, they end up doing X. A third possibility is that the inherent nature of economics is X, and that is what economists *should* do. When Rosenberg calls economics 'mathematical politics' (words he uses in the title of his book), and not an empirical science, he means mainly the third of these, in the sense that its methodology prevents economics from being an empirical science. He therefore calls for the development of another, alternative discipline that is an empirical science, and thus can provide policymakers with the information they need. Such a discipline cannot be founded on the folk psychology of desires and intentions of agents that economists use, and will have to reject the economists' theory of consumer choice.

He acknowledges that most neoclassical economists disagree, and that they claim that economics is an empirical science (Rosenberg, 1992, p.17), but he sees this more as a superficial posture than as a belief that dominates their work. Economists 'are not really much interested in questions of empirical applicability at all. Otherwise some of the attractive ... [alternatives to looking at factors other than the intentions of agents and at maximization] would long ago have elicited more interest from economists than they have' (Rosenberg, 1983, p.308). Moreover, 'anyone with much knowledge of the history of economic theory will agree that the discipline does not seek or respond to empirical data in the way characteristic of an empirical science – even a theoretically impoverished one' (Rosenberg, 1992, p.228). As a result, 'Nothing that would make empirical scientists give up a theory will make economists give up their theoretical strategy' (Rosenberg, 1992, p.236).

> Much of the mystery surrounding the actual development of economic theory – its shifts in formalism, its insulation from empirical assessment, its interest in proving purely formal, abstract possibilities, its unchanged character over a period of centuries, the controversies about its cognitive status – can be comprehended and properly appreciated if we give up the notion that economics any longer has the aims or makes the claims of an empirical science of human behavior. Rather we should view it as a branch of mathematics, one devoted to examining the formal properties of a set of assumptions. (Rosenberg, 1983, p.311)

To Rosenberg that is not necessarily bad. Being a mathematical science does not make economics worthless. On the contrary. He points out that economic theory has had a profound influence on political philosophy: 'Many philosophers have simply taken over the jargon and the agenda of welfare economics in order to express their problems and seek solutions to them' (Rosenberg, 1992, p.217). Economic theory has also benefited biology. Mathematical biologists, who are concerned with the equilibrium levels of various species, use the economists' analysis of the existence and stability of equilibrium (Rosenberg, 1992, p.194). Moreover, viewing economics as applied mathematics 'does economists more credit than several possible alternative explanations for its empirical weakness ... it renders the immense amount of sheer genius bestowed on the development of this theory its due. The explanation does not stigmatize the methods of economists as conceptually confused or misdirected' (Rosenberg, 1992, p.247), and it excuses the failure of economists as forecasters (Rosenberg, 1983, p.312).

At the same time, Rosenberg sees a substantial drawback to the mathematical character of economics. If economics is a branch of applied mathematics that deals with the logical implications of certain axioms, and does not try to provide a realistic description of the way economic agents behave, then something else is needed to fill the vacuum and provide guidance for policymakers. However, Rosenberg (1992, p.254) is skeptical that such a 'something else' can be developed.

Economics leaves such a vacuum because it fails fundamentally as an empirical science. Predictive success is a basic requirement for a successful empirical science, and economics lacks predictive success (Rosenberg, 1992, p.67).[1] Rosenberg does not deny that economics has some predictive successes, but he rightly points out that what matters is not the absolute number of correct predictions, but the proportion of predictions that turn out to be correct. Thus, while he concedes that Wade Hands (1984) might be right in saying that economics generates an ocean of correct predictions, it is not a science because it also generates an ocean of wrong predictions (Rosenberg, 1986, p.130). However, Rosenberg does not define or explain even in a vague way what he means by not enough predictive success.

Moreover, claims Rosenberg, economics (or microeconomic theory?) makes mainly generic predictions; that is, it predicts the existence of something in general terms, and does not provide information on its detailed characteristics. Such generic predictions are generally insufficient for empirical science. But he does not tell us how much detail is needed. If weather forecasts were to tell us only that tomorrow will be hotter than today, without saying by how much, they would still provide useful information.

A second criterion for a successful science, one that Rosenberg emphasizes strongly and calls 'the most innocuous epistemological requirement', is that the predictive power of its theories can be improved.[2] Economics fails by this criterion, too, because 'it never seems to acquire any more [predictive power] than it had at the hands of, say, Marshall. ... Economics has not substantially changed, either in its form or its degree of confirmation, since Walras, or arguably since Adam Smith' (Rosenberg, 1992, pp.67, 230). Economists cannot predict consumer behavior better than Adam Smith could (Rosenberg, 1992, p.54). Not only are 'at least half' of the predictions made by the theory of the firm disconfirmed, and the ones that are confirmed have serious difficulty, since 'economists have not been able to improve on them in a systematic way over the entire course of the history of the neoclassical theory of the firm' (Rosenberg, 1992, p.60).

Meanwhile, in macroeconomics, Keynesian theory has been rejected as the result of stagflation and the failure of fiscal policy, (Rosenberg, 1983, p.297). Other inadequacies of macroeconomics include the failure of fine-tuning, and that Keynes could demonstrate only the *possibility* of underemployment equilibrium (Rosenberg, 1992, pp.73–4). What is 'even more disquieting' for those who might think of economics as clearly a science is that 'a large part' of the profession has responded to the failure of Keynesian economics by returning to the 'microeconomic theories which it was sometimes claimed to supersede. ... This cycle brings economic theory right back to where it was before 1937' (Rosenberg, 1983, p.297).

The reasons for the failure of economic theory as empirical science are basic, and not problems that can readily be overcome. Micro theory starts from the preferences, intentions and beliefs of agents. It is folk psychology. It therefore cannot advance in its predictive power beyond what ordinary common sense tells us. Moreover, since there is no adequate way of measuring tastes, the assumptions that microeconomic theory makes about consumer behavior cannot be 'improved, corrected, sharpened, specified or conditioned in ways that would improve the predictive power of the theory. ... The intentional nature of the fundamental explanatory variables of economic theory prohibits such improvement' (Rosenberg, 1992, p.149). In addition, microeconomic theory is an extremal theory, that is a theory that relies on a variable reaching a maximum or minimum value, such as firms maximizing profits. Although such theories have been highly successful in other fields, they have a serious weakness: they cannot be modified when threatened with falsification (Rosenberg, 1992, p.232).

Furthermore, microeconomic theory is based on assumptions that are not accurate enough. Rosenberg is not protesting about the unrealism of assumptions in the naive way that Friedman (1953) has so effectively criticized. He acknowledges that a scientific theory must be abstract, that abstraction is inconsistent with descriptive realism, and that what matters is predictive success. His argument is that, precisely because the theory built on the assumptions of neoclassical economics lacks predictive power, we can say that the assumptions of microeconomic theory are too inaccurate. He draws an illuminating contrast between microeconomic theory and Euclidean geometry. A Euclidean triangle is an abstraction, that is, an unrealistic idealization, just as much as homo economicus is. But we can generally apply the Pythagorean theorem to real-world problems, because we can estimate the divergence of an actual triangle from the idealized triangle, and make allowance for this divergence. But it is a great deal harder to decide what allowance to make for the difference between homo economicus and homo sapiens.

Rosenberg focuses his discussion of the inadequacy of economics as an empirical science on two parts of microeconomic theory, consumer choice theory and general equilibrium theory, particularly on the former. He does concede that some economists, such as J.R. Hicks, have argued that economics does not try to explain the behavior of every individual household. Instead, what it tries to explain is the behavior of markets. As Hands (1991, p.117) points out, the most common use of microeconomics is to explain what results from the interaction of many agents, for example the determination of prices, and not what goes on in each agent's head.

Rosenberg rejects this defense of economics on several grounds. One is that many economists *do* try to analyse the behavior of individual agents. Another is that economics is precisely that science to which the task of explaining the economic behavior of individuals has been allocated (Rosenberg, 1980, p.93). A third reason is Rosenberg's (surprising) belief that:

> if our predictions of the behavior of individuals faced with individual choices are fated to be at best vague and imprecise, what can we expect when we aggregate individual behavior? It is improbable that we can improve on the accuracy of claims about the aggregation of individual choices without improvements in our accuracy about individual choice. ... Improvements in microfoundations are the best way to improve the accuracy of macropredictions. (Rosenberg, 1992, pp.129–30)

Moreover, defining economics to exclude the explanation of the behavior of each actual individual, and concentrating on the representative individual, does not improve our knowledge; it just passes a hot potato on to another subject (Rosenberg, 1992, p.121).

Rosenberg believes that economists 'lavish attention' on general equilibrium theory, not because of its factual adequacy, but because it provides an excellent argument in favor of markets, and because it is a theory that can be improved with further work. He criticizes general equilibrium theorists for arbitrarily defining economics as what can be done with general equilibrium theory (Rosenberg, 1992, p.203).

Roy Weintraub (1988) had responded to Rosenberg's previous criticism of general equilibrium theory by arguing that this theory should be treated as the Lakatosian hard core of economic theory that generates empirically progressive hypotheses in its protective belt. Hence, even though on its own it does not make any empirical predictions, it should not be criticized as empirically vacuous. Rosenberg now responds in several ways. First, he questions the usefulness of the Lakatosian methodology of scientific research programs (MSRP) on general grounds.[3] Second, he questions the extent to which the hypotheses in the protective belt of neoclassical theory have been empirically confirmed – as previously discussed, he believes that economists cannot predict correctly. Third, he responds to Weintraub's reference to specific papers that use general equilibrium theory with empirically progressive results by saying that they make only generic predictions of things that are obvious even without the theory. Fourth, he argues that general equilibrium theory gives only the illusion of empirical progressivity by changing the assumed conditions of the problem, that is by considering new problems with the same old theory, instead of improving the theory itself (Rosenberg, 1992, pp.96–107).

Since Rosenberg is a specialist in the philosophy of biology, as well as of economics, it is not surprising that he considers at length the possibility of defending economics by saying that, while it is dissimilar to the physical sciences, it is similar to the biological sciences. In this context he takes up Gary Becker's model of consumer theory in which all consumers have identical tastes, but differ in their production technologies, as well as Armen Alchian's approach in which evolutionary processes drive the economy toward the equilibrium position, because agents who make the wrong choices lose out to those who for right or wrong reasons somehow make the right choices. If Alchian is right, then an adequate theory of the behavior of individual agents is not needed, and much of Rosenberg's criticism of economics misses the point. But Rosenberg (1992, p.177) argues that the theory of evolution is not an appropriate model for economics. Among his reasons are that evolutionary theory lacks predictive power and that it is specific predictions, and not the type of generic predictions made by evolutionary theory, that economics should provide. Moreover, to say that evolution forces economic agents to adapt optimally to their environment ignores the fact that the environment changes over time, and also that evolution often results in quick and dirty solutions that are efficient only in the short run.

How valid is Rosenberg's critique

I believe that Rosenberg is mistaken on most of these points. After briefly evaluating the way he frames the question of what economics is, I take up his claim that economics has insufficient predictive successes. I then argue that Rosenberg's conclusion that economics is not an empirical science results, not only from his denigration of its predictive success, but also from his excessive emphasis on the theory of consumer choice. In a Cartesian manner he seems to insist that a scientific structure can be no stronger than its foundations, and it is this that predisposes him to see economics as a mathematical science. I then discuss Rosenberg's claim that economics does not respond to disconfirming evidence in the way that the genuine empirical sciences do. In doing so I will go along with Rosenberg, if only for the sake of the argument, in treating predictive power as the touchstone of science, a by no means uncontroversial position (see McCloskey, 1994, ch.16). I will not deal with some parts of Rosenberg's book, such as his discussion of biological analogies in economics and his criticism of McCloskey.

What is economics?

Rosenberg frames the question of what economics is in a problematic way because it assumes that economics has a single methodological foundation. Why should this be so if one defines economics along Marshallian lines as the study of the way humanity produces and distributes goods? Nor does the Robbinsian definition of economics as the study of the allocation of scarce means among competing ends necessarily require a single methodological foundation. On either definition economics could be a mixture of mathematical and empirical sub-disciplines. Nobody can deny that part of it is a mathematical discipline:

theoretical econometrics and most of the work on general equilibrium theory are obvious examples. But other parts, such as economic history and most of economic development, are empirical disciplines.

Presumably, Rosenberg would respond that those parts of economics that are empirical rather than mathematical have failed because at present they cannot predict, and there is little chance that their predictions can be improved. Hence they should be jettisoned, so that all that remains of economics is a mathematical science. Is he right?

Predictive success

Rosenberg's claim that economics fails to predict adequately is basic to his entire argument. More than that, if he could document this claim decisively, he would not only have put economics into its correct pigeonhole as a mathematical science, but would also have shown those firms and government agencies that now employ economists how they could save money. Furthermore, most students who now suffer through Econ. 1 could be relieved of this tiresome burden.[4]

As his previously cited discussion of economists' predictions shows, Rosenberg is by no means shy in asserting that economists cannot predict. But he is reticent in offering empirical evidence to support this claim. Previously, when Hands (1984) had challenged this assertion, Rosenberg (1984, p.127) had responded that he had not tried to establish the lack of predictive success, because he considered it 'beyond reasonable doubt'. But with his claim having been challenged, one would expect that in his subsequent book he would have tried to build a strong case. Instead he writes:

> It is easy to pile up Nobel laureates on either side of the question of whether economics has met the test of empirical progress. One side will include Leontief and Herbert Simon, holding that traditional economic theory leaves much wanting. ... [The other side] will include Samuelson, Friedman, Debreu and others. At this point the argument may take on an unproductive 'yes it does, no it doesn't' character since a manageable number of examples of success will not convince the doubters, and no argument short of an impossibility proof will convince the defenders of the traditional approach. Moreover, the parties to this dispute do not share a common criterion of predictive power or empirical confirmation because there is none. (Rosenberg, 1992, p.98)

Rosenberg's attempt to document his position by using outstanding economists as authorities is not convincing – he cites two who support him and three who contradict him. If that warrants any conclusion at all it is that we do not know whether economics 'has met the test of empirical progress'.

Moreover the authorities he cites as supporting his position fail to do so unequivocally. Neither Leontief nor Simon discusses whether economics has met the test for being an empirical science, at least in the publications cited in Rosenberg's bibliography (Leontief, 1971, 1982; Simon, 1987). What Leontief and Simon do is to complain, and rightly so, that bad practices leave economics 'much wanting', but that does not entail that it fails to be an empirical science. Someone could accept everything that Leontief and Simon say (as I am close to doing) and yet believe that economics has met the test of being an empirical science. Leontief is far from arguing, as Rosenberg does, that economics cannot be an empirical science unless it abandons its basic theory of consumer choice and its focus on agents' intentions and desires. What he proposes instead is that economists abandon their fascination with elegant models and allocate much more effort to gathering data.

Another problem with the passage just cited is that Rosenberg concludes that one cannot determine convincingly whether economics has sufficient predictive ability, because there is no clear standard against which to judge the predictive power that economics does have. If so, shouldn't he conclude that one cannot say whether economics is an empirical science, rather than that it is not an empirical science?

In presenting his own evidence on the deficiencies of economics, Rosenberg discusses in any detail only the theory of consumer choice and general equilibrium theory, and has very little to say about the more applied work that is the bread and butter of most economists' labor. Just about his only discussion of applied work consists of his previously mentioned remarks about macroeconomics. As I show in the appendix to this chapter, these fail to support his case. Apparently, he believes that the theory of consumer choice is so basic to economics that by showing that it is deficient he has brought down the entire superstructure of economics.

Rosenberg discusses not only the present status of economists' knowledge, but also whether economics is empirically progressive in the Lakatosian sense of adding to the empirically validated hypotheses in the protective belt. But that is not the same as asking whether economics generates correct predictions (see Hoover, 1994). A field may currently have many validated hypotheses that permit it to predict correctly, but may not be currently adding to this stock of hypotheses, and hence not be empirically progressive. Such a lack of progressivity does not invalidate its status as a theoretically organized set of valid empirical hypotheses, and hence as an empirical and useful science. Mechanics, being by now an essentially completed field, is not currently adding much to its stock of validated empirical hypotheses. Nonetheless, it is an empirical science and a highly useful one. In shifting the focus from the question whether economists can predict to the question whether their predictive capability is increasing, Rosenberg has confounded a stock and a flow.

Moreover, what is Rosenberg's evidence that economics is not currently adding significantly to its stock of empirically validated hypotheses? He does not document his assertion that economics has not advanced as an empirical science since Marshall and Walras.

If one takes the hard-nosed position that the burden of proof is on the author, one could therefore dismiss Rosenberg's book as based merely on an argument by assertion, an assertion that Rosenberg himself states cannot be tested. All the same, it would be too facile to dismiss his argument on these grounds. It is useful to know whether or not the current stock of empirical, non-obvious knowledge in economics is akin to that of an empirical science.

This is not an easy question to answer. Obviously, as Rosenberg (1992, p.67) agrees, some predictions of economists are correct. But how many correct predictions does it take to make a successful empirical science? Is it that the present value of the stock of economic knowledge exceeds the present value of expenditures made to acquire it? Or, despite the entanglements that philosophers have encountered in defining science, is it that some standard of 'science', however defined, is met? Moreover, how much should one subtract for wrong predictions? A further troublesome issue is how to weigh the importance of various predictions. In addition, one must decide how solid a confirmation is required. Furthermore, most of the predictions made by economic theorists are ceteris paribus predictions (cf. Mäki, 1993b). How should they be tested? Then there is the issue of what hypotheses should be considered. Since scientific knowledge denotes something beyond common knowledge, those predictions that non-economists can make without the assistance of professional economists, such as the downward slope of demand curves, or that hospitals will have lower costs if compensated under a prospective payments system than under a cost-based system, do not count. Where should one draw the line?

One area in which it is *relatively* easy to see whether economists can predict with some success is macro forecasting. Despite a widespread and journalistic impression to the contrary, economist's one-year-ahead GDP forecasts are fairly successful. They predict better than does a simple ARIMA model (see McNees, 1988; Zarnowitz and Braun, 1993). That does not necessarily mean that the theory embodied in econometric macro models is correct, because most forecasters combine the prediction of their model with their own judgement. And some of their judgemental adjustments may just be matters of common sense rather than of economic analysis. Moreover, inflation forecasts are not as accurate as GDP forecasts (Zarnowitz and Braun, 1993). Nonetheless, those who claim that economists cannot predict receive little support from the record of macroeconomic forecasts.

However, most predictions, at least those by academic economists, are not GDP forecasts, but are 'if ... then' predictions. Less information about their reliability is available. McCloskey (1994, p.232) cites two examples of theories in international finance that provide fairly successful 'if ... then' predictions: the theory of interest rate parity and purchasing power parity theory. That economists cannot predict asset prices does suggest a limitation of economics, but it is a limitation that economic theory explains, so that it is itself a significant contribution that economics makes. The same is true to a considerable extent of the Lucas critique, though if taken at face value it severely limits the scope of contemporary economics. But there is considerable disagreement about the empirical relevance of the Lucas critique.

It would be most useful to have several comprehensive surveys of how the 'if ... then' predictions of economists have performed, along the lines of Clifford Winston's (1993) survey of predictions of the effects of deregulation, a survey that showed these predictions to be fairly successful.[5] Without a reasonably large set of such surveys one can do little more than conjecture, but it does seem plausible that economists' 'if ... then' predictions are more accurate than the predictions of those who are not professional economists. If so, economics is an empirical and not only a mathematical science. To be sure, one might want to argue that the superiority of economists' predictions is not great enough to earn economics the title of 'science'. But that argument would have to be documented by empirical evidence, and one would also have to resolve the problem of the amount of predictive success required for economics to be a science. Debates about what is, and what is not, 'science' are futile, and what I am concerned with is only the choice between two adjectives, 'mathematical' and 'empirical'.

It is tempting to sidestep the problem that too few such surveys of predictive performance are available by pointing out that firms employ economists and purchase economic forecasts, something they would not do if economists could not offer reliable predictions (Hands, 1984, p.498). Rosenberg (1984, p.130) and Hausman (1992a, pp.181–2) have responded to this argument from market behavior by asking whether the fact that medieval kings employed astrologers and alchemists should be taken as evidence for the validity of astrology and alchemy. That is not a persuasive response. We now know that astrology and alchemy are nonsense, and that the medieval kings who hired astrologers and alchemists were mistaken. The information on which market behavior was based at that time has been overthrown by what we have learned since then. But that the market is not always right does not mean that the information it provides is not the best that is available at that time. Moreover, it is likely that businesses can evaluate the predictions that their economists provide much better than medieval kings could evaluate the predictions of astrologers.

All the same, for a quite different reason, the market argument for the predictive success of economics, though not entirely without merit, is weak because it cuts both ways: while some firms employ economists, others do not. To be sure, since it is costly to employ economists, one would not expect small firms to do so, particularly since they can obtain macroeconomic forecasts by subscribing to forecasting services, such as DRI. And all large businesses, according to Stigler (1991, p.46), do employ economists. But business economists do more than macro forecasting. Much of their work concerns microeconomic issues (Hershey, 1993). Hence, if their work is so closely related to what businesses need to know, one might argue that, if economists possessed great knowledge about the economy, many more firms would employ them. All the same, if economists lacked specialized knowledge, it is likely that far fewer firms than do so now would have their own economists. Hence the market argument has some, but only limited, import.

The market argument can be supplemented by looking beyond the business sector. The federal government, and to a much lesser extent state governments, employ many economists. Advocates of public choice theory may interpret this as just showing the political power of those whose interests can be advanced in the guise of economic analysis, or the bureaucrats' tendency to hire excess staff. But those who are less convinced by public choice theory will instead read it as showing the usefulness, that is the predictive capacity, of economics.

It may seem that some indirect information on the predictive capacity of economics is also provided by the extent of disagreement among economists. While unanimity among its practitioners does not necessarily denote that a subject is a successful empirical science, disagreement on most issues surely demonstrates that the subject is not a successful empirical science. But there are serious obstacles to applying this test. First, we do not know just how much disagreement is consistent with a subject being a successful empirical science. Second, disagreement among whom? Should one consider disagreement only among neoclassical economists? On the one hand, that seems the appropriate criterion because Rosenberg's discussion relates only to neoclassical economics. On the other hand, excluding members of other schools obviously biases the results. Third, to measure the extent of disagreement among economists one must weigh the various items on which economists agree and disagree. How does one obtain such weights? Fourth, much of the disagreement of economists on policy issues is due, not to disagreement about economic theory, but to disagreements on non-economic issues, such as political feasibility and metaphysical presuppositions (see Colander, 1994; Mayer, 1994b) and is therefore not relevant when gauging the extent of disagreement on economic theory. Cases in which disagreement is due to divergent views on non-economic issues are hard to isolate from those in which disagreement is due to disputes about economics itself.

The upshot of this discussion is that, not so surprisingly, in the absence of detailed empirical studies, one cannot justify strong claims about how well economists can predict. But the evidence from the success of GDP forecasts, and to a lesser extent the market argument, provide some, albeit fairly weak, evidence that economists can predict better than non-economists. On a casual, common sense level, reading newspaper editorials is likely to persuade at least economists that a knowledge of economics does enhance one's ability to predict economic events.

Rosenberg's other charge, that economics is not making any progress as an empirical science, and has made none for a very long time, is puzzling. He provides no documentation, and while it seems to follow from his claim that at present economists cannot predict, that claim itself is also undocumented. Most economists will find such a charge surprising. We now have econometric estimation, linear programming, inventory theory, the economics of information and uncertainty, modern finance theory, public choice theory, cleometrics and so on (cf. Hoover, 1995). Most of the field of macroeconomics developed in the last 60 years. Modern forecasting techniques allow us to predict better than in Marshall's day. As McCloskey (1994) points out, economic theory has improved with the systematic recognition of the need to include variables such as the prices of substitutes in the demand function, with the development of welfare economics and the theory of externalities, the introduction of habit formation and so on. Mathematical rigor and econometric techniques have raised the 'degree of confirmation' of economics at least to some extent. Even I, who am more skeptical than most economists about the claims for *great* progress in economics over the last few decades (see Mayer, 1993b), concede that considerable progress has been made.

What then accounts for Rosenberg's claims of no progress? One possibility is that he is not familiar enough with economics. But I believe that something else is involved, Rosenberg's view of the nature of economics.

The structure of economics and consumer choice theory

Rosenberg views economic theory as a tightly structured body of thought grounded in the theory of consumer choice. As already discussed, he believes that hypotheses about aggregates, such as markets or whole economies, must be built up from lower-level hypotheses about households, and can at best be only as reliable as these lower-level hypotheses. If one grants this supposition, Rosenberg's rejection of economics as empirical science becomes much more understandable, both because of the limited empirical content of consumer choice theory, and because of the problems this theory has encountered on experimental tests. But Rosenberg greatly overestimates the role that consumer choice theory plays in economics. To be sure, neoclassical economics is grounded in consumer choice theory, but this theory plays a much smaller role in the day-to-day work even of academic economists, not to speak of economists in government and business, than such a grounding might suggest. One reason is that consumer choice theory does not set many restrictions on admissible behavior. Hence much of the work of economists has to go beyond this theory.

The second reason is the positivistic revolution following Friedman's 1953 essay. In this approach empirically validated lawlike generalizations at any level of aggregation can serve, as long as they are consistent with consumer choice theory. Economics is no longer a purely deductive discipline. As Caldwell

(1992) remarked, this tends to confuse philosophers who study economics. They center their attention on the impressive formal models of economics, instead of on the 'true but innocuous general statements that actually account for both our discipline's glowing successes and for its most outrageous failures' (Caldwell, 1992, p.146). Similarly, as McCloskey (1994) points out, only about half the articles in the leading journals, and less than half in the lesser journals, are theoretical, so that philosophers who focus on economic theory miss much of what economists do.

Most practicing economists no longer defend their conclusions by claiming that they are correctly derived implications of assumptions, all of which are obviously valid. As Steven Payson (1994, p.152) recently put it: 'the prevailing logic among economists has been, "all models are wrong – some are useful."' The subject matter of economics is extremely complex, and the prime tool of science, experimentation, is of less help here than in the natural sciences.

Neoclassical economists are therefore driven to use the following roundabout procedure. First, you isolate two obviously important elements in the behavior of economic agents, self-interest and rational behavior, and use these as basic axioms, even though you know that human behavior is much more complex than that. You then add other assumptions, some of which are specific to the particular problem at hand, and deduce certain conclusions. If there are no errors in the deductive process these conclusions are valid for the hypothetical world for which the assumptions are valid. You then make the following audacious working assumption: since in economic behavior self-interest surely does play an important role, since, by and large, people behave more or less rationally, and since the other assumptions seem like sufficiently accurate approximations, the hypothetical world of the model maps sufficiently well into the real world for the conclusions to carry over, so that your model is a useful metaphor (cf. McCloskey, 1985, ch.5). You then look at the data to see whether this working assumption is legitimate.[6] In this process the assumptions that are added, the drawing out of their implications and the empirical testing is where the progress of economics takes place. In other words, it is in the Lakatosian protective belt that the real work goes on.

As an example of the difference between Rosenberg's perception of how to do economics and the typical economist's perception, consider the proportionality proposition of monetary theory that, ceteris paribus, changes in the growth rate of money eventually generate equivalent changes in the inflation rate. To evaluate this proposition a Rosenbergian economist would try to start with consumer choice theory to obtain a demand function for money. But she would notice that important elements of consumer choice theory have performed badly on experimental tests. She might therefore conclude that the proportionality proposition can be established only as an exercise in applied mathematics; that is, that she can write down certain axioms from which it can be deduced.

But if asked, say by the Federal Reserve, whether a 5 per cent increase in the monetary growth rate would cause a 5 per cent increase in the inflation rate, she would have to say 'I don't know.'

That is not the way most economists work. An economist with a strong empirical orientation would test the proposition simply by looking at past data. Someone with a more theoretical orientation would start with a demand curve for money, or with utility functions. Suppose he were told that the consumer choice theory that underlies his analysis has been disconfirmed. He would shrug his shoulders and reply that the irrationalities of individual consumers will average out. Suppose he is then told that this is not so, that, although some irrationalities cancel out, agents may have a systematic money illusion. He is likely to reply: 'Well, that *could* be the case. Let's develop the analysis on the assumption that there is no money illusion, and then test it against the data. If it is disconfirmed, well, then we may have to go back and add a term for a money illusion to the utility functions of agents'.

Given this pragmatic way in which most economists work, it is by no means obvious that economic analysis should start from the theory of consumer choice. If we follow Hick's suggestion and start with the market and its supply and demand curves, we would both bypass the experimental disconfirmations of consumer choice theory and make the theory's imprisonment in folk psychology that concerns Rosenberg irrelevant.

As already mentioned, Rosenberg rejects this solution, on three grounds. His first, that many economists *do* want to make statements about the behavior of individual agents, is hardly a compelling ground for claiming that neoclassical economics as a whole cannot be an empirical science. At most, one might say that to be an empirical science neoclassical economics has to jettison a part of its claimed domain.

Nor is Rosenberg's second reason, that economics is precisely that discipline that is responsible for explaining consumer behavior, compelling. Who assigned this task to economics, and by what authority? Is not consumer choice also studied by psychologists, sociologists and specialists in marketing? Besides, if economics cannot carry out a *part* of its assigned task, does that make economics unscientific? That medicine has not developed a cure for cancer does not mean that it is not an empirical science.

Rosenberg's third reason is that consumer choice theory is basic to neoclassical economics, because any false predictions it makes will be carried forward to predictions about aggregates, such as market demand curves, or the unemployment rate. Rosenberg presents no justification for this claim, and it is hard to see why it should be valid. A theory may predict the behavior of any particular consumer badly, and yet, as the law of large numbers tells us, it may predict the behavior of an aggregate of consumers well, just as Boyle's gas law does not account for the behavior of individual molecules, but does explain the behavior of gases. Whether economics can explain the behavior of aggregates better than the behavior of individuals depends on whether individual deviations cancel out, and that is an empirical issue.

So here is an empirical example. If one tries to explain the savings/income ratio of individual households by the standard economic variables, such as income and wealth, a regression will give an exceedingly poor fit, because it does not take into account the idiosyncratic elements that have a strong effect on the savings ratio of any particular household. But when one aggregates the data, by classifying the households, say by income, location or education, the idiosyncratic elements cancel out and the standard economic variables explain the savings ratio well. Such cancellation does not always occur, but whether it does in a specific situation is an empirical issue. Theories built up from the micro level are not necessarily better than those derived directly from macro relationships (see Chapter 4; Gilbert, 1991, p.141; Hoover, 1995).

Consumer choice theory plays two roles in economics. One is to serve as a check on the statements that someone makes, to see if they are consistent with rational utility maximization. If not, they are not necessarily rejected, but their author is required to offer a plausible explanation. Such an explanation can bring in factors other than those embodied in the folk psychology that Rosenberg criticizes, so that economics is not limited to such an extent that it cannot be an empirical science. To be sure, one might argue, as I will in the following chapters, that economists are too reluctant to search for and accept such explanations, but that reluctance is something that can be overcome, and hence not something that, in principle, prevents economics from being an empirical science.

The second role of consumer choice theory is to serve as a schematic or pedagogic device that simplifies the exposition of some important theorems. Hausman (1992b, p.79) characterizes this type of theorizing as follows:

> An absolutely crucial part of the scientific enterprise ... is the construction of new concepts, of new ways of classifying phenomena. Even extremely simple models, such as the model of a simple consumption system, provide such concepts. ... In defining a model of a simple consumption system and in proving that the individual's consumption will lie at the point of tangency between some indifference curve and the budget constraint, one is not making any claims about the world.

The theory of consumer choice fulfils such an organizing and pedagogic function. Indifference curves provide a convenient and telling way of illustrating such things as the welfare loss from rationing, and a backward-bending supply curve of labor. Such tasks can be accomplished by a thin theory, one that can be described as applied mathematics, since it does not try to provide either a realistic description of general consumer behavior or a useful way of predicting it, except for certain narrow aspects of behavior that are important for economics.

Given the little that it tries to do, introducing the complex psychology of consumer behavior would just add unnecessary complications. For a theory like this, evidence that preferences are intransitive is not disconfirming evidence, but irrelevant evidence. The cost of replacing such a thin theory, with a thicker, more realistic one is that economics would then no longer stand on its own feet, but would have to be based on psychology, which would greatly add to its complexity (see Hausman, 1992b). Certainly, there are also substantial advantages to such a switch, and in the next chapters I advocate it, but it is not required for economics to be an empirical science, and for many purposes it would just add unnecessasry complications.

The treatment of disconfirming evidence

A salient characteristic of empirical science is the way scientists respond to disconfirming evidence. To be sure, no knowledgeable person believes any longer in the old-fashioned story that a scientist abandons a theory, however powerful and previously well confirmed, as soon as any disconfirming evidence comes into view. But even so, a field that generally brushes aside disconfirming evidence cannot claim to be an empirical science. And this is how Rosenberg sees economics. Is he right?

He is right in the sense that it would be rare for the negative results on a single econometric test to eliminate a theory that economists regard highly, either because of its close tie to the main stem of economic theory or because it is technically sweet, or else because it has previously been strongly confirmed. But neither do physical scientists abandon such theories all that easily. And in economics consistent failure on many econometric tests is usually fatal to a theory's standing (cf. Chapter 9). Moreover, when the challenge to a theory comes from a dramatic natural experiment rather than from a subtle econometric test, economists are more willing to abandon a theory (see Lawrence Summers, 1991).

Empirical tests have induced economists to abandon numerous theories. In his *A Theory of the Consumption Function*, Friedman (1957) presented what was later called the 'proportionality hypothesis', that is the hypothesis that the percentage of permanent income consumed is independent of the level of permanent income.[7] It is the sort of hypothesis that one would expect economists to relish, because by being so greatly at variance with popular beliefs it shows the contribution that economic analysis can make, and because it simplifies our representation of the economy. But subsequently, when empirical tests overwhelmingly rejected it (for a survey, see Mayer, 1972) the proportionality hypothesis largely disappeared from the literature. While the other part of the permanent income theory, consumption smoothing, has survived, an extensive literature on excess consumption volatility has challenged it, and appears to have substantially reduced the standing of the theory. (For a survey of the debate, see Gilbert, 1991.)

The Keynesian–monetarist debate provides another example of the way economists respond to empirical evidence. It is an interesting example because it concerns a debate between two paradigms, one explaining aggregate demand mainly by the motives to spend and stressing the short run, the other explaining aggregate demand by excess cash balances and stressing the long run. Moreover, the two sides advocate conflicting policies and differ on issues that extend well beyond monetary economics (see Mayer *et al.*, 1978). Personality conflicts also play a role. So economists should be most reluctant to change their minds on this issue. Yet what happened? In the 1960s and 1970s the incoming data showed that velocity and the money demand function were surprisingly stable. As the monetarists had foretold, the Federal Reserve was pursuing wrong policies, and inflation accelerated. In addition, Friedman and Schwartz (1963a) provided massive empirical support for a monetarist interpretation of the Great Depression. If economists take empirical evidence seriously, monetarism should then have gained support. It did. And, what is at least as important, the mainstream Keynesian position moved substantially closer to monetarism.

Subsequently, in the 1980s, when the incoming data made it much harder to insist that the demand function for some readily measurable and controllable concept of 'money' was stable, when Fed policy improved, and when inflation became much less of a threat, monetarism lost much of its support. To be sure, this story does not conform entirely to the splendid picture of 'science' held by the naive. Political preferences and the graduate school one had attended seemed to play an unjustifiably large role in determining one's opinions. Moreover, both monetarists and Keynesians would argue that those on the other side were stubbornly adhering to their priors. While there is something to this complaint, the empirical evidence was certainly not being ignored; positions did change.

In the 1980s, there occurred a debate about whether anticipated and unanticipated changes in the money supply had substantially different effects. Economic theory suggests that unanticipated changes in the money supply should have relatively more effect on output and less effect on prices than do anticipated changes. By and large, the data refused to oblige. This evidence was taken seriously, and although the distinction between anticipated and unanticipated money has not entirely disappeared from the literature, it now receives much less attention than before.

Blaug (1991, p.510) lists several additional examples, such as Bowley's claim about constant relative shares and Hansen's secular stagnation thesis that many economists accepted in the 1940s. I conjecture that most readers can add examples of their own. In some other cases unfavourable empirical tests have not demolished the basic idea of the hypothesis, but have caused it to be reformulated in a substantially different and more subtle form. Examples include the accelerator theory of investment, money demand functions and the Phillips curve.[8]

Of course, there are also cases in which the empirical evidence plays a less heroic role. An example is the debate about Ricardian equivalence (see Chapter 5). In his survey of this literature Seater (1993, p.183) points out that the results reached by various investigators have an embarrassingly high correlation with their political views. This can be read as showing that these 'tests' are more debating artifices than serious scientific tests. But it can also be read as showing that in this particular case the results one obtains are so sensitive to minor differences in specification that they provide little reason for changing one's priors.

Thus the evidence does show that in applied economics hypotheses are far from immune to disconfirming evidence. Obviously, they are not always abandoned as quickly as they should be. That is so also in the natural sciences, though I suspect to a considerably smaller extent. One would expect economics to be worse in this respect because empirical tests are not nearly as conclusive in economics and (though I think that this is much less important) ideological influences inevitably play a larger role in economics. *Perhaps* it is also more difficult in economics to develop plausible rival hypotheses, and hypotheses are seldom abandoned until an alternative is available. But the difference between economics and the natural sciences in the extent of dogmatic adherance to disconfirmed hypotheses does not seem nearly as great as Rosenberg suggests.

Why then do economists not abandon the extensively disconfirmed theory of consumer choice? One possibility is that this theory is so basic a part of economics that abandoning it would bring too much of economics crashing down. But another possibility is that consumer choice theory is used in economics in such a thin way that the disconfirming evidence has little relevance for it.

Three other issues

Rosenberg criticizes economic theory for making only generic and not quantitative predictions. In doing so he is looking only at economic theory, and not at economics per se. Quantitative predictions abound in macroeconomics, with its surfeit of econometric models. In microeconomics, too, quantitative predictions are common. Economists, particularly business economists and agricultural economists, estimate many demand functions. Government economists, as well as many academic economists, produce quantitative estimates of microeconomic policies. To be sure, the formal theory of consumer choice does not make quantitative predictions, but then we supplement it with econometrics.

Even so, Rosenberg has a point when he complains about generic predictions. Economic *theory* does make only, or almost only, generic predictions. The standard reply is that we bring in econometrics to take us from these generic predictions to quantitative predictions. That is true, but one great difficulty in econometrics is precisely that we are often trying to test or apply theories that are too general. For example, the theory may suggest that the regressors should be lagged, but gives no indication of how many lags should be included in the regression, thus issuing a fishing license to the econometrician.

So it is a serious matter that economic theory makes almost only generic predictions. But Rosenberg has not shown that this prevents economics from being an empirical science. It would do so only if it prevented economists from making successful predictions. Rosenberg claims that this is the case but, as I have tried to show, it is a questionable claim.

Rosenberg is also too pessimistic when he says that, since economic theory is an extremal theory, it cannot be modified in response to disconfirming evidence. Surely consumer choice theory and the theory of the firm can be so modified, and much of the more exciting recent work on these theories has done precisely that. Consumer choice theory has been modified by allowing for choice under uncertainty, transactions costs have been introduced into various parts of economic theory, and economists, such as George Akerlof and Robert Frank, have enriched the utility function in ways that enable economists to explain some important types of economic behavior much better.

Rosenberg's discussion of the role that general equilibrium theory plays in economics is also unconvincing. Economists do not overvalue it because it justifies reliance on markets. Just the opposite, Frank Hahn who takes a critical view of markets (see Coddington, 1975, for a discussion) has used general equilibrium theory to argue that real-world markets do not have the virtues that economists ascribe to them. Nor is there any reason to think that general equilibrium theory is more improvable than other parts of economic theory. And while the few economists who specialize in general equilibrium theory have a natural tendency to view it as the essence of economics, there is little reason to think that other economists do so too.

A summing up

Rosenberg's thesis that economics is not an empirical science is vitiated by three major deficiencies. First, it rests on several claims that are unsubstantiated – that economists cannot predict sufficiently well, that their predictive capacity is not improving over time, and that they ignore falsifying empirical evidence. Second, Rosenberg sees economics through Cartesian glasses.[9] As a result he overemphasizes the role that consumer choice theory plays in economics. A third deficiency, one that originates in the other two, is that he assumes that any errors made in analysing household behavior are necessarily carried forward into the analysis of markets and of the macro economy.

That does not mean that Rosenberg's concern about the unrealism of consumer choice theory is without value. On the contrary, in the next chapter I will argue that economists should be more hospitable to a thicker theory of consumer choice. Nor does it deny that economists overemphasize formal theory at the expense of strenuous testing (see Mayer, 1993b). Hausman (1992a, p.101), who believes that the 'real methodological difference' between economics and the natural science is the smaller role of testing in economics, has remarked:

> Economists are so little involved with testing because, first, many are involved with non-empirical conceptual work. ... Second, even those who are interested in empirical theory are also relatively uninvolved with testing (in comparison with biologists or chemists) because, given the subject matter they deal with, they do not know enough to formulate good tests or to interpret the results of tests. If there is a cure, it can only come as a result of acquiring better experimental techniques and more detailed knowledge. This requires methodological reform. (Hausman, 1992b, p.190)

Much of the problem with Rosenberg's book arises from his attempt to cover all or most of economics with a single label. Some of economics has the characteristics of a mathematical science, but the greater part has the characteristics of an empirical science. More than half the papers published in the academic journals are empirical, and so is just about all the work of economists in business and government. Given the difficulty of delineating the economics profession, it is not clear what proportion of economists is employed in business. But using the Census definition 52 per cent of all American economists are employed in business and industry, 23 per cent in government at all levels and only 20 per cent in academia, with 5 per cent employed in 'other' activities (Klamer and Colander, 1990, p.7). Hence, if for some reason one were to insist on a single label for economics, it should be empirical science, not mathematical science.

Appendix: Rosenberg's critique of macroeconomics

The charges that Rosenberg brings against macroeconomics are puzzling. Why should macroeconomics be faulted because Keynes could demonstrate only the *possibility* of underemployment equilibrium? To start with, Keynes never claimed that underemployment was the only possible equilibrium, but just that full employment was only one of several possible equilibria. And even if in 1936 Keynes had tried unsuccessfully to show that underemployment is a unique equilibrium, why should modern macroeconomics, which most certainly does not assert this, be blamed for Keynes's failure?[10]

Why should macroeconomics, which can explain stagflation, at least in general terms, be blamed because old-fashioned Keynesian theory could not? Likewise, contemporary macro theory with its life cycle hypothesis, Ricardian equivalence and wealth effects can readily explain the failure of fiscal policy, insofar as this failure is due to a lack of strength, which is by no means certain.[11]

Rosenberg is right in saying that the inability to fine-tune the economy shows a weakness of macroeconomics, though a good part of the failure of fine-tuning is due to political problems. But the inability to fine-tune the economy does not invalidate the status of economics as an empirical science. We call chemistry an empirical science even though it has not found a cheap way to desalinate sea water. Instead, macroeconomics should be commended for having clarified the obstacles to successful fine-tuning. Moreover, although fine-tuning may not be feasible, there is good reason to think we do know enough to prevent extremely severe recessions.

Notes

1. Hausman (1992a, p.187) interprets Rosenberg as arguing only that economic theory, not economics per se, has made no progress. But that interpretation is inconsistent with Rosenberg's (1992, p.254) lament that economics does not provide policymakers with the information they need.
2. Rosenberg (1992, p.xiv). In stressing a science's progressivity Rosenberg is, of course, following Lakatos.
3. Rosenberg (1992, p.100) argues that the Lakatosian MSRP does not solve the demarcation problem because it uses the same methodological notions that had been tried unsuccessfully by its predecessors, and also because it would classify as science research programs in such obviously non-scientific fields as literary theory and painting. Not being a philosopher, I am not qualified to discuss this argument. But I disagree with both Weintraub and Rosenberg that general equilibrium theory should necessarily be called the hard core of neoclassical economics. Marshallian theory has at least as good a claim to that title (see Chapter 6).
4. However, it would not necessarily argue for reducing research grants to economics. That would depend on the elasticity of supply of good forecasts, and on the elasticity of demand for them.
5. To be sure, the tests are often compassionate rather than severe. But that is a matter of practice falling short of the ideal. The procedures I have sketched are not subject to the criticism of positivistic economics that Rosenberg (1976) presented in an earlier book. There he placed positivistic economics into the Procrustean bed of logical positivism, and then proceeded to chop its head off by showing that the terms of economic theory cannot be legitimately interpreted as theoretical terms.
6. Winston (1993, p.1286) summarizes his results as follows:

Economists were generally successful in predicting the direction and size of the effects of regulatory reform on prices and profits. They were less successful where deregulation led to substantial changes in firm's operations and technology. And their predictions did not adequately incorporate the effects of regulatory reform on service or foresee the extent of price discrimination in certain industries. In addition, they did not always anticipate the importance of supplementary government policies in ensuring deregulation's success, and were unable to foresee major changes in the external economic factors that dramatically affected some industries' performance and clouded assessments. ... Despite these problems the evidence clearly shows that microeconomists' predictions that deregulation would produce substantial benefits for Americans have been generally accurate. ... Their track record is good. Now if only *macro*economists could explain and forecast aggregate fluctuations!

7. This hypothesis also plays a role, albeit a lesser one, in the original presentations of the life cycle hypothesis of Modigliani and associates.
8. That these examples come from macroeconomics rather than microeconomics does not imply that microeconomic hypotheses are more resistant to disconfirming evidence. It just reflects the fact that I specialize in macroeconomics.
9. That is not surprising. Mäki (1993a) argues that a common failing of economic methodologists is that they overemphasize the importance of a well-defined economic structure connecting assumptions and implications 'or mathematical structure at the expense of less formal reasoning'.
10. Perhaps Rosenberg means something else, that Keynes's claim that there can be underemployment equilibrium has been refuted. But why should the correction of a mistake Keynes made almost 60 years ago, and that has long since been corrected, be counted as a failing of macroeconomics?
11. At least in the United States, much of the problem with counter-cyclical fiscal policy is political rather than economic.

12 A note on consumer choice theory

Economists frequently treat the neoclassical theory of consumer choice as the foundation of economics. That is legitimate in the sense that it is the starting point of micro theory. If the new classical reductionists are right (admittedly a big 'if'), it is also the foundation of macroeconomics (see Chapter 4). Economists have succeeded in building a powerful, and on the whole remarkably successful, superstructure on this thin theory of human behavior. Presumably because of these successes they often overlook the serious limitations of consumer choice theory. These limitations do not matter for formalist economics which merely develops the logical implications of certain axioms, axioms that may or may not correspond to actual conditions. However, for an empirical science economics that tries to predict or explain what actually happens, these limitations are more serious, though even here they do not argue for abandoning the theory, only for using it more cautiously.

Neoclassical consumer choice theory is traditionally (see Robbins, 1935) derived from two propositions, self-interested utility maximization and rational behavior.[1] Following Robbins and Mill, these are usually treated as self-evident propositions that no reasonable person should question. If someone does so, these doubting Thomases can readily be silenced by referring them to introspection and indubitable observation. Elaborate econometric evidence, or any other appeal to systematic predictive success, is not needed.[2] Surely no reasonable person would deny that people are – on the whole – rational. Madmen exist, but they are few and their behavior is of little interest to economists. Altruists exist, but the likes of Mother Theresa are too few to affect the behavior of markets.

Yes, all that is correct. It does establish that it is better to assume that people are swayed by self-interest than to assume that they are swayed by altruism, and that it is more reasonable to assume that they always behave rationally than that they always behave irrationally. But to pose such a choice between extreme assumptions misses the point. The consequential challenge to standard neoclassical theory comes from a theory that assumes only *some* altruism and *some* irrationality, say in 3 per cent of the decisions.

Neither introspection nor casual observations of our fellow-man rules out that challenge. Just the opposite. Few people's introspection would tell them that they never act from altruistic motives. Similarly, observation of other people's behavior tells us that, while self-interest is the main factor, it is not the only factor that motivates economic behavior. On an obvious level we observe that people contribute to charity, even those who do not believe in an after-life in which charity will turn out to have been a high-yielding investment. To be sure, owing to the small amount so contributed, it does not argue for extensive altruism. What is much more telling evidence for behavior that is other than purely self-interested is the limited extent of shirking on the job (cf. Simon, 1991; Akerlof, 1984, p.8). If employees did not feel a sense of responsibility and loyalty to their employers, productivity would surely be much lower than it is now, or else institutions, such as piecework or tipping by customers, would be much more widespread. To take an example close to home, most of us put more effort into class preparation than we can justify by the addition to our income that we can expect from such effort. Despite the well-documented relation between publication and professorial salaries (see Tuckman and Leahey, 1975), most of us (let us hope) would not publish a paper based on data we think are invalid, even if there is no chance of being caught.

It is tempting to reply that what seems like altruistic behavior is really utility-maximizing behavior in disguise, because people derive utility from altruism and from being honest, loyal and so on. But that answer will not do. Nobody challenges the assumption of utility maximization – if utility is defined broadly enough. But when the utility-maximizing assumption is put to work in economic theory the utility function is usually restricted to, at most, three arguments: income, leisure and risk. This narrow perception of the standard utility function is well illustrated by the way so many neoclassical economists dismiss out of hand the original Keynesian explanation of wage rigidity: that workers care about relative income, not just about their absolute income. They refuse to take Keynes's explanation of wage rigidity seriously, even though there is extensive evidence that relative income does enter the utility function.

The reason for relying on such a narrow utility function is, of course, tractability. A much broader utility function would not permit us to draw some important conclusions that we can draw with the present narrow function. For example, if we admit altruism, and the accompanying wish to treat people fairly, into the utility function, then if supply falls prices may not rise enough to clear markets. But the wish to obtain a certain set of conclusions is not a good justification for using a particular assumption, unless the conclusion has been independently confirmed. Hence, the thin utility function is usually not defended that way. Instead, what is often done is to start with the general proposition that agents maximize utility. Then, in the course of the argument, the terms 'income' or 'profits' are substituted for 'utility'.

A more defensible procedure would be to claim on positivistic 'as-if' grounds that a utility function containing only income, leisure and risk suffices to explain economic behavior. But, as discussed in the next chapter, there is ample reason to challenge this claim. It cannot be defended by citing the numerous and important cases in which it does suffice. It would be hard to deny that many such cases exist. But it is also hard to deny that there are other important phenomena that, so far at least, have not been explained by neoclassical theory.

The assumption of rational behavior raises a similar issue. Rational behavior, like self-interested behavior, is the norm, but there is a great difference between something being the norm and its being a self-evident truth that can be demonstrated by introspection and indubitable observation. Neither my observation of other people, nor reflections on my own past behavior, makes it self-evident to me that people always behave rationally.

The applicability of the rationality assumption depends upon the type of economics that is built upon it. If economists tried to establish only certain simple propositions, such as that with real income held constant demand curves slope downward, introspection might perhaps be an acceptable procedure, though not to resolute positivists. But once economics tries to go beyond simple propositions, and deals, for example, with behavior under uncertainty, it can no longer be grounded in self-evident propositions. It is not at all self-evident how people behave when faced with uncertainty. And even under certainty it is not self-evident that tastes are always stable enough for transitivity to be an empirically observable and hence an interesting condition. Nor is it clear how to incorporate the pleasure obtained on the one hand from variety, and on the other hand from following habits (see Koopmans, 1957, pp.136–7).

All this may seem obvious, even trite – and it is trite. But it has two implications that are often ignored. One is that economists should pay more attention to disconfirming empirical evidence than neoclassical economists usually do. If we cannot justify economic theory by the argument that it is rigorously derived from undeniable premises, but justify it instead by the consonance of its predictions with the empirical evidence, then we can hardly dismiss any instances in which the evidence contradicts the theory as something that is not worth bothering with. To be sure, since neoclassical theory has had much success we should not discard it because of a few disconfirming instances, but when those arise we may have to constrict the domain of the theory. For example, it is one thing to claim that the theory explains prices in auction markets well, quite another that it can explain wage setting, or that expectations *must* be rational, in the way that the term 'rational' is used in new classical theory.

The second implication relates to the status of a theorem that rigorously derives a particular implication of rational utility maximization. As a piece of logic or applied mathematics it is a contribution to the stock of knowledge, perhaps a valuable one. But as a piece of empirical science economics it is far from rigorous, and is not necessarily useful. Drawing an indubitable implication from assumptions that are themselves far from indubitable does not yield indubitable knowledge.

Where does this leave the popular methodological precept that one should start from first principles? Stanley Fischer, in a recent interview (Snowdon *et al.*, 1994, p.37), remarked about new classical economics: 'When it's just a methodological precept of trying to explain everything from first principles then I don't think there are any serious criticisms you could make of that – except that it's too often used as an excuse for not giving policy advice.' But there is another, more basic criticism. This is that by ignoring opportunity costs it generates a misallocation of scarce resources. It requires effort that the author could often spend better in testing the implications of her hypothesis. It also imposes on the reader's scarce time and, what is more, it detracts the reader's attention away from the question of whether the implications of the hypothesis are confirmed, or how plausible the rational maximization hypothesis is in this particular case. Since the first principles are not themselves firmly established, but are simplifications that fit well in some cases, but not well in others, these costs may outweigh the benefits.

None of this means that one must start with 'correct' assumptions (see Chapter 7). Nor does it deny that neoclassical economics frequently allows one to draw conclusions that are strongly confirmed. What it does mean is that such confirmation must come primarily from empirical tests of the implications.[3] Since empirical tests, while often highly persuasive, are seldom beyond question, it follows that – if interpreted as propositions about the external world – economics generally does not furnish rigorously derived results. One must either abandon the Cartesian dream of a rigorous economics, or else relinquish the goal of an economics that is an empirical science.

Many practicing economists seem to accept an amalgam of Cartesian, Robbinsian and positivistic methodologies. But these three elements cannot peacefully coexist. A Cartesian economics, if it is to apply to empirical science economics and not just to formalist economics, requires premises that are much more certain than those provided by Robbinsian introspection and casual empiricism. A positivistic economics requires that we test by the reliability of predictions and explanations, and not by introspection and casual empiricism. And it does not aspire to Cartesian certainty. So we must choose.

My own choice is positivism, in the loose, anemic sense of the term. Accordingly, in the next chapter I will sketch a positivistic evaluation of neoclassical theory relative to a new institutionalist theory.

Notes
1. Thus Robbins (1935, pp.79–9) wrote:

> The propositions of economic theory, like all scientific theory, ... are obviously deductions from a series of postulates. And the chief of these postulates are all assumptions involving in some way simple and indisputable facts of experience. ... The main postulate of the theory of value is the fact that individuals can arrange their preferences in any order, and in fact

do so. The main postulate of the theory of production is the fact that there are more than one factor of production. The main postulate of the theory of dynamics is the fact that we are not certain regarding future scarcities. These are not postulates the existence of whose counterpart in reality admits of extensive dispute once their nature is fully realized. We do not need controlled experiments to establish their validity: they are so much the stuff of our everyday experience that they have only to be stated to be recognized as obvious.

2.   In their explicit methodological statements many economists probably adopt a more positivistic stance, and base the legitimacy of economic theory in large part on its predictive success. Apriorism is no longer as popular as it once was. But it seems plausible that the combination of introspection and casual empiricism described in the text still plays a significant role in the acceptance of neoclassical theory.

3.   Empirical confirmation can be indirect. Suppose a hypothesis can be derived by a few steps that are logically compelling from another hypothesis that has extremely strong empirical confirmation. Even if the former hypothesis is not itself tested empirically, it is highly plausible.

13 Keeping poor relations at bay: economics as an isolated science

If French chefs resembled neoclassical economists, French cuisine would be more monotonous, for the chefs would use very few ingredients. They would also strenuously insist that food containing any other ingredients was not French. (Hausman, 1992b, p.260)

The natural sciences divide up their joint domain by levels of explanation. Physics explains phenomena on the atomic level, and chemistry on the molecular level. Biology applies the knowledge gained from chemistry, and so does geology. There are occasional disagreements between the practitioners of fields but, on the whole, it is a peaceful and cooperative enterprise. In the social sciences there is much less of a division by level, and much more overlap. Yet sociology, anthropology and political science coexist more or less peacefully, and carry on mutually profitable trades. But the queen of the social sciences, economics, takes a different view of man than sociology does (see Brunner and Meckling, 1977). Perhaps in large part for that reason, mainstream economics disdains imports from sociology, and usually also from the other social sciences, though like a good mercantilist it is more than willing to export to them.[1]

Is this disdain for the other social sciences justified, or is it just intellectual snobbery? In discussing the British class system someone has remarked that every group whose members can possibly claim the title of gentlemen draws the line between gentlemen and the hoi polloi just below itself. Is the splendid isolation of economics from the other social sciences no more than that, or is it justified by the particular questions that economists try to answer?

Daniel Hausman (1992b) presents a strong case that this isolation is unfortunate. Much of his important book, *The Inexact and Separate Science of Economics*, makes this point. He rightly treats the isolation of economics from psychology and sociology, not as a mere surface phenomenon, but as a basic methodological choice of economists. He argues that the driving principle of economic analysis is to determine the equilibrium that results from the market interaction of rational utility-maximizing agents. To introduce, as psychology and sociology suggest, motives other than utility (= income) maximization, or to allow for irrational behavior is, within mainstream economics, condemned as ad hocery.

Hausman's characterization of economics is surely correct. The charge of ad hocery is among the worst that a mainstream economist can hurl at a colleague.

133

But an even worse accusation is to call someone's theory 'sociological'. In the typical seminar, showing that the speaker's hypothesis is inconsistent with rational behavior would often be enough to sink it; even considerable empirical support might frequently not suffice to keep it afloat. To be sure, two factors ameliorate the situation. One is the existence alongside the mainstream of other streams, behavioral economics and institutionalism, new and old, where rational utility maximization is not the sine qua non. The other is that even in mainstream journals rational behavior can sometimes be ousted in favor of 'psychological behavior'. This is, of course, more likely if the author uses the standard tools of economic theory, our mantra being, 'what can be modeled is empirically important, what cannot be, is unimportant', or if the author has extraordinarily strong evidence that the rationality assumption is incapable of doing the job.[2] All the same, the advice one would give to a careerist graduate student is always assume rational utility maximization.

At first glance such a convention may seem bizarre. It is not just that economics uses as its default setting rational behavior, despite the extensive evidence for the existence of irrational behavior that psychologists have provided, but that economists are so reluctant to depart from this default setting. Both psychologists and experimental economists have confronted the theory of consumer choice with numerous well-documented anomalies (see the literature cited in Smith, 1991; Hogarth and Reder, 1987; Frey and Eichenberger, 1989; see also Kahneman *et al.*, 1982). But the theory just marches on with nary a tip of the hat. Hausman (1992b, p.244) is correct when he complains about the 'general complaisance' shown by most economists 'and their unwillingness to take seriously relevant psychological hypotheses'.

In defense of a thin theory
One way to justify the thin neoclassical theory of consumer choice is to claim that economics is a mathematical, that is a formal science. Hence, just as a geometrician is free to take as her axiom either that parallel lines do meet, or that they do not meet, so an economist is free to take rational behavior as his axiom, regardless of what psychologists proclaim to be realistic. But such reasoning can justify the acceptance of a disconfirmed theory of consumer choice only by formalist economists, and not by the more numerous economists who consider themselves empirical scientists.

Within empirical science economics one possibility is to say that in most circumstances that concern economists most people do try to maximize their incomes, and do so more or less rationally.[3] What various experiments and other empirical studies have established is that they do not do so under all circumstances. But a theory that is correct in most instances that we are interested in is useful, and may perhaps be the best we can provide. A social worker who counsels families that are unable to balance their budgets may well find the neoclassical theory of essentially choice with its strong rationality assumption unhelpful. But an economist who studies the behavior of Citicorp may find it helpful.

The role that welfare economics plays in economics provides a useful example. A basic assumption of welfare economics is that consumers are rational, at least to the extent that, if two commodity bundles cost the same, most of the time they will purchase the one they prefer. This does not require that they be fully rational. Economists who use welfare economics to advocate some policy change usually do so because they think that the resulting increase in welfare will be fairly large, so that the small losses that occur because consumers make the wrong choices will be swamped by much larger welfare gains. Similarly, on a practical level, the critical issue in evaluating the market allocation of resources is not whether consumers are perfectly rational, but whether their choices are superior to those generated by an alternative system (Coddington, 1975). And on a theoretical level, consumer choice theory does not provide an unequivocal basis for welfare economics in any case (see Sudgen, 1993).

Moreover, a theory that is as parsimonious as neoclassical theory should not necessarily be abandoned because a somewhat more accurate thicker theory has become available. The benefits of parsimony are not just simplicity of application and elegance. If we adopt a thick theory anchored in the latest findings of psychology, we may have to abandon it if subsequently psychologists change their minds. By using – perhaps on the 'as-if' principle – a theory so thin that it has very little psychological content we avoid this problem.

As Hausman (1992b, p.218) points out, the traditional theory of consumer choice also has the advantage of explaining the actions of agents in terms that makes sense to us because we can readily understand desires and intentions as determining actions. In addition, it might perhaps be the very thinness of economic theory that has made it useful to political philosophers and to biologists, who are not concerned with the behavioral detail that an institutionalist economist might want to see in the theory.

Another advantage of founding economics on a parsimonious assumption set is that it provides a valuable heuristic. A useful task that economics performs is to cut through ideological confusion and self-interested obfuscation to exhibit the underlying economic motives that drive both the actions and claims of various groups. In addition, it simplifies our picture of reality by demonstrating that a wide range of activities can be explained by a single motive. We can explain why most muggers are people with little education, without having to make the perhaps questionable argument that education improves moral character, simply by pointing out that whether or not street crime pays depends on opportunity costs. We can even explain such a 'sociological' phenomenon as the allocation of income with the Chinese patriarchal family, by invoking the theory of optimal taxation (Frey, 1992, ch.6). In Becker's hands economics has become an explanatory tool with an extraordinarily wide reach.

This use of economics requires that economists exert substantial effort in tracing phenomena to their roots in rational profit maximization. Such effort would not be forthcoming, at least to its present extent, if economists were to use a rich theory of human motivation, or were allowed to appeal to irrationalities whenever an explanation consistent with rationality was not readily available. As a result, a major contribution that economics now makes to the social sciences would be diminished. Put somewhat differently, a thin theory provides a barrier against undisciplined ad hocery. Without *some* such barrier appeals to irrationality and to more or less arbitrarily assumed peculiarities of the utility function would make it too easy to offer facile explanations. Insistence on a strenuous search for economic causes is a valuable heuristic that should be kept, though, of course, like almost everything else, it can be carried too far.

In listing these advantages of a thin theory of consumer choice I did not include three justifications that some other economists would have listed. One is the claim, rejected in the previous chapter, that the assumption of rational utility maximization is an assumption that we *know* to be correct by introspection.

The second is the argument that, without the strict rationality assumption, economic analysis is not feasible because, once we are willing to assume irrationality, we have no way of choosing between the vast number of alternative versions of irrationality. This, too, is incorrect. There are specific deviations from rational utility maximization that show up consistently in psychological tests, and at least some are amenable to a theoretical formulation, such as in prospect theory (see Tversky and Kahneman, 1982; Thaler, 1991, chs 1 and 2). For example, Benartzi and Thaler (1993) explain a major puzzle in finance theory, the equity premium (that is the much higher yield of stocks than of bonds) by two characteristics of agents. These are the mental accounting rules that they follow, and loss aversion, that is the principle, well established by experimental economics, that people are more sensitive to reductions than to improvements in their well-being to a greater degree than can be explained by the declining marginal utility of income.

Finally, I have not used Alchian's (1950) evolutionary defense: that those agents who make the right decisions for whatever reason not only survive, but obtain enhanced control over resources, while others drop by the wayside. It would be hard to deny that there is some truth to this.[4] But 'some truth' is not enough to vindicate neoclassical rational choice theory. The objections that have been raised against the evolutionary defense are cogent enough to make one doubt that it can justify a 100 per cent rationality assumption. In Chapter 11, I described Rosenberg's objections. In addition, Sidney Winter (1963) maintains that it is different firms that make the best decisions at different times, and also that economies of scale may inhibit the expansion of the firm that adapts best to a change in the environment. Moreover, as Geoffrey Hodgson (1993) points out, the evolutionary argument is hard to apply to consumers. Also research on 'noise' trades in financial markets has shown that such trades may be more profitable than trades based on fundamentals (see De Long *et al.*, 1993), while Russell and Thaler (1985) have shown that the existence of quasi-rational consumers can make a difference to equilibrium.

Similarly, one cannot use the evolutionary argument to claim that altruism does not affect economic behavior because in this world the good must lose out to the wicked. As Frank (1987) has demonstrated, an agent may benefit from having a conscience.

Disadvantages of a thin theory

It is true that one need not *necessarily* reject neoclassical theory because its assumption of rational income-maximizing behavior is disconfirmed by experimental tests. Friedman (1953) is largely right in saying that a theory should be judged by how well it explains and predicts those phenomena that it is intended to explain, and not other phenomena (see Chapter 7). But this does not mean that the theory's failure to account for the behavior of individuals on various experimental tests does not matter at all. It does matter, for two reasons.

First, if the theory predicted individual behavior on experimental tests correctly the theory would be more general, and hence at least somewhat better. Second, failure of the neoclassical theory on experimental tests creates some – though not necessarily a large – presumption that it will fail also on those tests that are more relevant for its intended uses. But defenders of neoclassical theory can argue that the small stakes in the experiments are insufficient to motivate rational thinking, that in the real world, unlike the situation in the experimental world, people can learn from experience, and hence adjust their behavior, and also that in the real world competition eliminates those who behave irrationally. There is experimental evidence that with higher stakes rationality rises (Frey, *et al.*, 1994). In rebuttal Thaler (1987, pp.96–7) points out that accurate learning requires 'timely and organized feedback', which may not be available. (I have already discussed the evolutionary argument that competition weeds out irrational agents.) The numerous failures on experimental tests should therefore not be brushed aside, though by themselves they do not make a compelling case for abandoning neoclassical theory.

What does matter much more, and indeed is the crux of the issue, is how well the neoclassical theory explains and predicts market behavior. In looking at its defects in that role one should keep in mind that finding some defects does not necessarily warrant abandoning the theory. It can fail in some situations, but be highly successful in others. And since there is no good alternative theory ready in the wings, the issue is more whether to modify or supplement it than whether to jettison it entirely.

A serious problem for neoclassical theory is the deficiency of efficient market theory. If rational income maximization is a reasonable assumption anywhere it is in financial markets with their sophisticated operators, highly organized institutions and large stakes. And yet the efficient market theory is beset by numerous anomalies. Stephen LeRoy (1989, pp.1609, 1614, 1616) reports in a survey article:

> The consensus now is that the anomalies pose a serious problem which cannot be shrugged off. ... However attractive (to economists) capital market efficiency is on methodological grounds, it is extraordinarily difficult to formulate nontrivial and falsifiable implications of capital market efficiency that are not in fact falsified. ... Cognitive psychologists have documented systematic biases in the way people use information and make decisions. Some of these biases are easy to connect, at least informally, with security market behavior. ... Economists have in the past confidentially assumed that these biases would disappear in settings where the stakes are high, as in real world securities markets. However, this line is beginning to wear thin, particularly in light of economists' continuing inability to explain asset prices using models that assume away cognitive biases.

Other papers, subsequent to LeRoy's, have found additional phenomena that contradict efficient market theory. In his introduction to a recent collection of papers on the behavioral theory of finance, Richard Thaler (1993, pp.xv, xvi) reports:

> A reading of the standard finance textbooks ... can create the impression that financial markets are nearly devoid of human activity. ... Since we know that there are indeed humans involved in financial markets, are the markets any different because of their presence? ... Indeed, the findings of the last two decades have been startling. Small firms, firms with low price–earnings ratios, or low ratios of market price to book value of assets, and losing firms all appear to earn higher returns than we would expect. There are also surprising calendar effects, most notably in January. Finally there is growing evidence that the capital asset pricing model β has no predictive power. ... These research findings, and the experience of the 1987 stock market crash, have made financial economists more cautious. If β does not matter, and stock prices can fall 20 percent in a day without any news, can we be sure that people are irrelevant?

None of this necessarily means that efficient market theory is useless. Presumably, it still predicts asset yields better than a random guess does. Moreover, much of the recent literature on efficient market theory has been a revisionist literature in the sense of highlighting the flaws of the received view, while ignoring its successes. It is certainly possible that subsequent research will resolve all the anomalies that now beset the theory. But saying: 'Oh well, all these nasty problems will eventually go away' is not a satisfactory answer. The poor performance of the rational income-maximizing model in financial markets therefore suggests that the neoclassical paradigm *may* face a Kuhnian crisis, at least for those economists who are not bedazzled by the blinding light of mathematical rigor.

Efficient market theory is not the only area in which neoclassical theory has encountered problems. Henry Aaron (1994) lists a host of observed behaviors that conflict with our standard theory of choice. From 1987 to 1990, Richard Thaler, with various co-authors, published a feature called 'Anomalies' in the *Journal of Economic Perspectives*. Among the anomalies they discussed were differences in the propensity to consume out of various types of increases in wealth, the winner's curse (that is, the tendency of winning bids to be unprofitable), the forward discount in the foreign exchange market and certain anomalies in people's intertemporal choices. Furthermore, Lawrence Ausubel (1991) investigated why, notwithstanding extensive competition, interest rates on credit cards have been so sticky. Despite a painstaking effort to explain it with conventional theory, he had to conclude that it was due to the irrationality of many customers who underestimate how likely they are to borrow, and hence pay little attention to the interest rate.

Another instance of something that is hard to explain by traditional neoclassical theory is the reluctance of households to purchase energy-saving models of durables despite the high rate of return on the extra cost. One *might* argue that this is consistent with rational behavior because households have a very high discount rate. One then has to explain why they hold low-yielding deposits. Friedman (1963) explains that by the imputed yield on liquidity that they obtain from deposits, but he offers no convincing evidence that this imputed yield is high enough to explain the discrepancy.

The rationality assumption and its implications are not the only places where the prevailing thin version of neoclassical theory has encountered problems. There is a growing realization that the traditional thin utility function may be inadequate for many problems, that a person's utility function contains the welfare, not just of his own household, but also of other, unrelated households. As Robyn Dawes and Richard Thaler (1988, p.188) point out, public television stations obtain funds from viewers, many people contribute to charities (see Chapter 12) and people tip even in restaurants they will never visit again, and they vote in presidential elections. One might respond that, while some people contribute to public television, many do not, that not tipping is ethically too similar to leaving without paying the bill, and that voting is both a ceremony and an opportunity for self-assertion that yields pleasure.[6] All the same, it is difficult to disagree with Jack Hirschleifer (1985, p.55) when he writes:

> But the analytically uncomfortable (though humanly gratifying) fact remains: from the most primitive to the most advanced societies, a higher degree of cooperation takes place than can be explained as a merely pragmatic strategy for egotistic man. The social contract seems to maintain itself far better than we have any right to expect,

given the agency and free rider problems involved in enforcing the contract against overt or covert violations.

An illustration of the importance of fairness and the associated notion of relative income comes from an opinion survey, taken in the greater New York City area, that asked the following question:

> Suppose the government wants to undertake a reform to improve the productivity of the economy. As a result, everyone will be better off, but the improvement in life will not affect people equally. A million people (people who respond energetically to the incentives in the plan and people with certain skills) will see their incomes triple, while everyone else will see only a tiny income increase, about 1 percent. Would you support the plan? (Shiller *et al.*, 1991, p.391)

Some 64 per cent said 'no'. Such a response is hard to reconcile with the popularity – among economists – of the Pareto criterion, but can readily be explained by considerations of relative income or fairness.

There is also considerable evidence that people have not abandoned the medieval notion of a just price. When asked whether it was fair for a manufacturer to raise the price of kitchen tables when demand had risen, but the cost of production had not, 70 per cent of the previously mentioned sample replied that it was not fair, and 41 per cent said that the manufacturer should not have the right to do so (Robert Shiller *et al.*, 1991, p.389). In another survey, Kahneman *et al.* (1986, pp.729–30) also found a strong emphasis on fairness in pricing, and concluded that the standard of perceived fairness is a dual entitlement standard:

> Transactors have an entitlement to the terms of the reference transaction [a relevant precedent, such as the price before a shortage developed] and firms are entitled to their reference profit. A firm is not allowed to increase its profits by arbitrarily violating the entitlement of its transactors to the reference price, rent or wage. ... When the reference profit of a firm is threatened, however, it may set new terms that protect its profit at transactors' expense.

The public's concern with fairness would not matter for price theory if firms did not respond to it. But they may do so, for two reasons. First, the managers themselves may believe in these norms and set prices accordingly. Second, they may be afraid that violating them would reduce profits by alienating customers. There is both survey and experimental evidence that customers are inclined to punish behavior that they consider unfair (see Kahneman *et al.*, 1986).

We could therefore find price and wage inflexibility in situations where, according to the thin neoclassical theory, wages and prices should be flexible. We could also find that firms sometimes respond to shortages, not by raising prices, but by formal or informal rationing, such as occurred during the West Coast gasoline shortage in 1920 (see Olmstead and Rhode, 1985).

More generally, Dennis Carlton (1989, p.939) in his comprehensive survey of the way markets clear concludes that it is not just prices that clear markets, but that other factors, such as 'a seller's knowledge of the buyers' needs' also play a role. However, Carlton (1986, p.638) also points out that the prevalence of non-price rationing could be due to uncertainty and to 'the cost of using the price system' instead of considerations of fairness.

When David Levine (1993) surveyed compensation executives to determine the role that wage norms and fairness play in wage setting, he, too, found that equity considerations are important. In another survey of firms, Blinder and Choi (1990), too, found that considerations of fairness of relative wages are very important in wage setting. George Akerlof and Janet Yellen (1988, p.45) report that: 'All textbooks on compensation consider it self-evident that the most important aspect of a compensation system is its accordance with workers' conceptions of equity. Workers who consider themselves ... unfairly treated are likely to shirk.'

Concerns about equity can also explain why tickets for certain concerts, sports events and so on, are sold out long ahead of time, rather than sold to the highest bidder, and why restaurants turn away potential customers. To be sure, Gary Becker (1991) has provided a neoclassical explanation: excess demand is a good way of advertising high quality, with consumers obtaining additional utility from knowing that other consumers have a high demand for the product. But as Thaler (1991, ch. 2) points out, that, unlike equity considerations, does not explain why tickets for events that have few repeat customers are sold at below market-clearing prices. It is therefore not surprising that in recent years many economists have built models around the notion of fairness (for references, see Snowdon *et al.*, 1994, pp.315–17).

None of this means that neoclassical theory is entirely untenable. One can generate auxiliary hypotheses under which it can be maintained, for example the existence of unidentified constraints that explain away the anomalies that plague efficient-market theory, a tendency of people to lie when asked about tipping or about their notions of just price, and a sufficiently high discount rate. But there comes a point at which the probability that all the auxiliary hypotheses that have to be maintained to preserve the theory is less than the probability that the theory is inadequate. What, after all, is the justification for the thin theory? It is essentially that it works well in many important cases. But a theory may explain some phenomena well and not others. If so, it is worth seeing if at a low enough cost it can be modified to extend its reach.

Thickening the theory
A reasonable starting point for modifying traditional micro theory is its basic assumptions of fully rational behavior and of a parsimonious utility function, because the theory has been developed primarily as a set of deductions from

these assumptions. As discussed in Chapter 7, realism of assumptions is not a necessary condition for a successful theory, but when a theory encounters serious problems, unrealistic assumptions are the obvious places to send the repair crew.

All the same, for many, perhaps most, problems the twin assumptions are useful heuristics. They not only allow us to make obvious statements, such as that demand curves slope downwards, but also to gain insights that non-economists lack, such as that under flexible exchange rates import barriers usually have only second-order effects on employment. But as economics develops beyond dealing with simple cases, and looks at more complex ones, such as behavior under uncertainty, or at the conduct of government agencies, more realistic and hence more complex assumptions *may* be useful.

Whether such greater complexity pays its way is an empirical issue, and not something that can be settled by assertions about what is or is not economics or what is realistic. But at the very least, the experimental evidence, as well as the deficiencies of efficient market theory, suggest that in complex cases the 100 per cent rationality assumption can lead to error. So can the assumption that a person's utility function contains only her own income, leisure and risk.

Altruism exists. Moreover, the self-centeredness that is said to be the bedrock of selfish actions generates, not just selfish behavior, but also concern about one's reputation, and that may induce people to act in a way that is observationally equivalent to altruistic behavior. A simple point, but one that is often ignored.

Beyond that, we should not insist so strongly that considerations of fairness play no role in wage and price setting. The empirical evidence suggests that fairness does matter. There is nothing inherently irrational about wanting to be treated fairly, quite apart from the higher income one may obtain that way, or wanting to treat others fairly. The demand for fairness and the wish to be fair are as legitimate tastes as any other.

Another way the thin theory needs to be supplemented, so that it can explain a wider range of observed market behavior, is to introduce relative income into the utility function. A classic puzzle in the theory of the consumption function is that, on the one hand, the savings ratio does not rise secularly as permanent income rises, but, on the other hand, in cross-section data the savings ratio does rise with permanent income (see Mayer, 1972). James Duesenberry (1949) resolved this paradox by including relative income in the utility function, so that a household's response to a rise in income depends upon whether the incomes of other households are also rising. In a fascinating book, Robert Frank (1985) discusses several other puzzles that can be resolved by including concern about status and relative income in the utility function. These include the flatness of the wage structure within firms, the scarcity of piecerate wages, and the greater emphasis that unions place on fringe benefits than on wages.

Adding relative income to the utility function represents a change that is entirely consistent with the spirit of neoclassical micro theory. It does, however, change welfare economics to some extent by modifying the Pareto criterion. Now a policy is an unequivocal improvement only if (1) it raises at least one person's income without lowering anyone else's income, and (2) it does not change anyone's relative income. That everyone's income thus has to increase proportionately is a much more severe restriction than that imposed by the standard Pareto criterion. But it raises no theoretical issues, and on a practical level it makes virtually no difference because it would be hard to imagine any policy affecting many people that satisfies the traditional Pareto criterion.

Apart from that, as Frank (1985) has shown, introducing relative income into the utility function extends the range of phenomena that microeconomics can explain. In macroeconomics it legitimizes Keynes's explanation of wage stickiness, which is the reluctance of workers to take a relative wage cut. Once one takes account of the substantial evidence for the role of relative income in the utility function, one must reject the new classicals' charge that Keynes's argument for wage stickiness is ad hoc. Indeed, the extensive evidence of the importance of relative income might tempt one to say that what is ad hoc is the new classicals' exclusion of relative income from the utility function.[7]

Finally, that economics is the most advanced of the social sciences should not prevent us from collaborating with other social scientists, both in the formal sense of collaboration and in the informal sense of paying attention to their work, or using their tools. Thus Gary Becker (in Swedberg, 1990) suggests that economists have much to learn from sociologists about the creative use of surveys, while Solow (1994, p.53) recently suggested that, in growth theory, 'the best candidate for a research agenda right now would be an attempt to extract a few workable hypotheses from the variegated mass of case studies, business histories, interviews, expert testimony ...'. And Arthur Denzau and Douglass North (1994) have made a strong case for paying attention to the work of cognitive scientists. Similarly, a recent survey article by Hausman and McPherson (1993) suggests ways of fruitfully collaborating with moral philosophers.

But while thus enriching our theory we should maintain as much as possible of the advantages of the prevailing thin theory. For some purposes the thin theory is adequate, and it should therefore be retained alongside the thicker theory that is needed for other purposes. There is nothing wrong with having two theories. Even when considering the same object, several different points of view may be appropriate. As I write this, I see an object that to a physicist is a particular combination of sub-atomic particles, to a chemist a specific combination of molecules, to me a comfortable armchair, and to a decorator an eyesore. Physicists use both Newtonian theory and relativity theory. Admittedly, they know the precise domain of application of the former, and hence know when to use it, and when to use relativity theory instead. Economists with a thin and a thick theory would not know exactly when to switch. But then, economics is not physics.

A reasonable procedure would be to look first for a thin theory explanation and to use a thick theory only if that fails (see Aaron, 1994). This would allow us to cut through the ideological fog and elucidate the underlying economic motive where it does exist. Admittedly, since there is prestige to be gained, at least among economists, by finding an underlying economic motive, there is a danger that such a motive will be found, even where it does *not* exist, or when it plays only a minor role. One needs to navigate carefully between the Scylla of being too indolent to find the economic motive that does exist and the Charybdis of being industrious enough to find it even when it does not exist.

This procedure of first trying a rational, maximizing solution privileges the neoclassical explanation. As a matter of general principle it is far from certain that this can be justified.[8] But one can defend it on the ground that there are many cases where no rational, maximizing explanation was obvious at first glance, but upon further search a very plausible one turned up.

Beyond that, one might justify privileging the neoclassical explanation purely as heuristic. If economists are permitted to rationalize what they otherwise cannot explain, by attributing irrational behavior to agents, or by adding additional arguments to the utility function, there is a great danger of ad hocery. Some disciplining mechanism is needed. A credible one is to allow an appeal to irrational behavior only under either of two circumstances. One is that the specific irrationality in question has been adequately documented either in psychological experiments or in other economic behavior. The other circumstance is that the irrationality is more plausible than another, closely related irrationality that has been well established in prior research. For example, suppose a certain type of irrational behavior has been shown to prevail among portfolio managers. It would then usually be legitimate to assume that individual investors are also irrational in this way. Similar rules could be applied to restrict the addition of new arguments to the utility function. That would avoid ad hocery.

Conclusion
Almost a generation ago George Stigler (1966, p.6) wrote:

> When we assume that consumers, acting with mathematical consistency, maximize utility, ... it is not proper to complain that men are much more complicated, and diverse than that. So they are, but if this assumption yields a theory of behavior, which agrees tolerably well with the facts, it must be used until a better theory comes along.

This is right. But the point at issue now is whether we are still limited to a theory that 'agrees tolerably well with the facts', or whether we can do better. Cognitive psychology and experimental economics have provided us with much information.

As Kenneth Arrow (1982, p.5) suggests, this information may allow us to understand situations in which the rationality assumption fails as a guide. Moreover, one can tell the following story. A long time ago economists achieved an immensely useful breakthrough by discovering that, despite their descriptive unrealism the rationality and income-maximizing assumptions provide great insights into economic behavior. For many years they assiduously exploited this insight, and their effort yielded much progress. But declining marginal productivity is inescapable. So the time has come to reorient not all, but some of our effort to analyzing situations in which the rationality and income maximization do not fully hold (for an example see Frey and Eichenberger, 1994).

I do not deny that it may well be a useful heuristic to treat appeals to irrationality or to a thick utility function with some suspicion. But such appeals should not be met with the hostility and the arrogant dogmatism with which mainstream economists have sometimes responded.[9] Thus Akerlof (in Swedberg, 1990, p.65) talked about:

> this taboo against ... introducing new topics into economics. Somehow there are certain frameworks that people are supposed to think in and which are acceptable. If you go outside these, then people don't know exactly how to deal with it. You'd think that people in this situation would be leaning over backwards and say, 'Well, this paper might have some merit to it and maybe we should publish it.' But people seem in fact more likely to do the opposite.

I am not recommending that mainstream economists jettison their thin theory, only that they be more open to behavioral economics and to the new institutionalism. There is no reason why there should be two separate schools, each with its own journals, trying to explain the same phenomenon.

Fortunately, a merging of the two schools appears to be already under way. The old institutionalists with their outright hostility to marginal analysis are eclipsed by the new institutionalists who are perfectly willing to use the neoclassical tools. At the same time the mainstream journals may be becoming more open to alternative views. Among the 15 regular papers and five 'shorter papers' (other than comments and replies) in the latest (as I write this) issue of the *American Economic Review* (December 1993), there are two papers (one a shorter paper) using survey results, one shorter paper demonstrating an irrationality in the stock market and one paper (discussed above), based on a survey of compensation executives, that shows the role of fairness in wage setting. In 1991, the *Economic Journal* devoted an issue to predictions of the future of economics by leading economists. A remarkable number, including some from whom one would not have expected this, foresaw a future in which economic analysis would be broadened by more emphasis on experimental economics, on psychological and sociological variables, and by a loosening of the rationality constraint (see Baumol, 1991; Bhagwati, 1991; Hahn, 1991; Malinvaud, 1991; Morishima,

1991; Pencavel, 1991; Plott, 1991; Roth, 1991; Schmalensee, 1991; Stiglitz, 1991 and Weiseman, 1991). Perhaps I am preaching to the converted. I certainly hope so.

Notes

1. The economist's attitude is sometimes reciprocated. Henry Aaron (1994, p.19) remarks: 'Practitioners of social sciences look on economists with a mixture of envy and contempt.' The contempt is for the economist's insistence on a view of human behavior they see as 'seriously incomplete'.
2. For examples of the use of standard theory, see Akerlof (1984) and Thaler and Shefrin (1981). For examples of the reliance on strong empirical evidence, see Ausubel (1991) and Shiller (1981).
3. A standard justification for including only agents' own income in the utility function is that this does not require the assumption that agents are selfish. An agent may strenuously maximize his income and then make large charitable contributions. What is assumed is not selfishness, but self-interestedness, that is the wish for autonomy and control over resources.
4. The evolutionary argument has come in for much unjustified, as well as justified, criticism. Correctly formulated, it states that competition among firms tends to drive out those who do not maximize profits efficiently, in the private, not social, sense of efficiency. It uses biological evolution merely as an analogy. Hence a showing that biological evolution is not always beneficial, or that there are some differences between survival of the fittest organism and of the fittest firm are besides the point.
5. Friedman referred to a discount rate of 33 per cent because that is what his permanent income theory required to be consistent with the data. He maintained that such a 33 per cent rate is more or less in line with rates paid on instalment contracts, small loans and so on. But at least for recent years a 33 per cent rate is substantially above the rate on credit card loans. Again, one might say that an imputed rate can account for the difference, because borrowing on a credit card reduces one's ability to borrow in the future. All the same, a 33 per cent rate seems highly implausible, particularly since there is other evidence indicating that the particular version of the permanent income theory that generated the 33 per cent rate is invalid (see Mayer, 1972).
6. In California there are no restrictions on voting by mail instead of in person. Yet most people vote in person. It is hard to believe that they value the extra time that this requires less than the cost of two first class stamps.
7. The ad hocery I am talking about is what Hands (1988) refers to as Popperian ad hocery, that is the making of a claim about the existence (or non-existence) of something that helps to establish the theory, when there is no plausible independent evidence substantiating the claim.
8. One might argue that, since economics is the most advanced of the social sciences, it should be privileged in this way, that any explanation that passes the stringent test of consistency with economic theory is more plausible than one that passes the much looser test of consistency with sociological theory. There is *something* to that, but not very much. It is true that the more advanced state of economic theory means that it is *on the whole* more difficult for a false hypothesis to be consistent with it than with the less developed sociological theory. But what is true on the whole is not necessarily true in every case, so that it is better to judge each case on its merits.

    Here is an example. Every time I visit my dentist I am told to floss more. Why? The more I floss, the less business my dentist has. A sociological explanation is that dentists internalize an ethic of healing, and hence give patients good advice, even though it reduces their incomes. A rival economic explanation is readily at hand: if my dentist did not urge me to floss, I would lose trust in him, and hence my demand curve for his services would shift inward. Is this economic explanation the more plausible? It has the advantage that an economist can cite numerous other examples of profit maximization, so that the economic explanation is certainly not ad hoc. But sociologists and psychologists can cite numerous examples of internalization of values, so that the sociological explanation is not ad hoc either. How can we tell which explanation is better?
9. One reason for the hostility may be ideological, though I suspect that this is only a subsidiary reason. To be sure, if agents are irrational the usual simple argument against government intervention is weakened (see Akerlof, 1984; Frank, 1985). But once we allow for irrational behavior we must also take the government's irrationality into account, and that argues against government intervention.

Glossary

Note: The following descriptions are intended to be simple explanations, and not formally correct definitions that would pass muster on a philosophy PhD exam. For more comprehensive, but readily accessible discussions see Blaug (1992, Part 1), Caldwell (1982, Part 1) and Hacking (1983).

Ad hocery denotes reliance on an arbitrary assumption that, if correct, would support one's hypothesis, but which lacks justification. Wade Hands (1988) has distinguished between what he calls 'Popperian ad hocery', that is assumptions that are ad hoc because they lack empirical support, and 'Lakatosian ad hocery', which is making assumptions that lack a basis in one's theoretical framework, such as price stickiness in the neo-Walrasian system. If allowed sufficient ad hoc assumptions, every theory can escape disconfirmation.

Cartesian vision refers to René Descartes' (1596–1650) belief that it would ultimately be possible to found all knowledge on indubitable deductions from self-evident propositions and sense perceptions. All scientific knowledge can therefore be unified and organized systematically with the help of mathematics.

Covering law model is a view of science according to which explanation consists of showing that the particular observation or principle that is to be explained can be deduced from one or several general laws that have previously been established. For example, the proposition that firms set prices so that marginal revenue equals marginal cost can be deduced from the two higher-level generalizations that firms act rationally to maximize profits, and that over the relevant segment marginal cost rises.

Falsificationism is a doctrine developed by Karl Popper to the effect that, for a theory to be considered scientific, it must, at least in principle, be falsifiable by some potentially observable events. That is, scientific theories must be testable and tested, not by looking for instances that confirm them, but for possible instances that disconfirm them. While popular in the 1950s and 1960s, this philosophy of science is no longer widely held, in part because it does not describe accurately what scientists actually do.

Instrumentalism views scientific theories, not as providing truth is some fundamental sense, but as devices ('inference tickets') that allow us to predict correctly. The flavor of instrumentalism is conveyed by the title of Nancy Cartwright's book, *How the Laws of Physics Lie*. In economics instrumentalism is usually identified with Friedman's (1953) famous essay on positive economics, though that is an oversimplification (see Mayer, 1983).

Lakatosian hard core and protective belt. According to Imre Lakatos, scientific research programs consist of a set of basic propositions that are not challenged and may not even be testable, called the 'metaphysical core'. These are used to generate a set of lower-level hypotheses in the 'protective belt' of the research program. It is in this protective belt that the action takes place, where the new discoveries are made that demonstrate the usefulness of the program, or where the program's hypotheses are refuted, thus inducing scientists to abandon it. For example, profit maximization is part of the metaphysical core of neoclassical microeconomics. The hypothesis that excess demand drives up prices is part of the protective belt.

Logical positivism is a doctrine that flourished in the early decades of this century, but has now fallen from favor. It attempts to distinguish scientific statements, whose truth can be tested by empirical observations (albeit often mediated by elaborate theories), from 'metaphysical' statements, such as value judgements, whose truth cannot be determined by empirical observation. It also categorizes all statements as either 'a priori' statements, whose truth results from the way their terms are defined, or as 'observation statements', or as a combination of the two ('synthetic statements') that make assertions about the world. The truth of the latter is ultimately established only by observation.

Popperian refers to the late Sir Karl Popper, who taught for many years at the London School of Economics, where he influenced a number of economists, such as Robert Lipsey. His main contribution is the use of falsificationism (see above) as the hallmark of scientific method.

Positivism argues that all knowledge of the external world is ultimately derived from sensatory perceptions. Many of the propositions of positivism are discussed in Chapter 3.

Realism takes two forms. Realism about theories is the view that the concepts used in valid scientific theories are descriptions of what actually takes place, and that the statements theories make are totally true, instead of being mere 'inference tickets', as the instrumentalists (see above) contend. Realism about entities asserts that entities, such as electrons, that play a role in scientific theories actually exist, and are not mere mental constructs used as an aid to scientific thinking.

References

Aaron, Henry (1994), 'Public Policy, Values, and Consciousness', *Journal of Economic Perspectives*, **8**, Spring, pp.2–21.

Acker, Mary *et al.* (1993), 'Petition to Reform Graduate Education', *American Economic Review*, **83**, December, pp.ii–iii.

Akerlof, George (1984), *An Economic Theorist's Book of Tales*, Cambridge: Cambridge University Press.

Akerlof, George and Yellen, Janet (1988), 'Fairness and Unemployment', *American Economic Review*, **78**, May, pp.44–9.

Alchian, Armen (1950), 'Uncertainty, Evolution and Economic Theory', *Journal of Political Economy*, **58**, June, pp.211–21.

Alogoskoufis, George and Smith, Ron (1991), 'The Phillips Curve, the Persistence of Inflation and the Lucas Critique', *American Economic Review*, **81**, December, pp.1254–75.

Alston, Richard, Kearl, J. and Vaughan, M. (1992), 'Is there a Consensus among Economists in the 1990s?', *American Economic Review*, **82**, May, pp.203–9.

Alston, Richard, Kearl, J. and Vaughan, M. (n.d.), 'Agreement and Disagreement among Economists: A Decade of Change', unpublished manuscript.

Anderson, Leonall and Jordan, Jerry (1968), 'Monetary and Fiscal Actions: A Test of Their Relative Importance in Economic Stabilization', Federal Reserve Bank of St. Louis, *Review*, **50**, November, pp.11–24.

Arrow, Kenneth (1982), 'Risk Perception in Psychology and Economics', *Economic Inquiry*, **20**, January, pp.1–10.

Ausubel, Lawrence (1991), 'The Failure of Competition in the Credit Card Market', *American Economic Review*, **8**, March, pp.50–81.

Backhouse, Roger (1991), 'The Neo-Walrasian Research Program in Macroeconomics', in Neil de Marchi and Mark Blaug (eds), *Appraising Economic Theories*, Aldershot: Edward Elgar.

Baumol, William (1952), 'The Demand for Cash: An Inventory-theoretic Approach', *Quarterly Journal of Economics*, **66**, November, pp.545–56.

Baumol, William (1991), 'Towards a Newer Economics', *Economic Journal*, **101**, January, pp.1–9.

Bear, Donald and Orr, Daniel (1967), 'Logic and Expediency in Economic Theory', *Journal of Political Economy*, **75**, April, pp.188–96.

Becker, Gary (1991), 'A Note on Restaurant Pricing and Other Examples of Social Influence on Price', *Journal of Political Economy*, **99**, October, pp.1109–116.

Beed, Clive (1991), 'Philosophy of Science and Contemporary Economics: An Overview', *Journal of Post Keynesian Economics*, **13**, Summer, pp.459–94.

Belloc, Hilaire (1918), *Cautionary Tales for Children*, London: Duckworth and Co.

Benartzi, Schlomo and Thaler, Richard (1993), 'Myopic Loss Aversion and the Equity Premium Puzzle', NBER Working Paper 4369.

Bernheim, Douglas (1987), 'Ricardian Equivalence: An Evaluation of Theory and Evidence', in Stanley Fischer (ed.), *Macroeconomics Annual*, pp.263–304.

Bernheim, Douglas (1989), 'A Neoclassical Perspective on Budget Deficits', *Journal of Economic Perspectives*, **3**, Spring, pp.55–72.

Bhagwati, Jagdish (1991), 'Economics Beyond the Horizon', *Economic Journal*, **101**, January, pp.15–22.

Blaug, Mark (1991), 'Afterword', in Neil de Marchi and Mark Blaug (eds), *Appraising Economic Theories*, Aldershot: Edward Elgar.

Blaug, Mark (1992), *The Methodology of Economics*, Cambridge: Cambridge University Press.

Blinder, Alan (1987a), 'Keynes, Lucas and Scientific Progress', *American Economic Review*, **77**, May, pp.130–36.

Blinder, Alan (1987b), 'The Rules vs. Discretion Debate in the Light of Recent Experience', *Weltwirtschaftliches Archiv*, **123**, (3), pp.399–409.

Blinder, Alan and Choi, Don (1990), 'A Shred of Evidence on Theories of Wage Stickiness', *Quarterly Journal of Economics*, **105**, November, pp.1003–15.

Bordo, Michael (1984), 'Comment on "Assertion Without Empirical Basis: An Econometric Appraisal of Friedman and Schwartz's Monetary Trends"', unpublished manuscript.

Brown, Vivienne (1994), 'Metanarratives and Economic Discourse', *Scandinavian Journal of Economics*, **96**, (1), pp.83–93.

Brunner, Karl (1981), 'The Case Against Monetary Activism', *Lloyds Bank Review*, **139**, January, pp.20–39.

Brunner, Karl (1989), 'Disarray in Macroeconomics', in F. Capie and G. Wood (eds), *Monetary Economics in the 1990s*, London: Macmillan.

Brunner, Karl and Meckling, William (1977), 'The Perception of Man and the Conception of Government', *Journal of Money, Credit and Banking*, **9**, February, (2), pp.70–85.

Buiter, Willem (1989), *Macroeconomic Theory and Stabilization Policy*, Manchester: Manchester University Press.

Butler, Samuel (1912), *The Notebooks of Samuel Butler*, London: Fifield.

Caldwell, Bruce (1982), *Beyond Positivism*, London: George Allen and Unwin.

Caldwell, Bruce (1991), 'Clarifying Popper', *Journal of Economic Literature*, **29**, March, pp.1–33.

Caldwell, Bruce (1992), 'Commentary', in Neil de Marchi (ed.), *Post-Popperian Methodology of Economics*, Boston: Kluwer Academic Publishers, pp.135–49.

Caldwell, Bruce (1993), 'Economic Methodology', in U. Mäki, B. Gustafsson and C. Knudson (eds), *Rationality, Institutions and Economic Methodology*, London: Routledge.

Carlton, D.W. (1986), 'The Rigidity of Prices', *American Economic Review*, **76**, September, pp.637–58.

Carlton, D.W. (1989), 'The Theory and Facts of How Markets Clear', in R. Schmalensee and R.W. Willig (eds), *Handbook of Industrial Organization*, Amsterdam: Elsevier.

Caudill, Steven (1990), 'Econometrics in Theory and Practice', *Eastern Economic Journal*, **16**, July–September, pp.249–56.

Coase, Ronald (1982), *How Should Economists Choose?*, Washington, DC: American Enterprise Institute.

Coats, A.W. (1987), 'Further Comments on McCloskey's Argument', *Eastern Economic Journal*, **3**, July–September, pp.305–7.

Coddington, Alan (1975), 'The Rationale of General Equilibrium Theory', *Economic Inquiry* **13**, December, pp.539–58.

Colander, David (1994), 'Vision, Judgment, and Disagreement among Economists', *Journal of Economic Methodology*, **1**, June, 43–56.

Cooley, Thomas and LeRoy, Stephen (1981), 'Identification and Estimation of Money Demand', *American Economic Review*, **71**, December, pp.825–43.

Cross, Rod (1991), 'Alternative Accounts of Equilibrium Unemployment', in Neil de Marchi and Mark Blaug (eds), *Appraising Economic Theories*, Aldershot: Edward Elgar.

Dawes, Robyn and Thaler, Richard (1988), 'Anomalies: Cooperation', *Journal of Economic Perspectives*, **2**, Winter, pp.187–98.

De Alessi, Louis (1971), 'Reversals of Assumptions and Implications', *Journal of Political Economy*, **79**, July/August, pp.867–77.

De Long, Bradford, Shleifer, Andrei, Summers, Lawrence and Waldmann, Robert (1993), 'Noise Trader Risk in Financial Markets', reprinted in Richard Thaler (ed.), *Advances in Behavioral Finance*, New York: Russell Sage.

Denzau, Arthur and North, Douglass (1994), 'Shared Mental Models: Ideologies and Institutions', *Kyklos*, **47**, (1), pp.3–31.

Dewey, John (1948), *Reconstruction in Philosophy*, Boston: Beacon Press.

Dotsey, Michael and Otrok, Christopher (1994), 'M2 and Monetary Policy: A Critical Review of the Recent Debate', Federal Reserve Bank of Richmond, *Economic Quarterly*, **80**, Winter, pp.41–60.

Duesenberry, James (1949), *Income, Saving and the Theory of Consumer Behavior*, Cambridge, Mass.: Harvard University Press.

Evans, Paul (1991), 'Is Ricardian Equivalence a Good Approximation?', *Economic Inquiry*, **29**, October, pp.626–44.

Fand, David (1970), 'Monetarism and Fiscalism', Banca Nazionale del Lavoro, *Quarterly Review*, **94**, September, pp.276–307.

Ferris, Timothy (1988), *Coming of Age in the Milky Way*, New York: William Morrow.

Feyerabend, Paul (1975), *Against Method*, Berkeley: University of California Press.

Fisher, Irving (1930), *The Theory of Interest*, New York: Macmillan.

Frank, Robert (1985), *Choosing the Right Pond*, Oxford: Oxford University Press.

Frank, Robert (1987), 'If *Homo Economicus* could Choose His Own Utility Function, Would He Want One with a Conscience?', *American Economic Review*, **77**, September, pp.593–604, New York: Macmillan.

Frey, Bruno (1992), *Economics as a Science of Human Behavior*, Boston: Kluwer Academic Publishers.

Frey, Bruno and Eichenberger, Reiner (1989), 'Should Social Scientists Care about Choice Anomalies?', *Rationality and Society*, **1**, July, pp.101–22.

Frey, Bruno and Eichenberger, Reiner (1994), 'Economic Incentives Transform Psychological Anomalies', *Journal of Economic Behavior and Organization*, **23**, pp.215–34.

Frey, Bruno, Pommerehne, Werner, Schneider Friedrich and Gilbert, Guy (1984), 'Consensus and Dissention Among Economists: An Empirical Inquiry', *American Economic Review*, **74**, December, pp.986–94.

Friedman, Benjamin (1988), 'Conducting Monetary Policy by Controlling Currency plus Noise: A Comment', *Carnegie–Rochester Conference Series on Public Policy*, **29**, Autumn, pp.205–12.

Friedman, Milton (1953), *Essays in Positive Economics*, Chicago: University of Chicago Press.

Friedman, Milton (1956), *Studies in the Quantity Theory of Money*, Chicago: University of Chicago Press.

Friedman, Milton (1957), *A Theory of the Consumption Function*, Chicago: University of Chicago Press.

Friedman, Milton (1963), 'Windfalls, the "Horizon" and Related Concepts of the Permanent Income Hypothesis', in Carl Christ (ed.), *Measurement in Economics: Studies in Mathematical Economics and Econometrics in Memory of Yehuda Greenfeld*, Stanford: Stanford University Press.

Friedman, Milton (1968), 'The Role of Monetary Policy', *American Economic Review*, **58**, March, pp.1–16.

Friedman, Milton (1972), 'Comments on Critics', *Journal of Political Economy*, **80**, September/October, pp.906–50.

Friedman, Milton (1988), 'Money and the Stock Market', *Journal of Political Economy*, **96**, April, pp.221–45.

Friedman, Milton and Schwartz, Anna (1963a), *A Monetary History of the United States, 1867–1960*, Princeton: Princeton University Press.

Friedman, Milton and Schwartz, Anna (1963b), 'Money and Business Cycles', *Review of Economics and Statistics*, **45**, February, pp.9–32.

Friedman, Milton and Schwartz, Anna (1982), *Monetary Trends in the United States and United Kingdom*, Chicago: University of Chicago Press.

Friedman, Milton and Schwartz, Anna (1991), 'Alternative Approaches to Analyzing Economic Data', *American Economic Review*, **81**, March, pp.39–49.

Garfinkel, Alan (1981), *Forms of Explanation*, New Haven: Yale University Press.

Gilbert, Christopher (1991), 'Do Economists Test Theories? – Demand Analysis as Tests of Theories of Economic Methodology', in Neil de Marchi and Mark Blaug (eds), *Appraising Economic Theories*, Aldershot: Edward Elgar.

Goldberger, Arthur (1964), *Econometric Theory*, New York: John Wiley.

Goodwin, Neva (1991), *Social Economics: An Alternative Theory*, vol.1, New York: St. Martin's Press.

Gordon, David (1987), 'Six Percent Unemployment Ain't Natural: Demystifying the Idea of a Rising "Natural Rate" of Unemployment', *Social Research*, **54**, Summer, pp.224–46.

Gramlich, Edward (1989), 'Budget Deficits and National Savings: Are Politicians Exogenous?', *Journal of Economic Perspectives*, **3**, Spring, pp.23–36.

Granger, Clive (1991), 'Reducing Self-Interest and Improving the Relevance of Economic Research', Discussion Paper 91–17, University of California, San Diego.

Hacking, Ian (1983), *Representing and Intervening*, London: Cambridge University Press.

Hahn, Frank (1971), 'Professor Friedman's Views on Money', *Economica*, NS, **38**, February, pp.61–80.

Hahn, Frank (1991), 'The Next Hundred Years', *Economic Journal*, **101**, January, pp.47–51.

Haley, James (1990), 'Theoretical Foundations for Sticky Wages', *Journal of Economic Surveys*, **4**, (2), pp.116–55.

Hall, Stephen and Milne, Alister (1994), 'The Relevance of P-Star Analysis to UK Monetary Policy', *Economic Journal*, **104**, May, pp.597–604.

Hallman, Jeffrey, Porter, Richard and Small, David (1989), *M2 per Unit of Potential GNP as an Anchor for the Price Level*, Washington, DC, Board of Governors, Federal Reserve System, Staff Study, **157**, Washington, DC.

Hammond, Daniel (1990), 'McCloskey's Modernism and Friedman's Methodology: A Case Study with New Evidence', *Review of Social Economy*, **48**, Summer, pp.158–71.

Hands, D.W. (1984), 'What Economics is Not: An Economist's Response to Rosenberg', *Philosophy of Science*, **51**, pp.495–503.

Hands, D.W. (1988), 'Adhocness in Economics and the Popperian Tradition', in Neil de Marchi (ed.), *The Popperian Legacy in Economics*, Cambridge: Cambridge University Press.

Hands, D.W. (1991), 'Popper, the Rationality Principle and Economic Explanation', in G.K. Shaw (ed.), *Economics, Culture and Education: Essays in Honour of Mark Blaug*, Aldershot: Edward Elgar.

Hands, D.W. (1992), 'Falsification, Situational Analysis and Scientific Research Programs', in Neil de Marchi (ed.), *Post-Popperian Methodology of Economics*, Boston: Kluwer Academic Publishers.

Hands, D.W. (1993), 'Popper and Lakatos on Economic Methodology', in U. Mäki, B. Gustafsson and C. Knudson (eds), *Rationality, Institutions and Economic Methodology*, London: Routledge.

Hausman, Daniel (1992a), *Essays on Philosophy and Economic Methodology*, Cambridge: Cambridge University Press.

Hausman, Daniel (1992b), *The Inexact and Separate Science of Economics*, Cambridge: Cambridge University Press.

Hausman, Daniel and McPherson, Michael (1993), 'Taking Ethics Seriously: Economics and Contemporary Moral Philosophy', *Journal of Economic Literature*, **31**, June, pp.671–731.

Havrilesky, Thomas (1993), *The Pressures on American Monetary Policy*, Boston: Kluwer Academic Publishers.

Hawking, Stephen (1990), *A Brief History of Time*, New York: Bantam Books.

Hendry, David and Ericsson, Neil (1983), 'Assertion Without Empirical Basis: An Econometric Appraisal of Friedman and Schwartz's *Monetary Trends in the United States and the United Kingdom*', in Bank of England *Panel of Academic Consultants*, London: Bank of England.

Hendry, David and Ericsson, Neil (1991), 'An Econometric Analysis of U.K. Money Demand in *Monetary Trends in the United States and the United Kingdom* by Milton Friedman and Anna Schwartz', *American Economic Review*, **81**, March, pp.8–38.

Hershey, Robert (1993), 'Economists Make a Comeback', *New York Times*, 23 September, p.C-4.

Hetzel, Robert (1990), 'The Political Economy of Monetary Policy', in Thomas Mayer (ed.), *The Political Economy of American Monetary Policy*, New York: Cambridge University Press.

Hirsch, Abraham and de Marchi, Neil (1990), *Milton Friedman: Economics in Theory and Practice*, Ann Arbor, Michigan: University of Michigan Press.

Hirschleifer, Jack (1985), 'The Expanding Domain of Economics', *American Economic Review*, **75**, December, pp.53–70.

Hodgson, Geoffrey (1993), 'Calculation, Habit and Action', in Bill Gerrard (ed.), *The Economics of Rationality*, London: Routledge.

Hogarth, Robin and Reder, Melvin (1987), *Rational Choice*, Chicago: University of Chicago Press.

Hollis, Martin (1985), 'The Emperor's Newest Clothes', *Economics and Philosophy*, **1**, pp.128–33.

Holmes, James and Smyth, David (1972), 'The Specification of the Demand for Money and the Tax Multiplier', *Journal of Political Economy*, **80**, January/February, pp.179–85.

Hoover, Kevin (1988), *The New Classical Economics*, Oxford: Blackwell.

Hoover, Kevin (1989), 'Scientific Research Program or Tribe? A Joint Appraisal of Lakatos and the New Classical Macroeconomics', in Neil de Marchi and Mark Blaug (eds), *Appraising Economic Theories*, Aldershot: Edward Elgar.

Hoover, Kevin (1994), 'Econometrics as Observation: The Lucas Critique and the Nature of Econometric Inference', *Journal of Economic Methodology*, **1**, June, pp.65–81.

Hoover, Kevin (1995), 'Why Does Methodology Matter for Economics?', *Economic Journal*, forthcoming.

Hutchison, Terence (1988), 'The Case for Falsification', in Neil de Marchi (ed.), *The Post-Popperian Legacy for Economics*, Cambridge: Cambridge University Press.

Hutchison, Terence (1992), *Changing Aims in Economics*, Oxford: Blackwell.

Janssen, Maarten (1993), *Microfoundations*, London: Routledge.

Johnson, Virginia (1994), 'Today I Dance "Firebird". Tomorrow, Layoffs', *New York Times*, 6 March 1994, p.H-35.

Kagel, John, Battalio, Raymond, Rachlin, Howard, Green, Leonard, Basmann, Robert and Klemm, W.R. (1975), 'Experimental Studies of Consumer Demand Behavior using Laboratory Animals', *Economic Inquiry*, **13**, March, pp.22–38.

Kahneman, Daniel, Knetch, Jack and Thaler, Richard (1986), 'Fairness as a Constraint on Profit Seeking', *American Economic Review*, **76**, September, pp.728–41.

Kahneman, Daniel, Slovik, Paul and Tversky, Amos (1982), *Judgment under Uncertainty*, New York: Cambridge University Press.

Kaldor, Nicholas (1970), 'The New Monetarism', *Lloyds Bank Review*, **97**, pp.1–18.

Keynes, J.M (1936), *The General Theory of Employment, Interest and Money*, New York: Macmillan.

Kirman, Alan (1992), 'Whom or What Does the Representative Individual Represent?', *Journal of Economic Perspectives*, **6**, Spring, pp.117–36.

Kitcher, Philip (1993), *The Advancement of Science*, New York: Oxford University Press.

Klamer, Arjo (1984), *Conversation with Economists*, Totowa, NJ: Rowman and Allanheld.

Klamer, Arjo (1987), 'The Advent of Modernism', unpublished manuscript.

Klamer, Arjo and Colander, David (1990), *The Making of an Economist*, Boulder, Col.: Westview Press.

Klein, Daniel (1994), 'If Government is so Villainous, How Come Government Officials don't Seem like Villains?', *Economics and Philosophy*, **10**, April, pp.91–106.

Kline, Morris (1980), *Mathematics: The Loss of Certainty*, New York: Oxford University Press.

Koopmans, Tjalling (1957), *Three Essays on the State of Economic Science*, New York: McGraw-Hill.

Krueger, Ann *et al.* (1991), 'Report of the Commission on Graduate Education in Economics', *Journal of Economic Literature*, **29**, September, pp.1035–53.

Kuhn, Thomas (1970), *The Structure of Scientific Revolutions*, Cambridge, Mass: MIT Press.

Laidler, David (1992), 'Issues in Contemporary Macroeconomics', in Alessandro Vercelli and Nicola Dimitri (eds), *Macroeconomics*, Oxford: Oxford University Press.

Leamer, Edward (1978), *Specification Search: Ad Hoc Inference with Experimental Data*, New York: John Wiley.

Leamer, Edward (1983), 'Let's Take the Con out of Econometrics', *American Economic Review*, **73**, March, pp.31–43.

Leeson, Robert (1994), 'A.W.H. Phillips M.B.E. (Military Division)', *Economic Journal*, **104**, May, pp.605–18.

Leijonhufvud, Axel (1992), 'Towards a Not-Too-Rational Macroeconomics', UCLA Center for Computable Economics, Working Paper 1.

Leontief, Wassily (1971), 'Theoretical Assumptions and Nonobservable Facts', *American Economic Review*, **61**, March, pp.1–7.

Leontief, Wassily (1982), 'Academic Economics', *Science*, **217**, 9 July, p.xii.

LeRoy, Stephen (1989), 'Efficient Capital Markets and Martingales', *Journal of Economic Literature*, **27**, December, pp.1583–1621.

Levine, David (1993), 'Fairness, Markets and Ability to Pay: Evidence from Compensation Executives', *American Economic Review*, **83**, December, pp.1249–51.

Lombra, Raymond and Moran, Michael (1980), 'Policy Advice and Policymaking at the Federal Reserve', *Carnegie–Rochester Conference Series on Public Policy*, **13**, Autumn, pp.9–68.

Machlup, Fritz (1950), 'Three Concepts of the Balance of Payments and the so-called Dollar Shortage', *Economic Journal*, **60**, March, pp.46–68.

Machlup, Fritz (1978), *Methodology of Economics and Other Social Sciences*, New York: Academic Press.

Machlup, Fritz (1991), *Economic Semantics*, New Brunswick, NJ: Transaction Publishers.

Mäki, Uskali (1993a), 'Economics with Institutions', in U. Mäki, B. Gustafsson and C. Knudson (eds), *Rationality, Institutions and Economic Methodology*, London: Routledge.

Mäki, Uskali (1993b), 'Isolation, Idealization and Truth in Economics', *Poznan Studies in the Philosophy of Science*.

Mäki, Uskali (1994a), 'Kinds of Assumptions and their Truth', unpublished manuscript.

Mäki, Uskali (1994b), 'Scientific Realism and Some Peculiarities of Economics', *Boston Studies in the Philosophy of Science*, forthcoming.

Mäki, Uskali (forthcoming), 'Reorienting the Assumptions Issue', in Roger Backhouse (ed.), *New Developments in Economic Methodology*, London: Routledge.

Malinvaud, Edmond (1991), 'The Next Fifty Years', *Economic Journal*, **101**, January, pp.64–8.

Mankiw, Gregory (1989), 'Understanding Real Business Cycles', *Journal of Economic Perspectives*, **3**, Summer, pp.79–90.

Mankiw, Gregory and Summers, Lawrence (1986), 'Money Demand and Fiscal Policy', *Journal of Money, Credit and Banking*, **18**, November, pp.415–29.

Mayer, Thomas (1972), *Permanent Income, Wealth and Consumption*, Berkeley, Cal.: University of California Press.

Mayer, Thomas (1980), 'Economics as a Hard Science: Realistic Goal or Wishful Thinking?', *Economic Inquiry*, **18**, April, pp.165–78.

Mayer, Thomas (1987), 'Replacing the FOMC by a PC', *Contemporary Policy Issues*, **5**, April, pp.31–43.

Mayer, Thomas (1989), 'Simulations with Econometric Models', *Methodus*, **1**, December, pp.13–14.

Mayer, Thomas (1990a), 'Minimizing Regret as an Explanation of Federal Reserve Policy', in T. Mayer (ed.), *The Political Economy of American Monetary Policy*, Cambridge: Cambridge University Press.

Mayer, Thomas (1990b), *Monetarism and Macroeconomic Policy*, Aldershot: Edward Elgar.

Mayer, Thomas (1993a), 'Friedman's Methodology of Positive Economics: A Soft Reading', *Economic Inquiry*, **31**, April, pp.213–23.

Mayer, Thomas (1993b), *Truth versus Precision in Economics*, Aldershot: Edward Elgar.

Mayer, Thomas (1994a), 'The Rhetoric of Monetarism', in P. Klein (ed.), *The Role of Economic Theory*, Boston: Kluwer Academic Publishers.

Mayer, Thomas (1994b), 'Why do Economists Disagree So Much?', *Journal of Economic Methodology*, **1**, June, pp.1–14.

Mayer, Thomas *et al.* (1978), *The Structure of Monetarism*, New York: W.W. Norton.

Mayer, Thomas and Spinelli, Franco (1991), *Macroeconomics and Macroeconomic Policy Issues*, Aldershot: Avebury.

McCallum, Bennett (1987), 'The Case for Rules in the Conduct of Monetary Policy: A Concrete Example', *Weltwirtschaftliches Archiv*, **127**, (3), pp.414–27.

McCallum, Bennett (1988), 'Robustness Properties of a Rule for Monetary Policy', *Carnegie–Rochester Conference Series on Public Policy*, **29**, Autumn.

McCloskey, Donald (1985), *The Rhetoric of Economics*, Madison: University of Wisconsin Press.

McCloskey, Donald (1991), 'Economic Science: A Search Through the Hyperspace of Assumptions', *Methodus*, **3**, June, pp.6–16.

McCloskey, Donald (1994), *Knowledge and Persuasion in Economics*, Cambridge: Cambridge University Press.

McLaughlin, Kenneth (1990), 'Rigid Wages', University of Rochester, Center for Economic Research, Working Paper No. 29.

McNees, Stephen (1988), 'How Accurate are Macroeconomic Forecasts?', Federal Reserve Bank of Boston, *New England Economic Review*, July/August, pp.15–36.

Meltzer, Allan (1986), 'Size, Persistence and Interrelation of Nominal and Real Shocks: Some Evidence from Four Countries', *Journal of Monetary Economics*, **17**, January, pp.161–94.

Meltzer, Allan (1987), 'Limits of Short-Run Stabilization Policy', *Economic Inquiry*, **25**, January, pp.1–15.

Milberg, William (1994), 'The Rhetoric of Policy Relevance in International Economics', unpublished manuscript.

Minford, Patrick (1991), 'Comment', in Thomas Mayer and Franco Spinelli (eds), *Macroeconomics and Macroeconomic Policy Issues*, Aldershot: Avebury.

Modigliani, Franco (1988), 'The Monetarist Controversy Revisited', *Contemporary Policy Issues*, **6**, October, pp.19–24.

Modigliani, Franco and Brumberg, Richard (1955), 'Utility Analysis and the Consumption Function', in K. Kurihra (ed.), *Post-Keynesian Economics*, London: George Allen and Unwin.

Modigliani, Franco and Friedman, Milton (1977), 'The Monetarist Controversy', in Federal Reserve Bank of San Francisco, *Economic Review*, Spring, pp.5–46.

Morishima, Michio (1991), 'General Equilibrium Theory in the Twenty-First Century', *Economic Journal*, **101**, January, pp.69–74.

Morrison, Denton, and Henkel, Raymond (1970), *The Significance Test Controversy*, Chicago: Aldine.

Musgrave, Alan (1981), 'Unrealistic Assumptions in Economic Theory', *Kyklos*, **34**, (3), pp.377–87.

Nelson, Alan (1992), 'Human Molecules', in Neil de Marchi (ed.), *Post-Popperian Methodology in Economics*, Boston: Kluwer Academic Publishers.

Niehans, Jurg (1978), *The Theory of Money*, Baltimore: Johns Hopkins University Press.

Nooteboom, Bart (1993), 'The Conservatism of Programme Continuity: Criticisms of Lakatosian Methodology in Economics', *Methodus*, **5**, June, pp.31–46.

Olmstead, Alan and Rhode, Paul (1985), 'Rationing without Government: The West Coast Gas Famine of 1920', *American Economic Review*, **75**, December, pp.1044–55.

Papell, David (1989), 'Monetary Policy in the United States under Flexible Exchange Rates', *American Economic Review*, **79**, December, pp.1106–16.

Patinkin, Don (1956, 1965), *Money Interest and Prices*, New York: Row Peterson.

Patinkin, Don (1971), 'The Chicago Tradition, the Quantity Theory and Friedman', *Journal of Money, Credit and Banking*, **1**, February, pp.46–70.

Payson, Steven (1994), *Quality Measurement in Economics*, Aldershot: Edward Elgar.

Pencavel, John (1991), 'Prospects for Economics', *Economic Journal*, **101**, January, pp.81–7.

Pesek, Boris and Saving, Thomas (1967), *Money, Wealth and Economic Theory*, New York: Macmillan.

Plosser, Charles (1989), 'Understanding Real Business Cycles', *Journal of Economic Perspectives*, **3**, Summer, pp.51–78.

Plott, Charles (1991), 'Economics in 2090: The Views of an Experimentalist', *Economic Journal*, **101**, January, pp.88–93.

Poole, William (1975), 'The Relationship of Monetary Deceleration to Business Cycle Peaks: Another Look at the Evidence', *Journal of Finance*, **30**, June, pp.697–712.

Pratt, John (1964), 'Risk Aversion in the Small and in the Large', *Econometrica*, **23**, January–April, pp.122–36.

Rappaport, Steven (1988), 'Economic Methodology, Rhetoric or Epistemology?', *Economics and Philosophy*, **4**, (1), pp.110–28.

Robbins, Lionel (1935), *An Essay on the Nature and Significance of Economic Science*: London, Macmillan.

Robbins, Lionel (1981), 'Economics and Political Economy', *American Economic Review*, **71**, May, pp.1–10.

Romer, David (1993), 'The New Keynesian Synthesis', *Journal of Economic Perspectives*, **7**, Winter, pp.5–22.

Rorty, Richard (1979), *Philosophy and the Mirror of Nature*, Princeton: Princeton University Press.

Rosenberg, Alexander (1972), 'Friedman's "Methodology" for Economics: A Critical Examination', *Philosophy of Social Sciences*, **2**, (1), pp.15–29.

Rosenberg, Alexander (1976), *Microeconomic Laws*, Pittsburgh: University of Pittsburgh Press.

Rosenberg, Alexander (1980), 'A Skeptical History of Microeconomic Theory', *Theory and Decision*, **12**, (1), pp.79–93.

Rosenberg, Alexander (1983), 'If Economics isn't Science, What is It?', *Philosophical Forum*, **14**, Spring–Summer, pp.296–314.

Rosenberg, Alexander (1984), 'What Rosenberg's Philosophy of Economics is Not', *Philosophy of Science*, **53**, pp.127–32.

Rosenberg, Alexander (1986), 'Lakatosian Consolations for Economics', *Economics and Philosophy*, **2**, pp.127–39.

Rosenberg, Alexander (1992), *Economics – Mathematical Politics or Science of Diminishing Returns?*, Chicago: University of Chicago Press.

Roth, Alvin (1991), 'Game Theory and Empirical Economics', *Economic Journal*, **101**, pp.107–15.

Rudner, Richard (1953), 'The Scientist *qua* Scientist Makes Value Judgments', *Philosophy of Science*, **20**, January, pp.1–6.

Russell, Thomas and Thaler, Richard (1985), 'The Relevance of Quasi Rationality in Competitive Markets', *American Economic Review*, **75**, December, pp.1071–82.

Samuelson, Paul (1947), 'The General Theory', in S. Harris (ed.), *The New Economics*, London: Dennis Dobson, pp.145–60.

Samuelson, Paul (1958), 'An Exact Consumption-Loan Model of Interest with and without the Social Contrivance of Money', *Journal of Political Economy*, **66**, December, pp.1187–1211.

Schmalensee, Richard (1991), 'Continuity and Change in the Economics Industry', *Economic Journal*, **101**, January, pp.115–21.

Seater, John (1993), 'Ricardian Equivalence', *Journal of Economic Literature*, **31**, March, pp.142–90.

Sheffrin, Steven (1989), *The Making of Economic Policy*, Oxford: Blackwell.

Shiller, Robert (1981), 'Do Stock Prices Move Too Much to be Justified by Subsequent Changes in Dividends?', *American Economic Review*, **71**, June, pp.421–36.

Shiller, Robert, Boycko, Maxim and Korobov, Vladimir (1991), 'Popular Attitudes towards Free Markets', *American Economic Review*, **81**, June, pp.385–400.

Simon, Herbert (1987), 'Rationality in Psychology and Economics', in R. Hogarth and M. Reder (eds), *Rational Choice*, Chicago: University of Chicago Press.

Simon, Herbert (1991), 'Organizations and Markets', *Journal of Economic Perspectives*, **5**, Spring, pp.25–45.

Sims, Christopher (1980), 'Comparison of Interwar and Postwar Business Cycles: Monetarism Reconsidered', *American Economic Review*, **70**, May, pp.250–57.

Sims, Christopher (1982), 'Policy Analysis with Econometric Models', *Brookings Papers on Economic Activity*, no. 1, pp.107–52.

Smith, Vernon (1991), *Papers in Experimental Economics*, Cambridge: Cambridge University Press.

Snowdon, B., Vane, H. and Wynarczyk, P. (1994), *A Modern Guide to Macroeconomics*, Aldershot: Edward Elgar.

Solow, Robert (1986), 'What is a Nice Girl Like You Doing in a Place Like This? Macroeconomics after Fifty Years', *Eastern Economic Journal*, **12**, July–September, pp.191–8.

Solow, Robert (1994), 'Perspectives on Growth Theory', *Journal of Economic Perspectives*, **8**, Winter, pp.45–54.

Spencer, David (1989), 'Does Money Matter? The Robustness of Evidence from Vector Autoregressions', *Journal of Money, Credit and Banking*, **21**, November, pp.442–54.

Stein, Jerome (1976), *Monetarism*, Amsterdam: North Holland.

Stigler, George (1966), *The Theory of Price*, New York: Macmillan.

Stigler, George (1991), 'The Direction of Economic Research', in G.K. Shaw (ed.), *Economics, Culture and Education: Essays in Honour of Mark Blaug*, Aldershot: Edward Elgar.

Stiglitz, Joseph (1991), 'Another Century of Economic Science', *Economic Journal*, **101**, January, pp.134–41.

Stiglitz, Joseph (1992), 'Methodological Issues and the New Keynesian Economics', in Alessandro Vercelli and Nicola Dimitri (eds), *Macroeconomics*, Oxford: Oxford University Press.

Strassmann, Dianna (1994), 'Feminist Thought and Economics, Or What do the Visigoths Know?', *American Economic Review*, **74**, May, pp.153–8.

Sudgen, Robert (1993), 'Welfare, Resources and Capabilities', *Journal of Economic Literature*, **31**, December, pp.1947–62.

Summers, Lawrence (1991), 'The Scientific Illusion in Empirical Macroeconomics', *Scandinavian Journal of Economics*, **93**, March, pp.129–48.

Suppe, Frederick (1977), *The Structure of Scientific Theories*, Urbana, Illinois: University of Illinois Press.

Swedberg, Richard (1990), *Economics and Sociology*, Princeton: Princeton University Press.

Thaler, Richard (1991), *Quasi Rational Economics*, New York: Russell Sage Foundation.

Thaler, Richard (1993), *Advances in Behavioral Finance*, New York: Russell Sage Foundation.

Thaler, Richard and Shefrin, Hersh (1981), 'An Economic Theory of Self-Control', *Journal of Political Economy*, **89**, April, pp.392–406.

Thornton, Saranna (1993), 'An Analysis of M1 and M2 Versions of McCallum's Rule', unpublished manuscript.

Tobin, James (1970), 'Money and Income: Post Hoc Ergo Propter Hoc?', *Quarterly Journal of Economics*, **84**, May, pp.301–17.

Tobin, James (1993), 'Price Flexibility and Output Stability: An Old Keynesian View', *Journal of Economic Perspectives*, **7**, Winter, pp.45–66.

Todd, Richard (1990), 'Vector Autoregression Evidence on Monetarism: Another Look at the Robustness Debate', Federal Reserve Bank of Minneapolis, *Quarterly Review*, **14**, Spring, pp.19–37.

Tuckman, Howard and Leahey, Jack (1975), 'What is an Article Worth?', *Journal of Political Economy*, **83**, October, pp.951–68.

Tversky, Amos and Kahneman, Daniel (1987), 'Rational Choice and the Framing of Decisions', in Robin Hogarth and Melvin Reder (eds), *Rational Choice*, Chicago: University of Chicago Press.

Viard, Alan (1993), 'The Welfare Gains from the Introduction of Indexed Bonds', *Journal of Money, Credit and Banking*, **25**, August, part 2, pp.612–28.

Walstad, William and Larsen, Max (1992), 'A National Survey of American National Literacy', The Gallup Organization, unpublished manuscript.

Weiner, S. (1986), 'The Natural Rate of Unemployment: Concepts and Issues', Federal Reserve Bank of Kansas City, *Economic Review*, January, pp.3–10.

Weintraub, Roy (1985), *General Equilibrium Analysis*, Cambridge: Cambridge University Press.

Weintraub, Roy (1988), 'The Neo-Walrasian Program is Empirically Progressive', in Neil de Marchi (ed.), *The Popperian Legacy in Economics*, Cambridge: Cambridge University Press.

Weintraub, Roy (1989), 'Methodology Doesn't Matter, but the History of Thought Might', *Scandinavian Journal of Economics*, **91**, (2), pp.477–93.

Weiseman, Jack (1991), 'The Black Box', *Economic Journal*, **101**, January, pp.149–53.

Winston, Clifford (1993), 'Economic Deregulation: Days of Reckoning for Microeconomists', *Journal of Economic Literature*, **31**, September, pp.1263–89.

Winter, Sidney (1963), 'Economics, "Natural Selection" and the Theory of the Firm', *Yale Economic Essays*, **4**, Spring, pp.25–71.

Woo, Henry (1990), 'Scientific Reduction, Reductionism and Metaphysical Reduction – A Broad View of Economic Methodology', *Methodus*, 2, (2), pp.61–8.

Woolf, Arthur (1992), 'Skills Economists Need in Government', in David Colander and Reuven Brenner (eds), *Educating Economists*, Ann Arbor, Michigan: University of Michigan Press.

Woolley, John (1986), *Monetary Politics*, New York: Cambridge University Press.

Woos, Joanna (1992), 'From Graduate Student to Liberal Arts Professor', in David Colander and Reuven Brenner (eds), *Educating Economists*, Ann Arbor, Michigan: University of Michigan Press.

Zarnowitz, Victor and Braun, Phillip (1993), 'Twenty Years of NBER-ASA Quarterly Economic Outlook Surveys: Aspects and Comparisons of Forecasting Performance', in James Stock and Mark Watson (eds), *Business Cycles, Indicators and Forecasting*, Chicago: University of Chicago Press.

Zevin, Robert (1992), 'Economists, Judgment and Business', in David Colander and Reuven Brenner (eds), *Educating Economists*, Ann Arbor, Michigan: University of Michigan Press.

Index

Economists of the Twentieth Century

Monetarism and Macroeconomic Policy
Thomas Mayer

Studies in Fiscal Federalism
Wallace E. Oates

The World Economy in Perspective
Essays in International Trade and European Integration
Herbert Giersch

Towards a New Economics
Critical Essays on Ecology, Distribution and Other Themes
Kenneth E. Boulding

Studies in Positive and Normative Economics
Martin J. Bailey

The Collected Essays of Richard E. Quandt (2 volumes)
Richard E. Quandt

International Trade Theory and Policy
Selected Essays of W. Max Corden
W. Max Corden

Organization and Technology in Capitalist Development
William Lazonick

Studies in Human Capital
Collected Essays of Jacob Mincer, Volume 1
Jacob Mincer

Studies in Labor Supply
Collected Essays of Jacob Mincer, Volume 2
Jacob Mincer

Macroeconomics and Economic Policy
The Selected Essays of Assar Lindbeck, Volume I
Assar Lindbeck

The Welfare State
The Selected Essays of Assar Lindbeck, Volume II
Assar Lindbeck

Classical Economics, Public Expenditure and Growth
Walter Eltis

Money, Interest Rates and Inflation
Frederic S. Mishkin

The Public Choice Approach to Politics
Dennis C. Mueller

The Liberal Economic Order
Volume I Essays on International Economics
Volume II Money, Cycles and Related Themes
Gottfried Haberler
Edited by Anthony Y.C. Koo

Economic Growth and Business Cycles
Prices and the Process of Cyclical Development
Paolo Sylos Labini

International Adjustment, Money and Trade
Theory and Measurement for Economic Policy, Volume I
Herbert G. Grubel

International Capital and Service Flows
Theory and Measurement for Economic Policy, Volume II
Herbert G. Grubel

Unintended Effects of Government Policies
Theory and Measurement for Economic Policy, Volume III
Herbert G. Grubel

The Economics of Competitive Enterprise
Selected Essays of P.W.S. Andrews
Edited by Frederic S. Lee and Peter E. Earl

The Repressed Economy
Causes, Consequences, Reform
Deepak Lal

Economic Theory and Market Socialism
Selected Essays of Oskar Lange
Edited by Tadeusz Kowalik

Trade, Development and Political Economy
Selected Essays of Ronald Findlay
Ronald Findlay

General Equilibrium Theory
The Collected Essays of Takashi Negishi, Volume I
Takashi Negishi

The History of Economics
The Collected Essays of Takashi Negishi, Volume II
Takashi Negishi

Studies in Econometric Theory
The Collected Essays of Takeshi Amemiya
Takeshi Amemiya

Exchange Rates and the Monetary System
Selected Essays of Peter B. Kenen
Peter B. Kenen

Econometric Methods and Applications (2 volumes)
G.S. Maddala

National Accounting and Economic Theory
The Collected Papers of Dan Usher, Volume I
Dan Usher

Welfare Economics and Public Finance
The Collected Papers of Dan Usher, Volume II
Dan Usher

Economic Theory and Capitalist Society
The Selected Essays of Shigeto Tsuru, Volume I
Shigeto Tsuru

Methodology, Money and the Firm
The Collected Essays of D.P. O'Brien (2 volumes)
D.P. O'Brien

Economic Theory and Financial Policy
The Selected Essays of Jacques J. Polak (2 volumes)
Jacques J. Polak

Sturdy Econometrics
Edward E. Leamer

The Emergence of Economic Ideas
Essays in the History of Economics
Nathan Rosenberg

Productivity Change, Public Goods and Transaction Costs
Essays at the Boundaries of Microeconomics
Yoram Barzel

Reflections on Economic Development
The Selected Essays of Michael P. Todaro
Michael P. Todaro

The Economic Development of Modern Japan
The Selected Essays of Shigeto Tsuru, Volume II
Shigeto Tsuru

Money, Credit and Policy
Allan H. Meltzer

Macroeconomics and Monetary Theory
The Selected Essays of Meghnad Desai, Volume I
Meghnad Desai

Poverty, Famine and Economic Development
The Selected Essays of Meghnad Desai, Volume II
Meghnad Desai

Explaining the Economic Performance of Nations
Essays in Time and Space
Angus Maddison

Economic Doctrine and Method
Selected Papers of R.W. Clower
Robert W. Clower

Economic Theory and Reality
Selected Essays on their Disparity and Reconciliation
Tibor Scitovsky

Doing Economic Research
Essays on the Applied Methodology of Economics
Thomas Mayer

Institutions and Development Strategies
The Selected Essays of Irma Adelman, Volume I
Irma Adelman

Dynamics and Income Distribution
The Selected Essays of Irma Adelman, Volume II
Irma Adelman

The Economics of Growth and Development
The Selected Essays of A.P. Thirlwall
A.P. Thirlwall

Theoretical and Applied Econometrics
The Selected Papers of Phoebus J. Dhrymes
Phoebus J. Dhrymes

Innovation, Technology and the Economy
The Selected Essays of Edwin Mansfield (2 volumes)
Edwin Mansfield

Economic Theory and Policy in Context
The Selected Essays of R.D. Collison Black
R.D. Collison Black

Capitalism, Socialism and Post-Keynesianism
Selected Essays of G.C. Harcourt
G.C. Harcourt

Time Series Analysis and Macroeconometric Modelling
The Collected Papers of Kenneth F. Wallis
Kenneth F. Wallis

Foundations of Modern Econometrics
The Selected Essays of Ragnar Frisch (2 volumes)
Olav Bjerkholt